## Advance praise for *Taken by Bear in Yellowstone*

"Bear attacks are multifaceted, fascinating, and often chilling events. Snow gives carefully researched and detailed first-person accounts of Yellowstone National Park's bear attacks. Her accounts and images inform and let readers draw their own conclusions. You get involved in tough decisions such as what was done with the sow grizzly with cubs that killed Brian Matayoshi in 2011 in a defensive attack. This bear was judged to have acted normally given the circumstances. Ms. Snow gives accurate advice regarding how to avoid a bear attack. If you want the details of Yellowstone's bear attacks told in vivid detail, Snow's book is the place to go."—**Stephen Herrero, author of** *Bear Attacks: Their Causes and Avoidance*

"Kathleen Snow's book reads like a series of crime scene reports, only they are not crimes. She uses careful and vivid detail to describe, incident by incident, 146 years of harrowing encounters between grizzly bears and humans in Yellowstone National Park, with a recap of earlier incidents dating back to 1870. These stories, usually told in the words of the people involved, are a non-judgmental but stark reminder of why we need to respect an animal that rightfully symbolizes the wildness in wilderness."—**David Knibb, author of** *Grizzly Wars, The Public Fight over the Great Bear*

"Kathleen Snow has done an outstanding job in putting together the details of many Yellowstone bear-human confrontations from numerous sources. She weaves the stories in both a comprehensive and compelling narrative. I have already referenced it during my lectures on bear attacks even while it has been in manuscript form. It is a must-have reference book for anyone interested in human-bear encounters."—**Steven P. French, M.D., author of "Bear Attacks" in** *Wilderness Medicine*

"Kathleen Snow has done an excellent job of chronicling the bear-human conflicts in Yellowstone with this book. She paints a picture of each event with her own prose and includes all the official transcripts detailing the events. This contrast between a writer's view of an incident and the stark forensic details of agency reports allows the reader to imagine each scene from different perspectives. It helps to soften the forensic evidence but also gives a glimpse of the stark reality that rangers and tourists have actually faced every time there is an incident. The bad news is that such incidents will probably always happen as long as we value wild bears and wilderness. The good news is that they rarely do happen, and bears in general go out of their way to avoid them."—**F. Lance Craighead, PhD, Executive Director, Craighead Institute, and author of** *Bears of the World*

"Valuable for its detailed collection of facts."—**Lee H. Whittlesey, Yellowstone Park historian and author of two books on Yellowstone**

"Kathleen Snow's exhaustive investigation into bear attacks brings home the message that Yellowstone is a wild, predator-rich ecosystem. While the details of these incidents remind us that our safety in bear country is not guaranteed, Snow provides the latest information on precautions to take to avoid a bear attack."—**Orville E. Bach, Jr., Yellowstone seasonal ranger and author of four books on Yellowstone**

# TAKEN BY BEAR
## IN YELLOWSTONE

More than a Century of Harrowing Encounters
between Grizzlies and Humans

### KATHLEEN SNOW

Guilford, Connecticut

An imprint of Rowman & Littlefield

Distributed by NATIONAL BOOK NETWORK

Copyright © 2016 by Kathleen Snow

British Library Cataloguing in Publication Information Available

**Library of Congress Cataloging-in-Publication Data is available on file.**

ISBN 978-1-4930-1771-3
ISBN 978-1-4930-2548-0 (e-book)

♾™ The paper used in this publication meets the minimum requirements of American National Standard for Information Sciences—Permanence of Paper for Printed Library Materials, ANSI/NISO Z39.48-1992.

*In memory of my husband*
*Francis X. Schumacher III*
*who loved Yellowstone*

# CONTENTS

# THE HOW AND WHY OF TAKEN BY BEAR IN YELLOWSTONE NATIONAL PARK

The most accurate way to learn about 146 years of bear-human encounters is to hear from those who were there: the victims as well as the rangers charged with finding and rescuing them—not in remembrance only, decades later, but in the moment and on the scene.

Here, told by those involved, is the first history of all grizzly-caused human fatalities inside park boundaries since Yellowstone's founding in 1872, and all known fatalities up to six miles outside of the park. I also included the most significant grizzly-caused injuries, as well as a chapter on black bears, with encounters dating back to 1870. I chose to exclude all but one of the many hunting-related grizzly-caused injuries adjacent to the park. For greatest accuracy, I chose to go to the original government sources (and not depend on others' interpretations). Events of the time, related by those at that time, are contained in the National Park Service archives and were made available to me through Freedom of Information Act (FOIA) requests honored by park headquarters employees. Each Yellowstone Park bear incident noted within this book has a Case Incident Record identified by number. Each of these records includes all related reports (sometimes handwritten), photographs, and documents. I used National Park Service photos, maps, and diagrams; ranger reports; victim and witness interviews; communications between rangers and Park Dispatch; and Board of Inquiry conclusions as primary sources.

I wish to thank Yellowstone superintendent Dan Wenk for his generous transparency in releasing to the public the Case Incident Records of the two 2011 fatalities within the park, along with the Investigation Team Reports of those fatalities (compiled by a panel of federal and state agencies, including Yellowstone Park). Wenk also released to the public the Investigation Team Reports of the two 2010 fatalities, which occurred within six miles of the park.

The remaining Yellowstone Park Case Incident Records have not been released publicly and were made available to me through FOIA requests. For their kind assistance I wish to thank former superintendent Suzanne Lewis, the park's FOIA coordinator, Ms. Kerrie Evans, and the park's bear management supervisor, Mr. Kerry A. Gunther, who has the incredibly complex task of protecting people from bears and bears from people in Yellowstone.

Any errors or omissions are my own.

# AUTHOR'S NOTE: TEN YEARS, THIRTY MILES FROM A DEATH IN YELLOWSTONE

In 1984 Brigitta Fredenhagen, a young Swiss woman camping alone in Yellowstone National Park's backcountry, was attacked by a grizzly bear while in her tent, killed, and partially consumed.

In 1974 I too was a young woman camping alone in Yellowstone's backcountry, not far from Brigitta's campsite as a bird flies. I survived, obviously. But when in 1984 I read of Brigitta's tragedy, I got out my old map of Yellowstone. The topological greens and browns blurred.

Brigitta and I had camped ten years and just thirty miles apart. And I had camped in a high-risk zone: beside the Mary Mountain Trail to Hayden Valley, where the garbage of Trout Creek Dump had drawn generations of grizzlies. In 1974 the dump had only been closed for three years. Once habituated, the bears kept coming, hungry now. And as a hitchhiker, I never received the pamphlets about how to camp in bear country as I entered the park. I knew I had been lucky, alone in the backcountry of Yellowstone. Perhaps a woman feels alone and vulnerable in a way a man may not. I had much to learn.

It was this need to learn which drew me to this book, about the subsequent and previous visitor experiences in Yellowstone, and about the wild innocence of its bears.

# PART I—2015, 2011, AND 2010: FIVE BEAR-CAUSED FATALITIES, TWO MAULINGS

2015—Day Hiker Killed in Park

2011—Two Day Hikers Killed in Park

2010—Day Hiker and Car Camper Killed Near Park, Two Mauled

# VICTIMS—HUMAN AND BEAR: LANCE CROSBY

*"It [a grizzly sow's attack] just goes on and on, it just seemed like an eternity.*
*And you just feel helpless."*
—TERRY EVERARD, BEAR ATTACK SURVIVOR[1]

*Author's Note:* As this book went to press, original government sources as used in succeeding chapters were not yet available. Yellowstone Superintendent Dan Wenk plans to release the *Federal Investigative Team Report–Crosby 2015* to the public in December 2015, including ranger reports and possible causative factors. Readers may go to kathleensnowbooks .com for a link to the report and to read this chapter's update.

## FATALITY—2015

*National Park Service—Yellowstone*

*Case Incident Record Number: to be released in Federal Investigative Team Report-Crosby 2015*

*Location: Less than half a mile from the Grand Loop Road between Lake Village and Fishing Bridge; atop Elephant Back Mountain Ridge half a mile from the Elephant Back Mountain Loop Trail*

*Date/Time: Thursday, August 6, 2015, time to be released in upcoming report. Body discovered Friday afternoon, August 7*

Among the creatures walking, crawling, or flying across Yellowstone National Park, he was just another being on the move, Lance Crosby might have thought. That sixth day of August 2015, a Thursday, Lance's off-trail progress caused other beings unseen by him to react to his human scent, sounds, and sight. One that reacted was a grizzly bear mother with two cubs born earlier that year. But she did not do anything unnatural, just unusual.

In Yellowstone both bears and humans have been occasional victims of each other. Both species are at the top of their respective food chains. The proportion of victims is very lopsided, however. It is mostly bears that have died (they are sometimes hit by vehicles or euthanized for behavior dangerous or costly to humans).

The air was fresh and cool that Thursday, August 6. Lance probably found the sun a pleasure as it warmed him. The Elephant Back Mountain ridge where he walked was flanked by lodgepole pines at least three hundred years old. The ridge top was not a trail but open and easy to walk nonetheless and popular with other park employees like himself. Park investigators later found "rock cairns, fire rings, and carved initials," on the ridge, said Yellowstone's Bear Management Supervisor Kerry Gunther in a telephone interview on October 26, 2015. "This is not remote wilderness," Gunther added. "Most use of this off-trail ridge area is made by local people who live there, who are out walking for exercise or exploring. The site of the attack is less than a half mile from the Grand Loop Road, and one mile from the nearest house."

As Lance walked the ridge, he must have been startled to see a grizzly bear with cubs. Or perhaps she was startled first. Was the grizzly mother defensive, curious, or predatory? Until the Investigative Report's analysis is completed, the circumstances remain unknown. This bear, according to Mr. Gunther's email of October 27, "was a new bear that had never been captured before. It had no known history as being involved in any other conflicts. It weighed 259.3 pounds (digital scale weight) and had 21.3 percent body fat, which is good for a female nursing two cubs for that time of year. Based on tooth wear she was fifteen-plus years old. One cub weighed 53.5 lbs. and the other cub weighed 41.3 lbs."

Lance was sixty-three, with a wife and two children. Since he both worked and lived in Yellowstone, he might have thought of this area so close to where he lived—a mountain ridge heavily used by other employees—as his backyard. On his way up to the ridge Lance may have paused at an off-trail overlook where he could view what early explorers called "the inland ocean"—Yellowstone Lake. This spectacular view has brought many visitors to Lake Village, where human development has transformed nature. Here stands Lake Hotel (resembling a southern plantation house painted pale yellow with white columns), the rustic Lake Lodge Cabins, plus restaurants, parking lots, and Medcor's Urgent Care Clinic.

Lance did not return from his walk the next morning. Lance's coworkers at Medcor, which staffs three clinics in Yellowstone, were expecting him as he was known to be conscientious and punctual. He was a registered nurse with a Master's in Science, and for five years he had worked Medcor's five-month season at Lake Village. Visitors' various emergencies—from drinking Calamine lotion instead of Kaopectate to heart attacks—kept Lance busy. In 2015, as Lance probably knew, there had been more people visiting and more bear sightings than ever before. "Yellowstone is on track to top four million visitors this year," reported park spokesperson Amy Bartlett. The magazine *Yellowstone Science* has stated, "Yellowstone and Grand Teton national parks have become the prime grizzly bear viewing destinations in the lower 48 states, contributing millions of dollars to local economies annually."[2] Bear management supervisor Gunther said that he had received 1,731 written reports of park bear sightings (both grizzly and black), as of September 30.

On August 7, that Friday morning, Lance's coworkers reported him missing. A park ranger discovered his body that afternoon, partially consumed and cached. A typical bear food cache is composed of a pile of dirt and vegetation that covers the food remains.

The grizzly that killed Lance, which was not tagged, was known to some photographers and park workers as "Blaze." After Lance's death, a wildlife photographer named Keith R. Crowley posted the following comments on the Internet:

The female Grizzly bear known by many park visitors as "Blaze" walks along the bank of the Yellowstone River in Yellowstone National Park, May 6th, 2014.
PHOTO © KENNETH R. CROWLEY

Last May, many fellow wildlife photographers and I watched another park employee have a close call with Blaze and her cubs. The employee was simply out for a run along the shore of Yellowstone Lake near the Lake Hotel.

He ran down the lakeshore, turned inland on a trail and ran to within 50 or 60 yards of Blaze and her then tiny cubs, all hidden in the chest high sage brush.

When the runner realized that there was a large group of photographers a couple hundred yards off and looking his way, he knew something was up. He wisely slowed to a walk and backed out of the area.

Blaze undoubtedly knew he was there, and she did nothing. Wild animals are unpredictable.

I approached the runner minutes later and asked if he knew there was a Grizzly sow with cubs in the area. He didn't. Until he saw us, he had no idea how close he was to potential disaster. He couldn't have. Had he not seen us, he told me, he would have continued his run right into her and the cubs.

That situation could have easily become another Yellowstone bear attack, and if it had, I doubt anyone present would have blamed the runner. Lots of park employees and park visitors run, jog, and stroll through that area each and every day. It's a well-established route that doesn't look like "Bear Country," and I have yet to see anyone carrying bear spray there.

Had Blaze attacked this young man, it would have just been a case of being in the wrong place at the wrong time. The internet would have blown up with accusations and insults, but those of us who spend much time there know how easily things can go wrong for no particular reason.

So, why is everyone so quick to blame Mr. Crosby?

Because this whole thing sucks and people need someone to blame, justly or not.[3]

Could the outcome for Lance Crosby have been changed? For this and all other human-bear encounters, Yellowstone publishes its own guidelines for safer travel in Grizzly Country (see Chapter 24). The guidelines emphasize the importance of carrying bear repellent spray and being ready to fire it, since a bear attack can occur in seconds.

But what should be done when a bear attack has occurred, and a grizzly has killed and consumed a person? In a Yellowstone news release about the Crosby attack, Park Superintendent Dan Wenk presented his and other park managers' view as such: "Our decision takes into account the facts of the case, the goals of the bear management program and the long-term viability of the grizzly bear population as a whole, rather than an individual bear." The decision was to euthanize the mother grizzly and place the cubs in a wildlife institution.

The park's actions were met with criticism. Yellowstone received hundreds of calls and letters denouncing the decision. One such person was Susan Roy of Florence, Montana, whose comments appeared in the *Missoulian* on September 6, 2015. "I'm sick of hearing," she wrote, "about people coming into contact with bears out in their natural setting, and then the bears are put to death because 'they tasted human flesh' or whatever reason the rangers can come up. News flash, folks—bears eat anything!"

Kerry Gunther provided a more in-depth explanation of the park's position on the matter. The decision, he said, "was not for punishment or retribution, but to prevent these bears from killing and consuming other park visitors or residents in the future. Bears are a very intelligent, highly adaptable species that quickly learn to exploit new food resources, especially foods that are easily obtained and contain concentrated sources of fat and protein. Since bears readily learn new foods and remember the locations, circumstances, and seasons foods are available, the possibility of these bears preying on people in the future could not be ruled out." He also pointed out since many recreationalists on National Park and Forest Service lands are allowed to carry firearms, "they may be more likely to use firearms instead of bear spray during surprise encounters, resulting in many more bear deaths in actual and perceived defense-of-life situations in the future." Lastly, Gunther contended that "society's willingness to protect grizzly bears and the large tracts of habitat necessary for grizzly bears to survive might be significantly diminished if bears were allowed to regularly kill and consume people."

Such decisions are among "the challenges of managing habituated grizzlies in national parks," as *Yellowstone Science* points out. All of Yellowstone's grizzlies could be considered to be habituated because they exist in a park that hosts close to four million visitors per year. This challenge is called co-existence, described in the more than a century of bear-human encounters detailed in the following chapters.

## 2

# EVERY HIKER'S WORST NIGHTMARE: BRIAN MATAYOSHI

*Until a grizzly charges you, you will never know if you are a "Stander"*
*or a "Runner."*
—STEVEN P. FRENCH, MD, CO-DIRECTOR WITH MARILYNN G.
FRENCH OF THE YELLOWSTONE GRIZZLY FOUNDATION

## FATALITY—2011

*National Park Service—Yellowstone*

*Case Incident Record Number: 112587*

*Location: South-Rim Canyon area, 1½ miles east of Wapiti Lake*
*Trailhead*

*Date/Time: Wednesday, July 6, 2011, 10:50 a.m.*

Brian Matayoshi did nothing out of the ordinary the day he died; perhaps that is what's most disturbing. He was a conscientious person enjoying a walk with his wife in Yellowstone Park. As for the grizzly bear that he encountered, it did not do anything out of the ordinary either.

The sun shone through light clouds that Wednesday, July 6, 2011, about 8:30 a.m., warming the air toward 75 degrees. Brian, a large man with black hair and black sunglasses, settled into the pleasant feel of his light-brown ankle-high shoes upon the soft dirt of the trail. He was fifty-eight, a retired pharmacist from California, enjoying Yellowstone for the fourth time with his wife, Marylyn, beside him. They had just left their vehicle at the Chittenden Bridge parking area, off the Grand Loop Road near the South Rim of the "Grand Canyon of the Yellowstone," as it is named. This was not remote wilderness. The parking area was paved and held other vehicles, and beyond it were picnic tables and restrooms.

Brian was not expecting to see a bear. Though while visiting California's Mammoth Lakes he and his wife observed black bears from trails and from roads, on their previous visits to Yellowstone they had never seen a bear, black or grizzly. The path Brian chose to follow that July morning began at the Wapiti Lake Trailhead and picnic area, where the trails receive intensive human use, both for day hikes and overnight camping. It was the second time that day Brian made a choice that may have inadvertently determined his fate. The first choice was to seek out a dirt trail.

———

After interviewing Brian's wife on July 7, 2011, Les Seago, assistant special agent in charge of the National Park Service Investigative Services Branch, wrote in his report that "Marylyn [Matayoshi] described she had wanted to hike the [canyon's] north rim, but Brian insisted they hike along a non-paved trail."[4] Unless otherwise attributed, what happened next is recorded in Yellowstone Park's Case Incident Record Number 112587, which contains accounts told by those involved, including rangers and witnesses in the moment and on the scene.[5] Superintendent Dan Wenk released this internal investigative file to the public, along with the federal and state multi-agency panel's *Investigation Team Report dated September 9, 2011.*[6] (Wenk made sure the family received a private preview before public release. All personal information was withheld.)

Marylyn Matayoshi described to Agent Seago how she and her husband departed Grand Teton National Park on July 5, drove their Honda into Yellowstone through its South Entrance, and checked in at site E151 at Grant Village's car campground. Their campground receipt noted a checkout date of July 10. They spent the rest of the day walking the boardwalks of Old Faithful and touring its visitor center, where they picked up a "Canyon Area Trail Guide" for "Grand Canyon and Falls of the Yellowstone."

On July 6 at the Wapiti Lake Trailhead, Brian's choice of trails to the south was restricted. Due to the presence of a wolf den, the Howard

Eaton and Sour Creek Trails were signed off limits as a "Wildlife Protection Closure Area." Brian chose to head east on the soft dirt of the Wapiti Lake Trail. Brian was notable to witnesses interviewed later that day for wearing a white T-shirt, white knee-length shorts, and white socks. He carried a red, black, and gray daypack with a GPS unit to avoid getting lost. The trail he and Marylyn followed roughly paralleled the course of the Grand Canyon of the Yellowstone itself, below its South Rim Drive leading to Artist's Point.

Brian and his wife weren't alone. This was the extended Fourth of July weekend, and Yellowstone Park reported its greatest influx of visitors so far in 2011. The visitors were also reporting more bear sightings in the backcountry and the front country. On the Grand Loop Road, in 2010, rangers had managed 435 grizzly-bear jams alone, as vehicles stopped and people poured out to view and photograph grizzlies feeding on native plants in roadside meadows.[7] A young grizzly was caught on video trying to cross the car-covered asphalt to the green of the other side. Once it had just been black bears along the roadsides. Now visitors driving through the park were occasionally seeing grizzlies as well.

The mother grizzly that attacked Matayoshi had never been in any trouble known to park personnel. For several weeks before the incident she and her two young cubs, one blond-headed, the other dark brown, had been foraging for forbs (most wildflowers are forbs), digging for starchy roots and tubers, and excavating insects around the Wapiti Lake Trailhead and its trails. Located in the northeastern part of the vast basin that is Hayden Valley, this area lies in the center of Yellowstone Park. As the *Investigation Team Report* later indicated, she "had been photographed several times and had likely encountered many parties of hikers during this time." Perhaps she was nervous because a male bear was also frequenting the area. She was six to seven years old, weighed 249.5 pounds, and would soon become known around the world as "the Wapiti sow."

Meanwhile, on July 6, Brian and his wife turned northeast from the Wapiti Lake Trail onto a branching trail to see Clear Lake, which Bill Schneider describes in his guidebook *Hiking Yellowstone National Park* as having a "bluish color and [is] surrounded by lodgepole pine and

Douglas-fir. The trail skirts the east side of the lake to a gurgling mud pot, one of the several thermal areas along this section of the trail."[8]

After taking photographs, the Matayoshis returned west to the junction with Wapiti Lake Trail and started east again to see Ribbon Lake. The hiking was rated as "Easy" and the elevation gain as "Minimal" in Schneider's book.

But soon their morning walk would include sighting a bear.

At 10:05 a.m. they topped a knoll and encountered a fellow hiker who showed them what he had spotted—what many park visitors come from all over the world hoping to see—a wild grizzly in its world. In this case Brian saw what can be every hiker's worst nightmare: a mother grizzly with two young cubs. Fortunately, the bears were below them and about three hundred to five hundred yards south of the trail, grazing and digging in the northeast Hayden Valley's open terrain.

In Agent Seago's report, he recorded that the Matayoshis "met [name of fellow hiker withheld] after hiking along the trail. He pointed out the sow and her cubs but to Marylyn the bears seemed like [distant] boulders." The report continued:

> [Fellow hiker] gave them his binoculars to use and talked about his attempt to hike to Ribbon Lake but he had to turn around due to the mosquitoes. Marylyn said [this hiker] seemed to know about the bears and she thought he described them as this year's cubs. Marylyn described the bears being in an open grassy area and beyond the bears was sand and bison. They watched the bears for approximately 10 to 20 minutes.

At 10:15 a.m. Marylyn photographed the bears. In the *Investigation Team Report*, Photo 1 shows the large mother grizzly as something like a dark speck in the grassy basin. But if you look closely, the bear's round ears are visible and her head is facing the photographer, as if she has noticed the hikers.

While Brian and his wife were still with the hiker whose binoculars helped them see the bears, nearby a group of twenty or so visitors hoping to see the Canyon wolfpack were using binoculars and spotting scopes from the vantage point of Grizzly Overlook, a car turnout along the Grand Loop Road. They spotted the Matayoshis and the third hiker, all of whom they erroneously thought had entered the Wildlife Protection Closure Area. They informed two rangers there who had concluded a wildlife talk.

One of the rangers, Kenneth B. Conway, noted the following in his Statement Form written on July 7:

> While on duty at Grizzly Overlook . . . visitors reported to me that a group of three was off trail and could be seen through spotting scopes. The time [was] approximately 10:00–10:30 a.m. The visitors also reported seeing sow w/2 cubs in the same area. I personally could see 3 people off trail in the spotting scope.

Conway radioed for two law-enforcement rangers to investigate. (*Note:* It was later determined that none of the hikers was in the wolf closure area, and that a small section of the Wapiti Lake Trail could be seen through binoculars and spotting scopes from Grizzly Overlook.)

But meanwhile the two concerned law-enforcement rangers headed for the Wapiti Lake Trailhead and began hiking east on the same trail Brian had taken to find the three hikers.

Marylyn told Special Agent Seago that their fellow hiker "and Mr. Matayoshi discussed the fact that the bears were far away and not near the trail." So Brian and his wife said goodbye and continued eastward to Ribbon Lake, the trail leading them away from open terrain and down into timber interspersed with thermal areas, where "the mosquitoes are bad," the hiker warned them. Behind a hillside they vanished from the hiker's view. The Matayoshis "continued hiking the trail to Ribbon Lake and Marylyn said she didn't think they walked very far," reported Special Agent Seago. During his interview with Marylyn he learned that "they crossed Hot Spring creek and hiked to an unknown body of water but had to turn around because of the mosquitoes. They did not encounter any other hikers."

Only one and a half miles from their waiting vehicle, the trail crossed a thermal plain (which consists of open ground with white mineral deposits of thermal activity), and they could see through a narrow band of trees into a green meadow. Suddenly—frightened and with his adrenaline surging—Brian saw the same grizzly for the second time that day. It had its broad head down and was foraging "within 25 yards of the trail and approximately 100 yards away from their position on the trail," noted the authors of the *Investigation Team Report*.

Seago's interview with Marylyn described what happened next:

> On their hike back, Marylyn thought Brian saw the sow first and was not sure if he saw the cubs. They turned around and started hiking back towards the unknown body of water. She said she and Brian kept looking back to watch the mother bear. She saw the sow's "head pop up and I told Brian. She [the sow] started coming at us and Brian said 'run.' We were running down the trail." Marylyn heard Brian yell and she turned to see the sow "hit him." Marylyn said the cubs were running behind their mother and they were growling. She did not think the cubs were far behind their mother when Brian was attacked. Marylyn said she was running when she went behind some downed trees and she didn't know how she ended up on the ground.
>
> Marylyn described she started to get to her knees in an attempt to take her camera off of her when she saw the sow look at her and started walking towards her location. Marylyn dropped to the ground. She felt a tug on her backpack then the bear was gone. Marylyn did not hear the sow make any noise when the bear came towards her.
>
> Marylyn walked over to her husband and attempted to use a jacket as a tourniquet on Brian's leg and heard a long breath escape from Brian. Marylyn said she tried to call 911 with her cell [21 times according to her phone log] but could not get a signal. Concerned the bear could be still in the area, Marylyn started to yell for help.

Only minutes before, at about 10:50 a.m. that July 6, other park visitors nearby heard the sounds of a bear attack in progress. They heard a bear roaring and people screaming. The following excerpt is taken from approximately seven minutes of 911 tapes connected to the bear attack on July 6 (the tapes were used by park officials to establish a timeline of the attack):

*First cell-phone call to Yellowstone Communications Center from a male hiker:* "We saw a mother grizzly bear and her two cubs. We heard humans screaming just ahead of us . . . I heard a man's voice making loud, like, animal noises—it sounded like he was trying to scare the bear. And I heard a woman screaming—it sounded like she was scared."

*Yellowstone Dispatch:* ". . . We have a couple of rangers up there along the trail there and they'll take a look at it." [Dispatch then contacts the two rangers who were already on the trail.]

*Second call from a different male hiker,* who said six hikers are now gathered together (including the hiker who earlier showed Brian and Marylyn the mother grizzly with cubs), [less than] two miles from the trailhead and just past the Wrangler Trail junction.

*Caller:* "Should we try to go in and get the person out? . . . All I can hear is the lady's voice now. There was a man as well, so I'm worried that the man may be injured . . . I'm a trauma surgeon so I can actually give this person medical assistance. But only if you guys say that we should go in."

*Dispatch:* "I don't want to send you into a dangerous situation . . . Stay where you're at. If you feel like you're in a safe spot, stay there. Ranger's about halfway up the trail to you. Hang up and he's going to try and call you."

Within a half hour of the incident, the two rangers previously summoned by the wolf watchers at Grizzly Overlook arrived at the scene, and did everything they could to find Brian and assist him if possible, and to help and comfort Marylyn.

To investigate the charges of three hikers in the wolf closure area, Park Ranger David Page had begun a patrol of the Wapiti Lake Trail along with Ranger Brian Speeg.

After Yellowstone Dispatch radioed the two rangers about the 911 calls of persons screaming, they accelerated their pace. Ranger Page wrote:

I was able to connect a cell phone call to [hiker name withheld] as I crested a knoll at about 1105 hours [11:05 a.m.]. I could see [the hiker] and a party of other hikers below me and continued to them. I briefly interviewed the group (six hikers) and they reported hearing two people, a male and a female, yelling and screaming and what sounded like a bear roaring. The yelling had continued a short time and then there was silence. After a while they could hear a lone female yelling for help.

A quick plan was made with the group. Four of the hikers had come upon the scene after the initial yells and none carried bear spray. [Name withheld] and a male solo hiker carried bear spray and had heard the initial yells. [Name withheld] also identified himself as a trauma surgeon. [Name withheld] reported seeing a sow with two cubs earlier in the area and just to the east of our location. He also reported that a couple had hiked in that direction earlier. The plan was for the group of four (who are from Britain) to stay together lower in the clearing and for [the other two] to follow Ranger Speeg and I as we continued east on the trail.

While formulating the plan I could hear faint yells from the east. As we approached the next meadow I could see a lone figure on the far side of the meadow. I called out to the lone person as we approached. I first asked if they were hurt and the person, later identified as M. Matayoshi, answered that she was not. As she answered, her head was down. I asked if there was a bear in the area and [she] answered no, not anymore. I asked if someone else was hurt and she said yes, that her husband was dead. I reached her shortly after this. I identified myself to her and she told me her name. She told me that her husband had been attacked by a bear and that he had been killed. She said that he was down the trail. She said that they had seen the bear in the meadow and that they tried to hike back east, but the bear had noticed them. She said the bear began to run at them from the meadow and that they started to run down the trail and yell. She said the bear caught them and hit her husband, B. Matayoshi. She said it was a bear with two cubs. She said that she had dropped behind a downed tree and that the bear had lifted her up by her day pack, dropped the pack, and then left the area. M. Matayoshi had dried blood on her clothing and body. M. Matayoshi had no apparent injuries and she denied being injured.

After the brief interview with M. Matayoshi, I asked [the two accompanying hikers] if they would stay with M. Matayoshi in the open meadow. They answered that they would stay with her. Ranger Speeg and I continued east on the trail from the meadow, crossing an open dry thermal area and entering a lodgepole tree area. Ranger Speeg carried bear spray out and in a ready position and I [had my] handgun out in a scanning position. After traveling a distance through the treed area, we came upon a body lying on the south side of the trail. The body, later identified as B. Matayoshi, appeared lifeless and had been partially covered with a shirt and light jacket. Ranger Speeg checked B. Matayoshi for signs of life. Breathing and carotid pulse were absent and his pupils were fixed and dilated. I continued to scan the area and no bears were seen. I then confirmed Ranger Speeg's observations and also observed early signs of lividity [post-mortem blood settling] at [11:30 a.m.].

Ranger Speeg and I then returned to the meadow and re-contacted M. Matayoshi. I confirmed with her that her husband had died. I told her that we did not see the bears in the area. I explained that our plan was to support her and to guard B. Matayoshi and remove him from the area. I also explained that we would have to investigate the scene and that this would take time. I asked her if she would like to hike out. She said no and that she would like to stay with B. Matayoshi. I told her we would accommodate her wishes as best we could.

To help Marylyn Matayoshi, two "family liaison" rangers headed in her direction. In her Supplementary Case/Incident Record dated July 10, Ranger Patti Murphee noted that "I was parked at the Wapiti Trailhead when dispatch notified Canyon patrol of a 911 call reporting someone yelling for help." As she and her colleague Ranger Derene headed into the area of the incident with medical equipment, they were charged by a large bull bison. They used their pepper spray, and the bison turned 90 degrees and ran until out of sight.

Murphee described what happened when they reached Marylyn Matayoshi:

I introduced myself to Marylyn and began my role as family liaison. I offered to hike out with her but she insisted on staying with her husband. We briefed Marylyn on what was going to happen and that it would be hours for the process to occur. She requested that she be able to go back and see Brian. Ranger Page and I explained what she would see but she still wanted to see her husband before anyone else arrived. Marylyn was taken to her husband and stayed there until the coroner team arrived and was then moved out of sight of the body. Marylyn and I were airlifted out to the helispot at the Canyon Corrals. We then went to the Canyon backcountry office and from there to Jackson Hole [Wyoming]. The communication center arranged for a room at the Antler Hotel for the evening of July 6.

I was with Marylyn from my arrival on scene until her family arrived in Jackson Hole at [10:00 p.m.]. The Matayoshis' vehicle was driven to the hotel in Jackson by Ranger [Mark] Plona.

Earlier that afternoon, Ranger J. Dennis Lojko acted as the coroner who pronounced death at the scene. In his Supplementary Case/Incident Record, he described what he found as follows:

Matayoshi was covered with a silver space blanket and two dark colored jackets . . . I pronounced Matayoshi dead at 1350 hours [1:50 p.m.] . . . There were visible injuries to the head, right arm, and right leg . . . The wound closest to the knee was approximately 6.5 cm long and 2.5 cm wide. It was located over the femoral artery . . .

Matayoshi was packaged in a body bag, carried on a stretcher approximately ¼ of a mile to a helicopter, and flown to the Canyon Government Corrals. He was then transported by ambulance to the Canyon Fire Cache [reexamined with two other medical personnel and consultation held with a forensic pathologist] . . . and then transported to Jackson, WY, by [name withheld] of Valley Mortuary . . .

On the State of Wyoming death certificate the manner of death was accidental. The cause of death was penetrating and blunt force trauma due to a grizzly bear mauling.

According to the *Investigation Team Report,* "The adult female grizzly impacted Mr. Matayoshi, knocking him down and subsequently biting and clawing him." The report's conclusion pointed out additional findings:

> He had no injuries on his hands or arms indicating that he was not facing the bear when he was attacked. He expired from his injuries at the location where he was first impacted by the bear. His most serious injuries included a bite puncture to his femoral artery causing extensive blood loss and a large contusion on his forehead extending into the scalp. No part of Mr. Matayoshi was consumed by the bear.

Nick Herring, Yellowstone's deputy chief ranger of operations, told Wyoming's *Cody Enterprise* on July 11 that "We don't have any indication the victim struggled."

On July 6, Yellowstone issued a news release in which Park Superintendent Dan Wenk said, "It is extremely unfortunate that this couple's trip into the Yellowstone backcountry has ended in tragedy. Our heart goes out to the family and friends of the victim as they work to cope with their loss."

A July 7 news release concluded that, after an initial investigation, "the sow grizzly acted in a purely defensive nature to protect her cubs. This female bear is not tagged or collared, and does not apparently have a history of aggression or human interaction. Typically, the National Park Service does not trap, relocate, or kill a bear under those circumstances. A Board of Review which will include interagency experts will be convened to review the incident." [The experts' findings are included in the *Investigation Team Report dated September 9, 2011.*]

———————

The news media in the U.S. and worldwide soon weighed in. When she spoke to Michael Sheridan of the *New York Daily News* on July 7, Diane Shober, director of the Wyoming Travel and Tourism agency, said, "This is a wild and natural park. At the same time, the likelihood of this happening again is small."

The *Daily News* described the attack in human terms [author's emphasis]: "A mama grizzly *brutally* attacked a husband and wife . . ." "The wife, who was also *assaulted* by the bear . . ."

"Bear Taunts Wife" headlined InternationalBusinessNews.com on July 7, implying that after killing her husband, the bear "teased" the wife by picking her up by her backpack, rendering her helpless, and only then releasing her.

CNN Wire, however, was more responsible in its reporting of the attack on July 7. "The grizzly bear that attacked and killed a man in Yellowstone National Park acted in defense, park officials said on Thursday, adding that they have no plans to kill the bear. . . . 'This bear is not marked in any way and has never been involved in another conflict in the area' said wildlife biologist Kerry Gunther [Yellowstone's Bear Management Supervisor]. 'We average only one injury per year and they are not usually repeat occurrences by the same bear . . . it was not predatory and we see no reason to take action against the bear.'"

Gunther told CNN Wire that bear hair and DNA samples were collected from the scene so that if another incident occurs they would know if the same bear was involved. He also told the *Cody Enterprise* on July 11 that "the age of the sow is unknown and she has never been trapped, tagged or otherwise 'handled by humans.' Her cubs are 'young of the year,' probably born in January or February."

Gunther sent the hair to a laboratory for DNA testing. (See the connection of this hair to the fatality noted in Chapter 3.) Ranger Lojko described this hair and other evidence in the *Investigation Team Report* as follows: "A pair of black Nike sunglasses [Brian's] that were broken during the mauling was collected off the trail as evidence. The sunglasses had 6–8 bear hairs on the bridge of the nose. The bear hair was collected and given to Kerry Gunther, Yellowstone National Park bear biologist."

Park spokeswoman Linda Miller told Reuters.com on July 7 that "Yellowstone rangers believe they know which grizzly was involved in the fatal mauling of a man who encountered the bears while walking the Wapiti Lake trail on Wednesday morning with his wife." She also indicated that the bear, as a mother of young cubs, had behaved defensively.

"Rangers were still keeping tabs on the sow and her cubs, Park Spokesman Al Nash said," the *Cody Enterprise*'s Mark Heinz reported on July 11. "The bears' last known location was inside a 10-square mile zone that was closed after the attack."

—◦—

Other people associated with the park including visitors seemed to side with the bear. Rick Hoeninghausen of Xanterra, which manages Yellowstone's accommodations including its campgrounds, told the *Billings Gazette* on July 8, "It's rare and tragic that this happened. We feel bad for the loss to the family." He said "the concessionaire had received only one or two cancellations for campground reservations after the incident. With more than 650,000 people visiting the park this month," Hoeninghausen called the cancellations "inconsequential."

Elizabeth Hoffman, a tourist from California, told the Associated Press on July 9 that she didn't think the bear should be hunted. "This is bear country. . . . It's got babies. If someone came after a human mother, I don't think that we'd take her from her children."

Park visitor Barbara Waxman, on her first trip to Yellowstone, disagreed with the park closure of the Grand Canyon's South Rim area due to the bear incident. "It's like not being able to see the Mona Lisa," the Baltimore resident told the *Missoulian* on July 10. "If they gave me the option, I'd go to that point [Artist's Point] in a second, grizzly bear or no."

—◦—

The Matayoshis' reaction to the bear encounter, and the bear's reaction to them are analyzed below in Ranger David Page's report dated August 3, 2011.

Matayoshis' reaction to the bear encounter:
- The Matayoshis' first sighting of the bear on their return hike was at a distance of approximately 100 yards and was through a thin line of trees in front of the meadow.
- Their first reaction was to hike back to cover and it did not appear that the bear was aware of their presence.

- M. Matayoshi stated that she wished they had not looked over their shoulders multiple times because that may have slowed them and the bear may have noticed that movement.
- The Matayoshis ran when the bear began to charge.
- The Matayoshis did shout and yell when the bear charged.
- B. Matayoshi remained standing just prior to the bear making contact.
- M. Matayoshi dropped to the ground, covered her neck, and remained silent.

The bear's reaction and known history:
- The bear began its charge from approximately 100 yards. Tracks from the bear and cubs were observed [in] thermal soil and crossed the trail at an angle to the north.
- At about 80 yards from the meadow the tracks suggested that the bear turned and may have stopped. There are bear cub tracks that lead to this area. This spot also is at a higher elevation than the trail and offers a slightly improved view down the trail corridor.
- The bear did not appear to continue to maul B. Matayoshi after he became quiet. This is based on M. Matayoshi's statement there was a period of quiet when she looked up and the bear was looking at her.
- The bear inspected M. Matayoshi and did not maul her.
- The bear and cubs departed the area rapidly.
- There is no evidence that the cubs participated in the mauling.
- There is no documented history of this bear having previous encounter with humans.
- A male grizzly bear (boar) had been sighted in the Wapiti Lake Trailhead area during the previous days. It is unknown if the sow had any encounter with the boar.

In the final section of the *Investigation Team Report dated September 9, 2011*, the authors concluded:

Although the bear initially saw the Matayoshis at an estimated 100 yards while it was adjacent to or perhaps within forest cover, the mother bear responded to the surprise encounter by proceeding toward them rather than fleeing. Adjacent forested areas would have allowed the bear to quickly disappear from their view if she had moved into the forest. What possibly began as an attempt by the bear to assess the Matayoshis' activities became a sustained pursuit of them as they fled running and yelling on the trail. In addition to the unfortunate circumstance of being at the wrong place at the wrong time, a possible contributing factor to the chase that ensued was that the victims ran from the bear while screaming and yelling. The bears left the area rapidly after the chase and attack. The bear was unmarked, had never been captured, and had no known history of conflicts with humans. The bear was not removed after the attack due to the fact that the encounter was characteristic of a surprise encounter.

Could the outcome have been changed? The importance of carrying and if necessary deploying bear pepper spray, as advised by the Park Service, is illustrated below.

Just four days before Brian Matayoshi's fatality, another couple on a hike had encountered a grizzly mother with a cub. This couple had driven into the Trout Creek turnout and informed a park ranger about their proposed off-trail hike into western Hayden Valley. This large, mostly open valley is considered prime grizzly habitat. Park personnel do not recommend that anyone hike off trail. However, this couple had hiked in Yellowstone for the past twenty years and felt comfortable doing so. Their first objective that day was to hike to Sulphur Mountain, which stands half a mile from the Grand Loop Road. Once there the couple spent forty-five minutes exploring Sulphur Springs, the nearby thermal area.

The weather was sunny and warm, and to take a break, they headed for the shade on top of a hill. What happened next occurred in only thirty to forty-five seconds, as estimated by the husband, and the outcome may have turned out differently had they not been carrying bear pepper spray.

The husband's account first appeared on July 2, 2011, on the Counter Assault.com pepper spray website and was picked up on July 13 by NBC Montana.com.

I heard that distinct "crack" of timber as I straightened back up. I immediately looked to my left, and here comes a Grizzly sow, at full speed 20 yards from me, running through the timber. I immediately started yelling as loud as I could at the bear as I reached for my bear spray. . . .

[Then he saw the cub.] [I] knew at this point it was going to be a life or death situation. Once the cub reached her, she bolted straight for me at full speed. I sent a burst of spray at her hoping this would make her run off, but no luck. At this point I had made the decision to stand my ground and take her on. There was nothing left to do. She closed to within 3 yards of me, right where I had laid my hiking poles down, when I adjusted for the wind direction, and then unloaded the whole can of spray on her.

Fortunately, at this second burst of pepper spray the grizzly mother and her cub turned and ran off, and the shaken couple drove to Canyon Village and informed three rangers that same day.

For this and all human-bear encounters, see also Chapter 24 "The Latest on Safer Travel in Bear Country," which includes Yellowstone Park's own guidelines.

# 3

# FOUND DEAD ALONG TRAIL: JOHN WALLACE

*It's hideously perverse that someone who loved nature so much would come to such an untimely end at the hand of nature.*
—JOHN WALLACE'S EMPLOYER

## FATALITY—2011

*National Park Service—Yellowstone*

*Case Incident Record Number: 114555*

*Location: Hayden Valley: Mary Mountain Trail, 5 miles west of Grand Loop Road*

*Date/Time: Thursday, August 25, 2011, approx. 3:00 p.m. +/- twelve hours*

*Discovered: Friday, August 26, 2011, approx. 6:00 p.m.*

The site where John Wallace was found on August 26, 2011—between Canyon Junction and Mud Volcano five miles west of the park's busy Grand Loop Road—turned out to be 8.1 miles from the site of Brian Matayoshi's death earlier that summer (see Chapter 2).

"Being in Yellowstone is like being in heaven," John told his wife by voicemail on August 24, 2011. Relatives of John reported his message on ABCNews.com, August 30. John, fifty-nine, from Michigan's Upper Peninsula, had arrived by himself to visit Yellowstone, and pitched his tent in the Canyon Village car campground. A very experienced outdoorsman, backcountry camper, and hiker who had previously hiked in Yellowstone a number of times, he stepped from his dark-green Jeep SUV that early morning of Thursday, August 25, to enjoy a day hike in Hayden Valley.

To look out as John did, over the vast basin that is Hayden Valley, its grasslands and sagebrush with patches of trees, is to peer across Yellowstone's geology, history, and many of the controversial subjects involving the coexistence of grizzly bears and humans. One of these is Hayden Valley's former Trout Creek Dump, closed in 1971.[9] A 1959 US Geological Survey quadrangle map shows the service road roughly paralleling Trout Creek, leading to a gravel pit and the large open-pit dump. Many of what are now considered "classic" Yellowstone grizzly photographs were taken at this dump, showing bears fattened into butterballs by preying upon garbage. The use of open-pit dumps in Yellowstone and the surrounding towns ended almost half a century ago, and today grizzlies forage and eat native foods including plants, elk, cutthroat trout, moths, berries, the high-protein seeds of whitebark pinecones, and bison.

That morning of August 25 at the Mary Mountain Trailhead, visitors reported seeing dozens of bison. The bison were swimming across the river near the Grand Loop Road turnout, where other cars besides John's were parked. But some bison were not seen: They were now two carcasses lying ahead near the hiking route John had chosen—the Mary Mountain Trail. In the interagency *Investigation Team Report dated January 30, 2012*, released to the public by Yellowstone superintendent Dan Wenk, it is recorded that "At the time of the fatality, there were 2 bison carcasses close to the trail, one of which was 330 meters southeast of the fatality site that had 16 bear beds around it [beds of trampled grass or dug dirt which bears rest upon during the hotter parts of the day]. The other bison carcass was near the trail about 1.5 miles away from the fatality site. Nine different grizzly bears, including a female with 2 cubs-of-the-year, were observed by a day-hiker on August 22 at this second bison carcass, 3 days before Mr. Wallace was killed [*note*: but not reported to park officials by the day-hiker until *after* the fatality]."[10]

What happened next is told by those involved in Yellowstone Park's Case Incident Record Number 114555,[11] an internal investigative file that Superintendent Dan Wenk released to the public, along with the *Investigation Team Report* noted above.[12]

———

At the Grand Loop Road turnout where John was parked, another visitor (later interviewed by Ranger Stephen Roper) reported that "she observed a 4x4 SUV parked in a pullout near the river at the Mary Mountain Trailhead." Roper's report in the Case Incident Record Number 114555 tells her description of the vehicle's driver, John Wallace:

> [Name withheld] stated she took note of a white male between 50 and 60 years old with light colored hair because he did not appear to be interested in the dozens of bison that were swimming across the river at this location. [She] stated there were several cars on the road and numerous people watching the bison, but this male did not even look at them. [She] stated she observed this male put on a lot of sunscreen and then a brightly colored back pack (possibly yellow) before walking west across the road into the Hayden Valley toward the Mary Mountain Trail.
>
> [Name withheld] stated she observed this male to be focused, methodical and purposeful as he tied his boots, prepared his day pack and went into and then out of his vehicle several times before departing. [She] stated it took the male at least 10 minutes to prepare and she believed he was going on a day hike since he had a smaller pack and no camping items with him that she could see (no tent or sleeping bag). [She] stated she did not observe this male to be carrying bear spray.

On this bright morning with light clouds, at about 7:30 a.m., John Wallace concentrated on his plans for his hike down into Hayden Valley. He wore a brown T-shirt with lettering that read "Reduce Your Paw Print. Planet Dog." Into his orange daypack he put a lidded plastic container of bread and cheese wrapped in a plastic bag, two drinking bottles, a protein bar, and among other items a brown denim long-sleeved shirt and a green rain-style jacket. He captured the start of his hike by taking photographs with his digital camera. The good weather he was enjoying would not last. By that afternoon heavy rain and hail would set in.

John's employer described him "as a quiet, easygoing man and conscientious worker who loved . . . the outdoors, particularly national parks," reported the Associated Press in a story that was also picked up by Forbes .com August 29. John's employer also said that:

> Wallace asked for vacation time to camp and hike at Yellowstone where he had visited before. "The possibility of encountering grizzlies never even came into our conversations," [the employer] said. Wallace treasured animals, including his two Australian shepherd dogs, one of which died last year. "It's hideously perverse to think that someone who loved nature so much would come to such an untimely end at the hand of nature. To me that sounded so unfair. It's shocking."

Exactly what happened that Thursday to John is only partially known. There were no witnesses. This is what we do know. John began his hike at the eastern end of the Mary Mountain Trail, which crosses the park twenty-one miles southwest and terminates at Old Faithful's Lower Geyser Basin. Behind him in his parked 1999 Jeep he left his Yellowstone pass to the Canyon campground, Site D82 registered through August 31, and in the rear passenger compartment his guidebook, *Hiking Yellowstone National Park* by Bill Schneider, marked by John at the Hayden Valley entry.

"The trail starts right at the north edge of Hayden Valley," writes Schneider, "and follows Alum Creek (which has several interesting thermal features along its course) along the forest edge on the northernmost reaches of the wildlife-rich valley." His description continues:

> The trail stays in the open all the way. The first few miles of the trail are not well defined, but you can follow orange markers to stay on course. For some reason, this trail stays marshy all summer, so be prepared for wet feet.
>
> Also, bison use this area extensively, so the bison trails are often better than the official trail. Watch for orange markers, and if you don't see them, you're probably off the main trail.
>
> This is prime grizzly habitat, which is why you can't stay overnight in this area. It's also why you should be especially careful not to disturb

or get too close to any bear you see—both for your safety and the bear's welfare.[13]

The day before, on August 24, John was looking forward to hiking once more in Yellowstone, the park he loved. Perhaps he had not yet chosen to hike the Mary Mountain Trail. From Cody, Wyoming, he drove toward the park's East Entrance on Route 20/16/14/North Fork Highway, passing Forest Service signs about recreating in "grizzly country." One sign at Mile Marker 23 Forest Service Outpost at the side of the road, about what to do in an encounter with a grizzly, stated the following:

### PLAY DEAD
AS A LAST RESORT, ASSUME THE
CANNONBALL POSITION, COVERING
YOUR NECK AND HEAD WITH
YOUR HANDS AND ARMS.

At Canyon Village Campsite D82, under the trees, John used his outdoor experience to create a neat and almost homelike environment. He pitched his simple, small green tent, placing inside his sleeping bag and a pillow with a flower-covered case. When he left the next morning, August 25, for his hike in Hayden Valley, his forty-five-foot clothesline held his drying purple towel. He had hung up the orange seat cushion for his striped chair. His white rope hammock awaited his return, slung between two trees.

Five days before, a Mary Mountain Trail hiker (with two partners) on August 20 reported seeing bears. He gave a written statement to rangers about seeing both tracks and a grizzly. "During our morning ascent to Mary Lake, frequent bear tracks (appeared to be grizzly) were seen in the dust of the trail," the Old Faithful maintenance employee said. The hiker pointed out additional observations:

These tracks were of various sizes (mid to large) and appeared to be fresher than the boot prints on the trail. The tracks indicated that multiple bears were using the trail although not necessarily at the same time. Along Nez Perce Ck the tracks were quite large and very fresh; closer to Mary Lake during the steeper ascent the tracks appeared older and somewhat smaller. All tracks appeared to be traveling east. No fresh bear scat was observed.

Approximately 5–6 (?) miles from the Alum Ck trailhead [Mary Mountain Trailhead] we saw 3 hikers ½ mile to the east of us looking at something below the trail. We were on a knoll and we watched through binoculars as the 2 men and 1 woman walked 10–15 yds below the trail and examined something on the ground. We couldn't tell at that distance what they were bent over and examining. After several minutes they slowly returned to the trail and began walking east. As we approached the site they had been examining, we saw an old bison carcass where they had been standing—head, horns, hide and bones were clearly identifiable. No meat was visible.

I scanned the area including the ridge above and saw nothing unusual. We did not leave the trail to examine the bison carcass more closely. About ¼ to ⅓ mile E we stopped on another rise above Violet Ck. We saw the 3 eastbound hikers meet with 2 westbound hikers and stop and talk for 4–5 minutes—pointing west up the trail. The groups separated and continued hiking. We did not see the 3 again. The two hikers passed by us as we snacked while sitting on the rise/ridge and asked us if we had seen "the bear." We said, "No," but we explained to them about the carcass. They indicated they were hoping to see "the bear."

After 20 minutes, we began descending to Violet Ck. Halfway down the slope, a mid-sized grizzly (200–250 lbs) came running out of the cleft of Violet Ck to our west and ran up the far slope angling away from us at an initial distance of 120–140 yds. He/she was running hard with his/her mouth open and tongue visible and kept looking back down the slope the way it had come. Its rump was very wet as if it had been lying in the creek. It didn't acknowledge our presence and only slowed as it crested the ridge. We did not see the bear again on our hike . . .

At approx 1730 [5:30 p.m.] we reached the Alum Ck trailhead. As we prepared to depart, the previously mentioned 2 hikers (a man and a woman) reached the trailhead. When asked if they had seen the bear, they responded by saying they had seen "the cub" but not "the sow." In response to their query, we said we had seen a lone grizzly which definitely was not "a cub." They hurried on to their vehicle. At the trailhead we noted a "Bear Frequenting Area—8/18/2011" sign posted at the trailhead sign.

On Thursday, August 25, at about 7:30 a.m., eager to start his Mary Mountain Trail day hike, John locked his Jeep Cherokee, leaving in its rear a manila envelope containing a 2008 Yellowstone trip planner and a 2009 Yellowstone backcountry campsite reservation. He probably felt the security of the other vehicles parked there, and the prospect of other hikers on the trail. John adjusted his blue brimmed hat and began walking west on the trail, wearing a red bandanna, T-shirt, light brown cargo-style long pants, and ankle-high laced leather hiking boots, size 10. He carried a whistle. The temperature was 49 degrees, rising to 71 degrees by 12:56 p.m. Sometime that morning, before the afternoon rain and hail, John probably stopped along the trail for something to eat and a drink of water. Perhaps he sat down. The trail through dry grasslands and sagebrush had entered a more timbered area. Downed and dead trees were strewn like matchsticks. The scene was located in a depression. A log lay across the soft dirt of the path.

John unbuckled the belt of his daypack, took the pack off, and unzipped the main compartment, removing a protein bar and one of his two bottles of liquid. He unwrapped and ate half of the protein bar (leaving the other half neatly wrapped), and drank one of his two bottles of liquid, plus a quarter of the remaining bottle.

Then he was attacked by a grizzly, from the front or from behind. Was it a defensive attack—a mother defending her cubs from perceived harm? Was it a predatory attack—simply a hungry, opportunistic bear? John fought for his life, at one point facing the bear and receiving self-defense wounds on his hands and arms. "The majority of his wounds appear to have been postmortem, however," wrote Thomas L. Bennett, MD, of the company Forensic Medicine and Pathology in Billings, Montana. The bear prevailed. The bear (or other bears) fed upon his remains.

John was not the only hiker to choose Hayden Valley's Mary Mountain Trail. The next day, in the early afternoon of Friday, August 26, two other hikers found a tragedy—a human body, which they thought might be male because of the hiking boots' size. The two hikers, struggling to process their harrowing find, left immediately to inform Ranger Mark Plona at the Canyon District backcountry office.

"Myself and my father," the young woman hiker's handwritten statement noted, "left on the Mary Mountain Trail (canyon side) at approximately 7:30 a.m. on Friday, August 26." Her words, signed by her at 1:40 p.m., are contained in Yellowstone Park's Case Incident Record Number 114555. The young woman described what she and her father found:

> We hiked, took some photos, and our plan was to continue to Mary Lake. I was hiking a little in front of my dad. The trail started to go into some timber and there were 5 or 6 birds circling above the area. I climbed over a log that was across the trail and that is when I saw a plastic clear drink container with some pink liquid in it and what I thought was a backpack. As I got closer I realized there were boots sticking out, legs, and the upper part of the body was covered with dirt.
>
> I ran back towards my dad and told him and then he came down to look as well. We stayed away from the body about 5–10 yards. We then turned around and left quickly because we were afraid there might be a bear in the area. We returned to the trailhead and drove to the Ranger station. We arrived back at the trailhead at 1:20 p.m.[14]

Ranger Plona also interviewed this hiker's father at 2:10 p.m., and Plona's report states that the father "believed, from his past hunting experience, a bear was feeding on the body and had covered the remains with dirt." Plona's interview of the father, who expressed concern for his and other hikers' safety, continued:

> He feared for his safety and immediately left the area. While hiking back to the trailhead, about 3–4 miles from the trailhead, [name

withheld] saw two male and 1 female individual[s]. He observed the individuals from several hundred yards with binoculars. The individuals were naked and "having a good time." [Name withheld] did not make contact with the group. About 10 minutes from the trailhead [name withheld] contacted two French males. He advised the two they had found a body far down the trail. The two males said they were only hiking a short distance and continued west on the trail.

Another hiker's statement (also from August 26) noted a "buffalo carcass just past Mary Mt. trailhead in Hayden Valley." This hiker wrote that he had:

—arrived 6:30 a.m. approx 7:40 fog lifted; watched nearly black large grizzly on carcass for about ten min. Grizzly left carcass went up ridge, came back to carcass for approx ten min—ran up over low ridge then appeared above Mary Mt. trail went up into trees about 8:15. Watched carcass rest of day didn't appear by 5:21 p.m.

Also on August 26 other hikers' statements noted the large number of hikers on the trail. "There were 4 people in front of me and 2 behind," one interviewed hiker wrote.

The search for the reported body began at about 2 p.m. Ranger David Page, team leader, wrote in his Supplementary Case/Incident Record that he implemented trail and area closures. "After retrieving personal and investigative equipment, I met with the helitack crew at the Canyon helicopter landing zone . . . The decision had been made to insert a search team by helicopter to the reported location on the Mary Mountain Trail to locate the body." Page noted that:

On the flight in the trail was checked from the air and two passes along the trail were completed . . . The aerial search did not produce any sightings of the body, bears, or hikers in the area. We located a meadow that we believed would be west of the described approximate location of the body and landed. A second flight dropped off the remaining search team members at this location.

The team began hiking the trail towards the east, searching the trail and areas to both sides of the trail. Occasionally boot tracks and bear tracks could be seen in the trail . . . ([Snake District Ranger Matthew] Vandzura later attributed the boot tracks to be those of the deceased). After traveling about 2 miles, the team observed at a distance what appeared to be the limbs of a human body lying in the trail. This observation was confirmed as a deceased human body utilizing binoculars at about 1800 hours [6:00 p.m.]. Injuries and trauma to the body were visible that would not be conducive to life.

Upon arrival, the investigative team saw that the body was surrounded by grizzly bear tracks, five bear scats (droppings), and some bear hair. Ranger Page wrote that "The body was approached from the west to avoid the trail and possibly disturbing remaining tracks." Page described what he found:

The body was lying with the feet clad in leather hiking boots, in the trail. The upper body was extending away from the trail to the west at roughly a 90 degree angle. The upper body, starting near the waist and extending to the head, was covered in dirt and some plant material that had been dug from around the upper body. One arm was partially visible.

A short distance from the head of the body, a red handkerchief and a brimmed hat was located. Beyond those two items, a whistle and small piece of plaid cloth was found. The small piece of cloth was later identified as a piece of the victim's boxer type underwear. All of the items contained what appeared to be blood on them . . .

Small logs (small diameter tops of fallen trees) that lay between these items and the body had what appeared to be blood stains on them as if something had had contact with the logs. There appeared to be at least one partial bloody/dirt soiled bear track on one of the downed trees. Although a partial track, it appeared it may have been from a medium sized bear. Two areas of pushed down vegetation extended from the body in a westerly direction. The pushed down vegetation appeared to be a path made recently by animals that came and went from the body.

Ranger Roper wrote, "The on-scene team stated the male body they located matched basic features of a picture of Wallace's Michigan driver's license (provided by Yellowstone National Park Dispatch). The on-scene team also informed me that they located a key to a Jeep [found registered to John Wallace] in the pants pocket on the body. The on-scene team informed me that the body had been partially consumed by an animal and partially buried (by approximately two inches of dirt)."

Ranger Page's report noted that he returned on August 27 "to the fatality site via helicopter with a team to continue the investigation and to begin a bear trapping operation." Page described what the team did next:

After being flown to the site, we first checked on a bison carcass that was observed during a flight into the scene. This carcass was about 330 yards from the fatality site. The carcass was of a large bull bison and was estimated to be about a week old. There were obvious signs that the carcass had been fed on by grizzly bears. There were numerous bear scats, tracks and bear paths in the area of the carcass.

There was a bear path in a draw that led back to the fatality site. Along the bear path, a day bed was discovered in a grassy area below the fatality site. This day bed was approximately 120 feet from the fatality site . . .

Upon arriving at the fatality site, small bear tracks were observed on the trail and on the disturbed soil where the body was discovered. The track size was of a cub of the year. *These tracks were new from the time that we left the area the night before, at about [8:00 p.m.]* [emphasis added].

[Special Agent Justin] Ivary positioned a remote camera with the fatality site and trail in view. I collected bags of dirt [with bear hairs in it] from where the body was discovered.

The fatality site, and area surrounding the site, was searched for additional bear hair evidence...

[Bear Management Biological Technician Travis] Wyman discovered what appeared to be a recent day bed digging on the edge of lodgepole pine regrowth. The day bed was in line from the bear path and was about 220 feet from the fatality site. Near this day bed site, Wyman discovered additional blood soiled tracks on downed logs. These tracks appeared to be from a medium sized bear and a cub of the year due to their size.

These blood soiled tracks would have occurred from the time of the fatality to the time we arrived at the site at [6:03 p.m.] on August 26, 2011. After [8:00 p.m.] on August 26, 2011, with the removal of the body, there would not have been any blood, fluids, or rain to mix with soil to allow the described tracks to be left on the downed logs.

The autopsy confirmed that the bear had killed Wallace, as detailed in the *Investigation Team Report*. "Mr. Wallace received multiple puncture wounds over the upper right part of his body including bite marks on his right hand plus scratches, lacerations, and punctures of his right forearm, consistent with self defense and facing a bear. Superficial scratches also occurred on the upper left part of his body." The *Report*'s analysis contained the following:

On his back, he had several bite marks that appeared to be opposing pairs of canines. The canine bite marks on his back were wide apart, suggesting that the bear's jaw was wide open when they were inflicted. The wounds on his back were also accompanied by bruising indicating they were inflicted when Mr. Wallace was still alive. There were significant injuries to the left side of his head, including a laceration at the left corner of his mouth and a severe laceration to his left ear. There were areas of significant bruising on his upper left arm and over his right hand and forearm. This bruising is indicative of wounds suffered while Mr. Wallace was still alive. The conclusion of the Coroner was that Mr. Wallace died of severe injuries received during an attack by a large animal, with death from blood loss (exsanguination).

The Park Service closed to hikers "The Mary Mountain Trail, the Cygnet Lakes Trail, and the section of the Hayden Valley west of the Grand Loop Road," an August 27 Yellowstone news release noted. "An aerial search of the area Saturday morning failed to turn up any current bear activity."

"The next step is to see if we can find a bear, and then determine if that is the bear involved in the incident," Yellowstone spokesman Nash was quoted on SeattleTimes.com August 29. "That might help them figure out why this attack happened at all."

A Yellowstone news release on September 2 reported that "Daily reconnaissance flights over the area have resulted in very few bear sightings." The news release also described bear trapping efforts:

> The three bear traps previously set out in the area have been moved to different locations, and five additional traps have been deployed in an attempt to capture grizzlies in the area. Results of DNA tests of hair samples taken from the attack site and from any bears that may be captured in the area will aid the ongoing investigation into the circumstances surrounding this fatal attack.
>
> Sunny skies with daytime highs in the 60s could result in a large number of visitors to Yellowstone during the Labor Day holiday weekend.

Superintendent Wenk told the Associated Press that "'We know of no witnesses' to the attack." Wenk's additional comments were picked up on Forbes.com August 29 as follows:

> "We think we provide visitors with pretty good knowledge and techniques to keep them safe in the backcountry. Unfortunately, in this case it didn't happen that way." Rangers set traps and plan to kill the bear if they can establish through analysis that it was the one that attacked Wallace, Wenk said. There was too little information to know if it was a defensive attack or not, so Wenk said, "We're going to err on the safe side of caution since we'll never really know the circumstances in this case."

The "Matayoshi" bear, with two cubs of the year, that killed Brian less than two months earlier, in what was determined to be a defensive attack, had been allowed to continue its life in the backcountry. "Park spokesman Al Nash said it was possible the same bear also was behind the latest attack," MLive.com (Michigan News) reported on August 29, "and that DNA from hair samples collected at both scenes would be compared to make that determination." The Michigan News report quoted Nash further:

"We will be able to definitively answer that question once DNA tests on the hair samples have been completed," Nash said. The July mauling [Matayoshi] occurred near the start of the Wapiti Lake Trail, several miles from the scene of last week's attack, a distance within the roaming range for grizzlies, he said. The female grizzly from July's incident is not the only suspect.

———

Mr. Kerry Gunther, Yellowstone's bear management specialist, analyzed the bear's behavior August 30 for BozemanDailyChronicle.com. "It's just one of those rare things where we'll probably never know why." Gunther considered other contributory factors:

He [Gunther] said it's been a good food year for bears. And besides these fatalities [Matayoshi and Wallace], there has been only one other conflict in the park involving bears. In that case, a grizzly was euthanized for aggressively approaching and charging a man [see details of that grizzly below].

Gunther did note, however, that more people are living in and moving to the Greater Yellowstone ecosystem, and park visitation has been increasing. Plus, over the past decade, the bear population has increased by about 4 to 7 percent. Currently, about 600 bears live in the ecosystem.

"More bears, more people, more interactions," Gunther said.

In an effort to curtail bear/people interactions, a Yellowstone news release on August 2 reported that "An aggressive, habituated

grizzly bear conditioned to human foods was captured and euthanized by Yellowstone National Park staff on Monday morning,
August 1."

For the past three years, the 4 year old, 258-pound male bear had been
unsuccessfully hazed at least 25 times from the Lake Village, Bridge Bay
Campground and Fishing Bridge developments. On July 30, the bear
aggressively approached and then charged at a man sitting along the
Storm Point Trail on the north edge of Yellowstone Lake.

The man threw his pack at the bear, which stopped the bear's
charge. However, the bear then tore into the man's pack and ate the
food inside. The sub-adult male bear was healthy and had 14.8% body
fat, normal for this time of year.

Due to the bear's history of associating people with food, repeated
visitation to developed areas within the park and numerous unsuccessful hazing attempts, the bear posed a threat to the safety of park visitors.
Efforts to relocate food-conditioned bears have also generally proven
unsuccessful because the bears simply return to the areas from which
they were removed.

Reuters reported on the same grizzly as above on August 2. "Rangers
have taken the rare step of capturing and killing a grizzly bear deemed
a threat to human safety in Yellowstone National Park after the bruin
menaced a hiker without any apparent provocation." The report noted
further that:

The confrontation marked the latest in a string of incidents in which
the same grizzly showed aggression toward people in its search for food
at campgrounds and other developed areas in the park, officials said in
a statement.

"This grizzly crossed that threshold and made direct and aggressive contact," Yellowstone spokesman Dan Hottle said. "It will never
be known if it was coming after (the man) for the food or to take him
down."

On September 2, the Associated Press reported that Yellowstone officials had "captured a grizzly bear Friday near the site where hikers found the body of a Michigan man who died from a bear attack last week." The JacksonHoleNewsandGuide.com picked up the report, which further stated that:

> Officials will likely test a hair sample from the 25-year-old, 420 pound male grizzly to determine whether it killed John Wallace, 59, of Michigan, officials said.
>
> "We did capture a bear this morning," Yellowstone spokesman Al Nash said by phone Friday from Mammoth. "It is the only bear we have captured."
>
> Officials will fit the bear with a tracking collar and release the animal pending results of the test, Nash said. If hair samples match those found near Wallace's body, Yellowstone officials previously said they will track down and kill the bear.
>
> "We're going to collar it so that it can be located again," Nash said.
>
> The grizzly was released because the park does not have a good facility to hold bears for an extended period, Nash said.
>
> Nash wasn't sure how close the capture site was to the location where Wallace's body was found. Two hikers found his body Aug. 26 about five miles up the Mary Mountain trail north of Old Faithful.
>
> "Certainly he's in the area because we set up the traps in that area, specifically," Nash said. "We recognize that bears can travel a great distance."
>
> There were no eyewitnesses to the attack in the Hayden Valley area, and a DNA match alone won't be conclusive in determining whether a bear was responsible for the attack or happened upon the body afterward, Nash said. That means additional evidence would be needed to make that conclusion, which may be difficult.
>
> "The Hayden Valley is an area that is typically known for a significant amount of bear activity, so we may never capture and positively identify the bear or a bear that was involved in this incident," Nash said of the section of the park. "We're working with the hope that we can ultimately resolve this attack, but we may not be able to do so."

The Mary Mountain trail and others nearby in the Hayden Valley section remained closed Friday as Yellowstone officials prepared for a busy Labor Day weekend filled with holiday visitors. With the exception of the bear that was trapped Friday, wildlife managers have had little luck capturing bruins in the area. Yellowstone National Park and Interagency Grizzly Bear Study Team personnel now have eight grizzly traps in place along and around the Mary Mountain trail.

By September 27, Yellowstone Park officials had captured seven grizzly bears near the Hayden Valley scene of John Wallace's death. "But none had been linked definitively to the attack, park officials said Tuesday," reported the Associated Press. The AP further reported that:

> Superintendent Dan Wenk said DNA analysis continues on evidence gathered from the park's Hayden Valley. . . . a park official indicated Tuesday that efforts to unravel what happened have been complicated by the poor condition of some of the DNA samples collected.
>
> Those samples yielded inconclusive laboratory results that could make it more difficult to connect the attack to an individual bear, said Yellowstone bear biologist Kerry Gunther . . .
>
> Yet so far there's no evidence to say any of those bears at the scene were among the grizzlies captured in the month since the attack.
>
> The seven captured bears were fitted with radio collars and released so they can be recaptured later if necessary.
>
> "All we have is pieces. We just don't know how they fit yet," Wenk said. "There are multiple bears in the area of Mr. Wallace. We'll never know which bears caused the fatality, which bears were investigating the activities, which bears were there two days before or two days after."
>
> On Tuesday Wenk said park officials will consider killing any bears that can be linked to the scene and also have a history of run-ins with humans.
>
> "We're going to have to make all those decisions individually," he added.

On October 3rd Yellowstone announced the capture of a grizzly bear sow and two cubs:

[The bears] have been linked to the scene of the recent mauling death of a hiker in the Hayden Valley. Results from genetic (DNA) tests obtained from bear hair and scat samples indicate the 250-pound, 6 to 7 year-old sow was present at the scene on the Mary Mountain Trail where hiker John Wallace's body was recovered August 26.

This is the same bear that was responsible for the death of hiker Brian Matayoshi during a defensive attack on July 6 on the Wapiti Lake Trail. Rangers and an Interagency Board of Review determined Mr. Matayoshi's death near Canyon Village on the Wapiti Lake Trail resulted from a defensive attack by the sow protecting her cubs. "We will more than likely never know what role, if any, the sow might have played in Mr. Wallace's death due to the lack of witnesses and presence of multiple bears at the incident scene," said Superintendent Dan Wenk. "But because the DNA analysis indicates the same bear was present at the scene of both fatalities, we euthanized her to eliminate the risk of future interaction with Yellowstone visitors and staff."

The adult female grizzly was captured on Wednesday, September 28. Her two cubs were captured Thursday, September 29 and placed in the Grizzly & Wolf Discovery Center in West Yellowstone, Montana. The sow was euthanized on Sunday morning, October 2. Grizzly bear cubs typically adapt successfully to captivity. Adult bears that are removed from the wild do not adapt well to captivity.

Capture operations, reconnaissance flights, and DNA sampling and testing will continue through the fall. Any future management decisions will be made on a case by case basis for any additional bears that are captured and provide a DNA link to the scene.

Park Superintendent Wenk, at a luncheon appearance, addressed the Cody, Wyoming, Chamber of Commerce on the continuing dilemma. "We'll never know which one of the bears killed him," Wenk remarked. A Reuters report on the address was picked up by wnep.com:

But Yellowstone officials decided that the bear [the Wapiti Trail bear that killed Brian Matayoshi] should be destroyed because of its involvement in a second fatal encounter with a park visitor.

"The bear management program in Yellowstone National Park is far too important than to risk it on one bear," Wenk said.

◦—◦

The *Investigation Team Report* concluded that the Matayoshi and Wallace attacks were probably linked, but stopped short of confirming that the Matayoshi bear was definitely culpable in both attacks:

> The presence of bloody adult and cub tracks suggests that the adult female that killed Mr. Matayoshi and one of her offspring were likely involved in the consumption of Mr. Wallace's body. However, there could have been other bears involved in the consumption of Mr. Wallace . . .
>
> There is no evidence indicating what bear(s) killed Mr. Wallace, nor is there evidence to determine if the attack was defensive or predatory in nature.

◦—◦

What is the nature of grizzlies? Filmmaker Werner Herzog believes that the "nature" of nature itself should be understood as less than kindly to people. "What I'm trying to say in the [*Grizzly Man*] film, through [Tim] Treadwell [who with his girlfriend lived among and was killed by Alaskan brown bears] is about this New Age romanticization of wild nature," Herzog told *Outside* magazine in August 2011. "When you look out at the universe at night and you look at the stars, you know that there is a huge mess out there, and it's very hostile and very inhospitable. There is no such thing as the harmony of the earth."[15]

◦—◦

John's employer told BozemanDailyChronicle.com that the library where "Wallace was a maintenance worker has a small staff of 15." The news website further learned the employer and staff's plans to honor John:

They plan to close the library the day his services are held and are considering the possibility of a memorial garden for Wallace. The garden would go between the building and the waterway [where boats leave for nearby Isle Royale National Park, a place Wallace loved].

"I can't believe it's actually happened," [the employer] said. "Somebody I talked to last week is not here and won't be here again."

# 4

# FINAL EXPEDITION
# (6 MILES FROM PARK): ERWIN EVERT

*The bear had a "Large open wound behind [its] left shoulder, 3" x 2"
at widest. Numerous scars and fight wounds on head and neck. Both
old and new."*
—ACCOUNT OF BEAR TRAPPING IN INVESTIGATION TEAM REPORT

## FATALITY—2010

*National Park Service—Yellowstone*

*US Forest Service Law Enforcement Agents*

*Wyoming Game and Fish Department, Park County Wyoming Sheriff's
Office*

*Location: 6 miles outside Yellowstone Park's East Entrance*

*Shoshone National Forest, Kitty Creek Trail #756*

*Date/Time: Thursday, June 17, 2010. Body first found 6:15 p.m.*

*Recovery completed approximately 12:18 a.m. on 6/18/10*

Three paths intersected in a tragic accident of time and place near Yellowstone Park's East Entrance on June 17, 2010: those of a hiker, a field crew from a multi-agency bear study team, and a large male grizzly—trapped, anesthetized, and then set free. A fatality of this sort had never before occurred.

About 12:45 p.m. that day, Erwin Evert, age seventy, set out to hike on his long-beloved, at least three times weekly, expedition. He adjusted his prescription glasses and pulled a blue knit hat snugly down around his ears (the weather was windy and spitting snow). He wore jeans and a blue sweater, black socks and tennis shoes, and a black jacket. He tucked a gold-color pocket watch in his front pants pocket.

Erwin left the private cabin his family owned in the Kitty Creek Drainage, six miles east of Yellowstone, to trek the Shoshone National Forest's Kitty Creek Trail. Erwin, a botanist who was now white-bearded but wiry and strong, had dedicated his life to studying nature, and was familiar with bears and their terrain, which here was wooded and brushy.

The trail, #756, which he had hiked since 1971, roughly parallels the contour of a small part of Yellowstone's eastern boundary, beginning just south of Highway 14-16-20, which connects Cody, Wyoming, with Yellowstone's East Entrance. Rated "moderate" in difficulty, Kitty Creek Trail is ten miles long with elevation from seven thousand to ten thousand feet. From its start at Buffalo Bill Camp, the trail winds south/southwest following the Kitty Creek Drainage, enters the Washakie Wilderness, passes 10,964-feet-tall Howell Mountain, and ends at Flora Lake.

Erwin had a hiking circuit he typically followed, starting out on Kitty Creek Trail and then traveling up on a ridge above, or reversing the order and returning home via the trail to the cabin where his wife awaited him.

What happened next, unless otherwise attributed, is recounted by personnel from Yellowstone National Park, the US Forest Service Law Enforcement Agency, Interagency Grizzly Bear Study Team, Park County Wyoming Sheriff's Office, and Wyoming Game and Fish Department. The *Investigation Team Report dated July 16, 2010* (*Fatality of Erwin Evert from a bear attack in Kitty Creek on the Shoshone National Forest on June 17, 2010*) has been released to the public.[16]

Earlier that day, about 7:30 in the morning, a two-person field crew from the Interagency Grizzly Bear Study Team (IGBST) rode horses and led two pack animals toward their three previously set bear-trapping sites at Kitty Creek. The IGBST is an interdisciplinary group of scientists and biologists who monitor and research grizzlies in the Greater Yellowstone

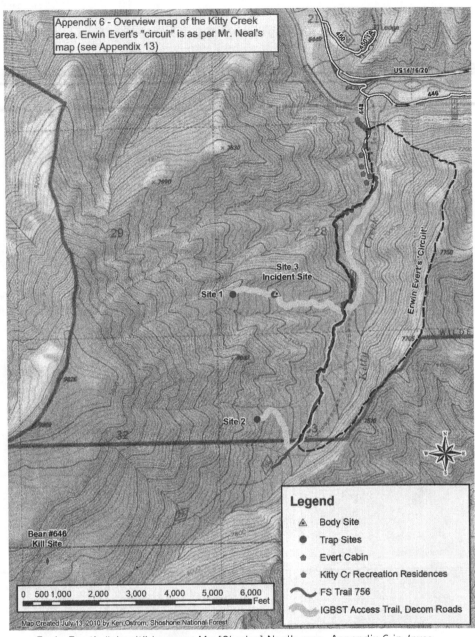

Erwin Evert's "circuit" is as per Mr. [Charles] Neal's map. Appendix 6 in *Investigation Team Report dated July 16, 2010*. MAP CREATED JULY 13, 2010, BY KEN OSTROM, SHOSHONE NATIONAL FOREST

Ecosystem. At the first site checked, the field crew found a large male grizzly with its right front foot successfully caught in a "pail set" (a snare secured to a large tree and baited with an animal carcass). They darted and anesthetized the bear for study purposes, including taking biological samples, followed by fastening a radio collar for the first time around its neck. The bear (designated #646) and its movements near and possibly through Yellowstone Park could now be monitored by tracking radio signals.

"The darting and handling were uneventful," the field crew wrote in the *Investigation Team Report*:

> However 2 [additional] hard doses [of anesthetic] were given [due] to the length of time for tooth pulling and some recovery signs that were earlier than expected . . .
>
> It was decided . . . that after handling this particular male grizzly bear that the site would be pulled and shut down. This meant all snares pulled and trapping closures signs would be removed . . .
>
> At 12:30 p.m. I decided that we needed to leave the male grizzly (646) since we had another snare [site] still that needed to be checked. At this point 646 had his head up and was swaying side to side but would respond to stimulus such as clapping or yelling.
>
> On our ride down to connect to the main trail to our upper site we encountered no human activity.

The large male grizzly bear, which was frequenting the area, had never been caught before, and so had a history unknown to humans. Its color, "blond tips on back, blonde girth band, dark legs" was noted in the *Investigation Team Report*.

Beginning at 9:06 a.m. the grizzly was rendered immobile with an injection of Telazol and examined, estimated to be eight to ten years old, and was weighed on a sling scale (425 pounds). Tooth, blood, hair and tissue samples were taken, upper lip tattooed, and ear tags placed both right and left. Tooth examination showed "upper and lower right canines intact. Upper left canine broken & rounded (old). Bottom left canine broken & rounded, old chip hanging by gum, removed. Incisors flattened across, upper show heavier wear. Molars have moderate flattening."

Also noted was a "Large open wound behind left shoulder, 3" x 2" at widest. Numerous scars and fight wounds on head and neck. Both old and new. Treated with Furacin [antibiotic]." At 10:48 a.m. the bear was observed coming out of its immobilized state and described as: "Licking, blinking." At 12:30 p.m. the bear was "holding head up, swaying. We left the site."

The field crew had injected the grizzly with Telazol to render it immobile and permit its examination. Commonly used in bear captures, Telazol is "a combination of two drugs, a dissociative anesthetic drug, tiletamine, with the benzodiazepine anxiolytic [anti-anxiety] drug Zolazepam" for muscle relaxation.

What did this drug combination cause the bear to experience? Obviously this is unknown, but it is hoped the bear experienced nothing. In humans, the veterinary anesthetic tiletamine is known to off-label users seeking a recreational "high." This human "high" is described by one user on the Internet's Erowid Experience Vaults as "more like an Angel Dust high than it is to the Ketamine experience." (Ketamine is also a veterinary anesthetic.) Tiletamine's effects in humans are reported to include a variety of unpleasant experiences, testified to by this first-person account on the Internet:

> The recovery phase lasted what seemed like forever. My head felt like it had gone through a cheese grater and then placed on a merry go round. Motion sickness, headache, general dysphoric malaise that just kept going and going. The peak/plateau seemed to last for perhaps 1.5–2 hours and the recovery/re-entry phase lasted some 4–6 hours or more.

The following Monday, June 21, Chris Servheen, grizzly bear recovery coordinator for the US Fish and Wildlife Service (who has a doctorate in wildlife biology), told a caller from NationalParksTraveler.com that the bear probably was not reacting to having been drugged. "It doesn't wake up really mad. We've heard repeated references to human emotions with bears here. They don't hold a grudge, they're not mad or anything like that. They wake up. It's a dissociative drug, so they're completely unconscious during the time that they're handled, and they wake up and they're not in any kind of retribution state of mind or any such thing. That's all human emotions."

*Note:* Chapter 10 of this book details the 1983 human fatality by a grizzly that had been captured nineteen times and drugged twelve times using Sernylan (street name "angel dust"). Afterwards there was some speculation that the drug may have made the bear more aggressive. Telazol is considered a much safer drug for bears than Sernylan.

Regardless, when the field crew packed up to leave the large male grizzly, it was stirring. "Spontaneous blinking will occur," notes an International Veterinary Information Service paper. "Bears will show chewing movements and paw movements. They will start to lift their head, and may attempt to raise themselves with their forelimbs."

The field crew's report noted that the bear was recovering well from the Telazol.

Wind conditions at the capture site that day were persistently blustery, and could have contributed to the bear not easily hearing or smelling an approaching hiker like Erwin Evert.

At about 1:15 p.m. the field crew moved on and found a second trapped grizzly at the Upper Kitty Creek site, a previously trapped four-year-old female. The *Investigation Team Report* included the team's explanation of what happened next: "At 5:10 p.m. we left GB628 [grizzly bear 628] standing and we proceeded down the trail and back to the truck. Upon leaving this upper site we pulled the closure sign and shut that site down."

⌐⌐

The hiker, Erwin Evert, was very knowledgeable about the Yellowstone area, an outdoorsman whose summer base-camp since 1971 was his family's cabin among thirteen others in the Kitty Creek Drainage. His Yellowstone-area botanical research spanned thirty-nine years, during which he shared more than forty-eight thousand of his plant specimens with the Chicago-area Morton Arboretum, and Laramie, Wyoming's Rocky Mountain Herbarium. Further, he had just achieved a career-long goal: his 750-page book, *Vascular Plants of the Greater Yellowstone Area*, complete with maps, was published.

"That morning Evert informed his daughter [by phone] of his plans to hike up the ridge east of the creek and then return via the Kitty Creek Trail," Evert's friend and *Grizzlies in the Mist* author Chuck Neal told the Wyoming newspaper *Powell Tribune*, as reported online on June 22, 2010. According to Scott Steward, sheriff of Park County, Wyoming, "Evert's outing was supposed to last about three hours."

"He put on his stocking cap," his wife, Yolanda Evert, told the *Chicago Sun-Times* "because we'd had snow flurries that morning, and it was a little windy. He said he'd be home in a couple of hours. I didn't even give him a hug or anything because it was such a usual trip."

By 4:00 p.m., "his wife said she headed out toward the hiking trail head and called out, 'Erwin! Erwin!' An hour later he still hadn't returned—which was odd, his wife said—because he knew she had prepared an early dinner for him. 'I had deviled eggs, marinated beef and rice ready for him,' Evert said. 'I had the table all set.'"

"At approximately 6:15 p.m.," the field crew noted in their account, "while riding past the lower cabins (closer to the NF River & Hwy) [North Fork of Shoshone] we were contacted by an elderly woman (Mrs. Evert). She asked if we had seen anyone hiking while we were riding."

We said no that we had not. Mrs. Evert said that her husband had gone hiking and was gone longer than expected. Mrs. Evert then asked what we were doing and I responded grizzly bear research and that we were conducting capture efforts in Kitty Creek. After telling this to Mrs. Evert she mentioned that her husband (Mr. Erwin Evert) had told her that he had seen our trapping closure signs before. Upon hearing this from Mrs. Evert I thought it would be prudent to ride back up the trail to our Middle Creek site [the large male grizzly] to see if I could see any sign of Mr. Evert . . .

I entered our site (yelling considerably) and found Mr. Evert laying next to a tree. I yelled his name "Erwin" a great deal and observed no response. I then trotted Lemon [the horse] around the site to make sure a bear was not in the immediate area. Upon doing this I rode within a few feet of Mr. Evert and could see that he was face down and the back of his head had considerable trauma . . . I could not see any breathing and one leg looked to be damaged as well. I did not dismount off of Lemon to check Mr. Evert for vital signs. I was concerned for my own safety and was very convinced that Mr. Evert was indeed dead. I then trotted Lemon back to the first cabin and asked the man there to call 911.

Erwin's wife, Yolanda, is further quoted in her *Chicago Sun-Times* interview (reported online June 25, 2010). "About 15 minutes later, the horseman who'd galloped away, returned. He came down, and I said, 'Did you find him? Did you find him?' Yolanda Evert recalled. He said, 'I found him. He's gone.' And then he put his head down and got off of his horse. I almost fell apart."

Erwin's daughter, [name withheld] of Louisiana, was interviewed by the *Billings Gazette*. "I've been on every single mountain in that whole drainage with my father. We've encountered bears many, many, many, many, many times," she said. "We've never had any incidents with bears, because none of the bears have been harassed, or baited or snared."

The daughter, the *Gazette* continued, "said her father had seen a sign days before the attack warning people about the research. But the Park County sheriff's deputy who recovered Evert's body reported seeing no signs in the area, Sheriff Scott Steward said. [The daughter] said she believes researchers removed the signs as they left, leading her father to believe there was no longer any danger."

The Park County Sheriff's Office responded to the report of a grizzly attack. Their June 18th press release summarized their findings:

At this time, it appears that members of IGBST had captured the bear and tranquilized the bear for research purposes, put a radio collar on the bear and then packed up their equipment and left the area. At some point Evert wandered into the capture area where he was fatally wounded. Evert was not armed nor was he carrying bear spray.

On June 18th The U.S. Forest Service issued a closure order for the Kitty Creek Drainage. Game Wardens, U.S. Fish and Wildlife Agents and USFS Law Enforcement Agents are diligently searching the area for the bear with the aid of an electronic tracking device. If located the fate of the bear will be determined by U.S. Fish and Wildlife Agents.

The death of Erwin Evert was the first fatal attack at a site where researchers had trapped and released a bear. However, "We have a lot of bears and we have several attacks a year," Park County sheriff Scott Steward told "Mail Foreign Service" (dailymail.co.uk) on June 21, 2010. "I recommend [people] always be prepared in many different aspects whether it be survival gear and in this particular instance, personal protection."

On Friday, June 18, wildlife officials used a radio tracking device to locate the bear, homing in on the signals emitted by the collar the field crew had placed on it. Grizzly Coordinator Servheen told the *Billings Gazette* on June 19 that "the bear was initially near a road where it might have been captured, but it later began moving deeper into the wilderness, where it could later shed its radio collar and become exceptionally difficult to locate." The interview continued:

> DNA testing of genetic material from the bear that was left on the victim matched blood drawn from the bear when it was tranquilized Thursday, said Servheen. He said he decided late Friday to authorize killing the bear if it could not be captured, because experts could not definitively determine whether the animal's actions were natural and defensive or aberrant and unusually aggressive. [Servheen told NationalParksTraveler.com that "The grizzly also did not view the botanist as food, for after mauling the man—removing what threat it might have perceived—the bear left the area without consuming any part of him."]

The *Gazette* reported that "Servheen said he and other agency officials agreed that 'the best thing to do for the safety of the public is to remove the bear. . . . We regret the whole idea of having to remove a bear, but we just wanted to be sure. I stand by that decision to remove him,' Servheen said . . .Wildlife officials used a helicopter and radio tracking gear to locate and shoot the bear Saturday morning."

The Kitty Creek area where Erwin Evert lived was reopened to the public on Monday, June 21, 2010. Those living there and those researching grizzlies there came together in a way that no one intended. Coexistence is not just a problem for grizzlies and people, but for those persons whose interests in grizzlies diverge.[17]

The Investigation Team recommendations stemming from Evert's death may be reviewed in the document of July 16, 2010: Recommendations of the Investigation Team Based on the Investigation of the Fatality of Erwin Evert from a Bear Attack on June 17, 2010.[18]

# 5

# MAN AS PREY (5 MILES FROM PARK): KEVIN KAMMER

*Words cannot describe what it's like to hear someone attacked by a bear.*
—CAMPER DON WILHELM

## FATALITY AND TWO MAULINGS—2010

*National Park Service—Yellowstone*

*Gallatin National Forest*

*Montana Fish Wildlife and Parks, Park County Wyoming Sheriff's Office*

*Location: 5 miles outside Northeast Entrance to Yellowstone Park*

*Soda Butte Campground in Gallatin National Forest–East Half*

*Date/Time: July 28, 2010, between approximately 2:00 a.m. and 4:00 a.m. (three attacks)*

In the early morning hours of July 28, 2010, Kevin Kammer became prey to a grizzly bear. At the time he was asleep in a tent, with many others sleeping nearby in a car campground five miles outside the Northeast Entrance to Yellowstone Park.

To become prey is to become an animal hunted or killed for food. "For most of Yellowstone's history," Paul Schullery wrote in his 1997 *Searching For Yellowstone*, "we have studiously and sometimes explicitly denied that bears even were predators, although they have by now killed at least five people in the park and injured many hundreds of others."[19]

At Soda Butte Campground that night of July 28, people slept closely together, with twenty-four of twenty-seven sites for car camping filled. Only one mile from Cooke City, the campground was located right off Highway 212. The campground, within the Gallatin National Forest, was particularly attractive, with stands of spruce visually screening most of the sites from each other. Two loops of campsites, the eastern Upper Loop and the western Lower Loop, spanned one thousand yards. Beside the strip of campsites Soda Butte Creek flowed downstream from east to west, making a loud rushing sound. Heavily timbered hills rose on the creek's opposite bank.

The time was about 1:45 a.m. Along the campsite loops, eighteen families from Colorado, Texas, Canada, and other locales had pitched their tents beside their cars, while six others had parked their trailers. They were long since asleep.

What happened next, unless otherwise attributed, is recounted by campground witnesses, other victims, two hospital surgeons, and bear specialists. The events were investigated by a federal and state interagency team. *The Investigation Team Report dated August 13, 2010—Bear Attacks in the Soda Butte Campground on July 28, 2010* has been released to the public.[20]

That night at Soda Butte Campground, campers enjoyed ten acres of amenities: picnic tables, drinking water, restrooms, and facilities for the disabled. At each campsite stood four bear-resistant garbage containers, and a bear-resistant food storage box. All sites in the campground were later found to be in compliance, with no food or garbage left out or in tents. Numerous signs informed those present that the area was frequented by grizzly bears.

But how many of these campers knew that two years before, in this same Soda Butte Campground at 3:00 a.m. (July 18, 2008), an Oregon man inside his tent with a companion reported that "he awoke that night when something bumped his feet and then head-butted him." His account told what happened next:

[Steven] Bartley sat up and began to unzip his tent, and a bear bit his right hand. He was unable to see the animal in the darkness. "It was just over so fast," Bartley, from his hospital room, told the *Billings* (Montana) *Gazette* [picked up by FoxNews.com on July 19]. "I was just going nuts, screaming at the top of my lungs. When that's happening, you'll do anything—swing, kick." His yelling woke up nearby campers, and the commotion apparently caused the bear to run off . . . He received about a dozen puncture wounds to both hands, some deep lacerations and a broken bone below his thumb that required surgery.

"I can't think of anything more scary in your life," the man said, according to KPAX-TV in Missoula, Montana. The *Billings Gazette* reported that the motorcyclist's "tent was crushed and the bear returned later that morning, crushing another tent . . . Five days later, Montana Fish Wildlife and Parks trapped a young adult female grizzly [450 pounds] at the site of the incident. That bear was sent to a research center in Washington State University."

Three weeks before the Kammer incident, a July 6, 2010, Yellowstone Park Bear Sighting Report noted one sow grizzly and three large, yearling cubs along a park section of Soda Butte Creek, "walking and grazing." The sighting was in the park's Lower Barronette Meadow, and caused a bear jam of vehicles pulling over to watch. The report cited the distance between the observers and the bears as 130 yards, and noted that the bears moved away upon noticing the humans watching. Barronette Peak is seven miles west of Yellowstone Park's Northeast Entrance.

Just a week before Kammer died, another park report described the same four bears just outside the park, but this time the adult bear charged. A woman wrote that she was "jogging ¼ mi. from NE station toward Silver Gate. Bears came out of woods on road. Mom stood up & cubs ran on side of road toward me. Mom charged & I screamed 'Hey Hey Hey' & she stopped. She ran to the woods on the right and I ran back to NE station."

On July 27 forty-eight-year-old Kevin Kammer of Michigan drove his car into the Soda Butte Campground. He registered for the campground's Lower Loop, the westernmost, and was given Site #26 to park and camp for the night. He had come "west to fulfill a lifelong dream: fly-fishing in Yellowstone National Park," the Associated Press later reported. "Kammer, a stay-at-home dad with a wife and four children, was an avid outdoorsman and kayaker."

Kevin set up his small orange and yellow tent, which was composed mainly of an insect screen with a rain-fly stretched across it. Waist-high willows grew about thirty feet down-slope, and forty-five yards farther came the rushing sound of Soda Butte Creek.

Sometime after dark he crawled into his sleeping bag, rested his head on his camp pillow, and fell asleep, alone.

In a tent toward the campground's other end, the Upper Loop at Site #12, the Wilhelm family from Texas—Paige and Don (a wildlife biologist) and their two sons—woke at approximately 2:00 a.m. to disturbing sounds just a few campsites away. From upstream to the east, someone screamed. Then they heard more noise, of indeterminate origin, followed by silence.

Don "thought the first scream was just teenagers, maybe a domestic dispute in the middle of the night," he told the Associated Press. "He tried to go back to sleep, stifling thoughts that a beast might be lurking outside his family's tent."

Five to fifteen minutes later he heard a woman's continuing screams, this time from downstream to the west, as if trouble were following the creek. It came from the site right next to them, #11.

Don's wife, Paige, told the AP: "First she said, 'No!' Then we heard her say, 'It's a bear! I've been attacked by a bear!'" A grizzly had bitten an entry hole on the south-facing side of the woman's tent, leaving a "fragment of what appeared to be a broken tooth from the offending bear (appeared to be from a larger canine tooth, fragment had a black cavity track through the fragment,)"[21] and was now biting her left upper arm, her left lower arm, crushing an arm bone, and biting her left leg.

About her agony, Don told the AP: "Words cannot describe what it's like to hear someone attacked by a bear."

An ominous silence followed. "Then they [the Wilhelms] heard a bear come by their tent, making a huffing sound," reported the *Billings Gazette*. The parents immediately reacted:

They hustled their sons, ages 12 and 9, into their minivan and drove to the woman's campsite, where they could see her lying in her sleeping bag [amid her flattened tent], her arm bloodied. Unsure if the animal was still in the area, they were afraid to get out and go to the woman. They drove through the Upper Loop of the campground, honking their horn, looking for help and hoping to scare the bear away, Wilhelm said.

The woman was fifty-eight-year-old Canadian camper Deb Freele. She later told the Associated Press, "Something woke me up, and a split second later, I felt teeth grinding into my arm." She tried to make out what this was:

> "I realized, at that split second, I was being attacked by a bear, but I couldn't see it. It was behind me and I screamed. I couldn't help it—it's kind of like somebody else was screaming. And then it bit me harder, and more. It got very aggressive and started to shake me." She kept screaming but then realized that if she didn't do something, she was going to die. "I decided at that point, the only other thing I knew to do was to play dead, and I just went totally limp, got very quiet, didn't make a sound. And a few seconds later, the bear dropped me and walked away." She said the bear was silent. "I felt like he was hunting me."

At the same time the Wilhelms in their minivan were finding help, a truck sped away with a young man on the seat inside, bleeding from a bear bite to his leg. His girlfriend was the first person who had screamed that night. He was twenty-one-year-old Ronald Singer from Colorado, who had been camping at Site #16 with his girlfriend's family in two tents, including a puppy dog in his tent.

After the family reached safety at a nearby motel, the girlfriend's father called 911:

> ***911 Operator 2:*** "9-1-1 emergency, what is the location of your emergency?"

*Caller 2:* "My daughter's boyfriend got bit by a bear, just a little bit ago. There's another lady down there, screaming. I don't know if she got bit or not."

*Operator 2:* "And it was a bear?"

*Caller 2:* "And it was a bear. We're sitting right in front of Super 8 [motel in Cooke City] right now."

*Operator 2:* "OK, you can just stay at the Super 8 and if we need to get a hold of you we can get a hold of you there."

*Caller 2:* "OK, what do I do with the guy that's bit in my car?"

*Operator 2:* "You can just hang out there. We're gonna page out an ambulance to come and check him out. And then we're gonna get rangers on the scene to check out this bear. If anything else worse happens give me a call right back."

The bear had torn through one of their two tents and bitten into Ronald Singer's lower left leg. Singer punched the bear several times in the nose until it let him go. His surgeon summarized his wounds to Mark Bruscino (Wyoming Game and Fish) as "1 laceration 5 cm in length, 1 laceration 7 cm in length, deep muscle damage associated with the bite, tooth divots to the bone, no nerve or vascular damage."

The bear or bears then had apparently moved downstream, toward the west, from Site #16 to Site #11, Deb Freele's tent. Her surgeon summarized her injuries to Mark Bruscino as "wounds to her left arm as 1 laceration 15 cm in length to the upper arm with deep muscle damage, 3 other small lacerations to the upper left arm, 8 lacerations on the lower left arm, 1 fracture to the ulna bone with no bone exposure, no nerve or vascular damage. The bite to the left leg caused no lacerations or punctures."

Interestingly, during these two presumably predatory nighttime tent attacks, Singer fought back while Freele played dead. The bear broke off the attack both times.

"It was like a nightmare, couldn't possibly happen," Paige Wilhelm told the AP. But the list of victims was not at an end. From the campground's Lower Loop at Site #26, beside which stood the dark shape of Kevin Kammer's car, there was silence.

The multi-agency panel in its *Investigation Team Report* wrote that "The third attack was on Mr. Kevin Kammer and occurred at campsite #26, approximately 600 yards downstream (west) from campsite #11 where Mrs. Freele was attacked. This attack was fatal."

Kevin Frey of Montana Fish Wildlife and Parks wrote, "Talking with the couple that was camping in Site #25, the man stated, 'I did not hear a woof, growl, moan, whimper . . . nothing,' which is understandable due to the loud creek noise, night-time and sleeping. The bear(s) would not have been disturbed at Site #26 by the human injury/rescue activities that occurred in the upper portion of the campground."

The investigating panel estimated that, after the first attack that night on Singer, "In as little as 10 minutes' time, the bear(s) could have been to Site #26/Kammer." The report detailed Kevin Kammer's discovery:

Mr. Kammer's body was not discovered until 0421 hours [4:21 a.m.] when law enforcement personnel drove through the lower campground loop to clear it of all campers. By the time Mr. Kammer's body was discovered [by a Park County (Wyoming) Sheriff's Office deputy and a Yellowstone National Park ranger], the bear(s) had consumed a significant portion of his torso. This occurred at his campsite and where the body was found approximately 10 yards toward the creek from his campsite. Evidence indicated that the victim was killed within 4 feet of his tent. His tent was a small tent primarily of insect screen with a full weather fly stretched over it. Evidence indicated that the victim had been attacked in this tent and had been pulled by his head and shoulders through a hole ripped in the insect screen of his tent. Campers at the campsite adjacent to Mr. Kammer's site (approximately 60 yards away) never heard any activity and were only awakened when the Sheriff's Department drove through the lower loop of the campground to clear the area of campers.

In all 3 attacks, the bear bit or ripped through the tent fabric or the insect screen of the tent. In some cases, the bear apparently reached under the rain fly and bit through the tent or the insect screen of the tent to reach the campers inside.

## • *Capture of the Bears*

At the tent of the fatality victim, there were several identifiable bear prints on the tent and on the fly of the tent. These prints were of 2 different sizes: 1 set of larger prints and numerous sets of smaller prints. No tracks were visible on the ground due to hard-packed dirt and vegetation. Several bear scats containing vegetation were found in the area of the victim's body. These scats were of different sizes, appearing to be from an adult bear and at least 1 smaller bear. Bear hairs were collected for DNA analysis in the areas of the fatality and from the victim's body. The investigation crew searched the adjacent willows and riparian zone but halted their search at the edge of the upslope timber on the other side of the creek for fear of driving the bears out of the area. On the morning of July 28, 2010, a special aerial radio telemetry flight was conducted in the general vicinity of Cooke City and the Soda Butte Campground to search for radio-collared bears. No radio-collared bears were found in the area . . .

Culvert traps were immediately set in the area of the fatal attack. The largest culvert trap was set within 6 feet of where the victim was killed. The trap was baited with bighorn sheep meat and the fly from the victim's tent was draped over the culvert. ["The other two traps were baited with whitetail deer quarters and all traps had a chunk of watermelon on the floor under the trigger. The victim's tent was set back up in the exact location it had been during the attack."] At approximately [3:30 p.m.] on 28 July 2010, traps were baited and human activity at the campground ceased with the collection of all camping equipment by campers or agency personnel. At approximately [6:00 p.m.], a door was heard closing on a culvert trap. It was visually confirmed using binoculars that an adult grizzly bear was in the culvert trap that was closest to the fatality site and which had been covered with the fly from the victim's tent.

At [7:29 p.m.] the adult bear was immobilized and was found to be an adult female grizzly bear. Blood, hair, and tissue samples were collected for DNA analysis. The upper right canine tooth was recently broken and this break matched the part of a canine tooth recovered from Mrs. Freele's tent.

Personnel watching the area verified that 3 smaller grizzly bears were moving in the willows at the edge of the stream. The adult female was placed back into the culvert trap to recover from immobilization and 2 other culvert traps were all moved within 40 yards of the yearling activity area to maximize capture of the yearlings . . .

It is not clear if the yearling offspring accompanying this female participated in the attacks but the evidence indicates that they participated in the consumption of the third victim.

The *Investigation Team Report* concluded that the DNA evidence proved that the mother bear, estimated to be ten to fifteen years old, led her family in this predatory attack. In addition, as in forensic dentistry establishing the guilt of humans, "The right canine on the upper jaw of the bear had been recently broken and was missing a portion of the tooth. The right canine on the upper jaw had what appeared to be a black hole or cavity near the center of the tooth. (Similar characteristics of the tooth fragment found in victim #2 tent at campsite #11)."

The female bear was euthanized, and the three yearlings sent to a nonprofit zoo for—as the Investigation Team phrased it—"permanent removal from the wild." The cubs were described by the team as "Bear No. 1–Runt Female cub, Bear No. 2–Dominant Female cub, and Bear No. 3–Male cub." The last to be caught had elicited sympathy before capture because, reported the Associated Press, it "could be heard nearby through much of the day, calling out to its mother and eliciting heavy groans from the sow, which periodically rattled its steel cage."

The Investigation Team's panel noted that the three young grizzlies were "observed eating fruit and meat as soon as in [the zoo] holding area."

"In summary, the attack involving an adult female grizzly bear and her 3 yearlings on 3 separate people in the Soda Butte Campground on 28 July 2010 cannot be clearly explained or understood," the Investigation Team reported. The summary provided possible causative factors:

The adult female and her offspring were nutritionally stressed due to their primarily plant-food diet ["92% of the grizzly bears in the Yellowstone ecosystem consume a higher proportion of meat in their diet than did this female"], and the adult female had a moderate intestinal parasite load which contributed to her poor nutritional status. However, their body size and condition were not outside the range of normal values for grizzly bears in the Yellowstone Ecosystem. It is clear this bear had obtained few if any human-related foods prior to the attack and therefore was not food conditioned to seek human use areas as sources of food."

On August 17, BozemanDailyChronicle.com's Daniel Person took up the question. "An in-depth investigation into the diet, health and behavior of a grizzly bear that killed one man and injured two others in a campsite just outside Yellowstone National Park offers frustratingly little explanation of why the bear and her three yearling cubs went on the deadly rampage in the early morning hours of July 28."

"It's disturbing to everyone, not knowing why this happens or what caused it to happen," added Kevin Frey, a bear specialist with the Montana Fish, Wildlife and Parks. "It's always been said how unpredictable bears can be, and this is the worst case scenario in regards to unpredictability," Frey said.

Commenting on the tragedy, Kevin's brother-in-law Jim Howard told the Associated Press that "He [Kevin] could've just as easily been hurt in Grand Rapids riding down the road, there could've been a car accident or something. I think it's important for people to live their lives and to do what they want to do and what they dream about doing.

"I mean, yeah, in retrospect I wish he hadn't gone, but I was glad he was pursuing his dream and pursuing what he loved to do."

# PART II—BECOMING PREY: FOUR MORE FATALITIES, ONE PROBABLE FATALITY

# 6

# WOMAN AND NATURE: BRIGITTA FREDENHAGEN

*I walked to the tent and saw rip marks in the tent fly near the door.*
—Park Ranger Mark C. Marschall

## FATALITY—1984

*National Park Service—Yellowstone*

*Case Incident Record Number: 842913*

*Location: Backcountry Site 5W1, White Lake*

*Date/Time: Monday, July 30, 1984, 11:00 p.m.*

Brigitta Fredenhagen had never been to Yellowstone Park before. She hoped to experience its natural web of life by hiking and camping in its beautiful (but wild) backcountry.

She, her brother, and sister-in-law were all from Switzerland. She had educated herself about Yellowstone and carried a hiking guide. She attached to her backpack two "bear bells," whose ringing could warn bears of her approach on the trail. A Board of Inquiry later found that she "had apparently received and followed all safety recommendations."

That morning, a Monday, July 30, 1984, Brigitta, her brother, and sister-in-law arrived at the Pelican Valley Trailhead at 11:00 a.m. That night a thunderstorm would boom and flash, but for now Brigitta saw sun and wildflowers, smelled wild mint and pine. From the trailhead, the three hiked 3.3 miles to the Pelican Creek Bridge, and then another 2.5 miles to the Astringent Creek Bridge. Brigitta settled into the rhythm of her lug-sole boots—size 5½—striking dirt, feeling the strength of her legs, conditioned by many other hikes and backpacks, for she was an experienced outdoorswoman.

That night, alone, she would set up her tent in Backcountry Site 5W1 at White Lake. But it was still day, and she felt the security of her brother and sister-in-law hiking alongside her. She carried a pale-green paperback, *Yellowstone Trails*, by Yellowstone Lake District ranger Mark C. Marschall. After Brigitta disappeared, Ranger Marschall was one of the park personnel to join the search for her.

His guidebook notes:

> The trails in the Pelican Valley area should be especially attractive to those hikers interested in viewing wildlife. But if the thought of viewing a grizzly bear isn't especially attractive to you, then maybe you should consider a different area. Grizzly bears are drawn to Pelican Valley for its relatively lush plant growth of grasses, sedges and forbs. Sightings aren't uncommon, though encounters between bear and people are rare."[22]

On the far side of the Astringent Creek Bridge, as at so many junctures, Brigitta made a choice that may have determined her fate. As she had planned, there where the Astringent Creek–Broad Creek Trail started northward, she chose to hike north alone.

She turned to her brother and sister-in-law, and said goodbye. She watched them hike back toward the Pelican Valley Trailhead and their rented car because unlike her—as they explained the next day, July 31, to Lake District ranger Timothy P. Blank—they had not brought their backpacking gear with them. From that point on Brigitta would be hiking—and planned to camp tonight at the site she had registered for, near Broad Creek—alone.

She was a colorful figure on the trail, her red backpack carrying all that she needed to camp overnight. Her food supplies—a comforting thought—included "instant noodles, smoked ham in a plastic sack, dried peaches, two slices of bread, two granola bars, tea leaves, powdered milk, cereal, and liquid tea in a metal container." She wore leather boots with sturdy Vibram soles, blue-beige jeans, brown jacket, and a yellow and gray blouse. She saw much beauty along the way and recorded it with her 35mm camera and lens; the film was later found and developed.

At the end of the day Brigitta focused the lens on her cookstove set up in the fire ring fifty feet from her tent, and made a final exposure.

Brigitta's Yellowstone journey began on July 25, 1984, when she boarded an airplane from Paris to New York City. Her birthplace and residence was Basel, a Swiss city on the Rhine River, home of pharmaceutical companies and the annual Art Basel, one of the world's most prestigious art shows.

On July 26 she flew from New York to Denver to meet her brother and sister-in-law. The excitement of an adventure in the American West brought them together, and they rented a car, driving from Denver up through Grand Teton National Park, whose mountain faces were reflected in Jenny and Jackson Lakes.

On July 28 their family group of three drove into Yellowstone through the South Entrance, and (according to later interviews with the family) received a park map and safety brochure, documented in Brigitta's possession by the aforementioned Ranger Blank. The three set up camp in the public campground at Grant Village and then drove around to see the sights: West Thumb Geyser Basin, Thumb Paintpots, and Yellowstone Lake's "Fishing Cone"—named because so many visitors, including the Washburn party in 1870, once caught fish and cooked them, still on the hook, in the steaming water within the cone.

On July 29, Brigitta's family group drove to the Grand Canyon of the Yellowstone—twenty miles long and fifteen hundred feet deep—admiring the lower falls' plunging water and sprays of mist. Then, by herself—to obtain a backcountry camping permit for the following day—Brigitta walked into the Canyon Ranger Station.

What happened next is narrated in the Case Incident Record by the park professionals who were directly involved. "[A]t approximately 12:15 p.m. a young lady entered the office area and began looking at a large

Yellowstone topographical map, which is mounted on the east wall of the Canyon Ranger Station Office," reported Law Enforcement Specialist Floyd Klang, after interviewing Ranger James G. Youngblood on July 31. Youngblood was on duty at the ranger station and helped Brigitta with her backcountry permit. Klang continued:

Ranger Youngblood described the young lady as pretty, 5'3" to 5'5" tall, 120 pounds, dark, wavy shoulder length hair, wearing blue jeans and a knit pullover shirt or blouse . . . he handed Ms. Fredenhagen a pre-assembled package of backcountry informational brochures . . .

Youngblood called the backcountry office, located at Mammoth, and received a confirmation to issue Ms. Fredenhagen a backcountry camp-site permit for site 5-B-1, for the night of July 30, 1984. The number of this permit was designated as 847N806 . . . The trail that Ms. Fredenhagen planned to use is commonly known as the Astringent-Broad Creek trail and she was planning on beginning her hike at a trailhead in Pelican Valley, located approximately 3 miles east of Fishing Bridge.

Ranger Youngblood . . . wrote the following information on the backcountry permit: Broad Creek, Bears, Firearms, H20, Food, Fires . . . he gave Ms. Fredenhagen the following verbal information:

"The bears in Yellowstone National Park are dangerous, that she should not attempt to approach them, hang her foodstuffs in a tree and well away from the campsite area, don't have any foods or foodstuffs near the tent or sleeping equipment and generally keep a clean camp."

"Firearms are not allowed in Yellowstone backcountry."

"Do not drink stream or lake water, boil her water for at least 15 or 20 minutes."

"Make certain that all fires are out."

"It is dangerous to travel alone – take extra precautions, if she should get hurt, like breaking a leg one might be in big trouble."

"A lot of women in this area do not hike during their period." . . .

Ms. Fredenhagen asked questions concerning locating the camp-site and the trail. Ranger Youngblood advised Ms. Fredenhagen that the trail was marked with a sign with the campsite number printed on it. Ranger Youngblood advised Ms. Fredenhagen that the Wapiti trail was boring and that she would have a much more enjoyable trip if she would loop around to the east and return via the Pelican Trail and return to the originating trailhead.

Ranger Youngblood stated that Ms. Fredenhagen appeared to be very intelligent, that she spoke near perfect English and that she did not appear to have any difficulty in communicating with him.

Brigitta had now obtained the necessary permit to camp the night of July 30 at the remote Backcountry Site 5B1, at Broad Creek. After her overnight camp alone, she would hike the connecting Wapiti Lake Trail to Canyon, where she would rejoin her brother and sister-in-law at the Grand Canyon of the Yellowstone.

That night, July 29, Brigitta, her brother, and sister-in-law slept in the public campground near Norris Geyser Basin, where hot springs spread acres of greens, blues, and yellows, as vivid as dreams.

Tomorrow they would hike into the wilder world of Yellowstone's backcountry.

<hr>

The next morning, to begin their hike, the three Swiss visitors drove past Fishing Bridge toward Pelican Valley. Pelicans could be seen on Yellowstone Lake, near where the three parked their car. Just past Indian Pond, and four miles north of the islet called Pelican Roost, the Pelican Valley Trail began.

At 11:00 a.m., with two "bear bells" on her pack, Brigitta signed the trail register where, in International Orange, a new placard read: "Warning—Grizzly Frequenting Area Traversed by This Trail, Be Alert." In fact, grizzlies sometimes traveled *on* human trails—the paths of least resistance—especially in the seldom used (by humans) evenings, nights, and dawns.

Brigitta, her brother, and sister-in-law followed the trail for two miles, emerging into the broad expanse of Pelican Valley. "The area is ideal grizzly habitat and you will probably spot several droppings and diggings along the way," warned writer Orville E. Bach Jr. in the 1979 edition of his book *Hiking the Yellowstone Backcountry*, a book Brigitta may have read. Bach advised the following:

Make noise and remain alert as you traverse the valley. Coyotes are frequently sighted throughout the valley searching for small game. At the 3 mile point you reach Pelican Creek and a junction with the old fire road used to provide access to forest fire areas. Pelican Creek moves along rather slowly. The water is not very cold and therefore makes poor drinking water. There are good populations of cutthroat in this stream, however." [no longer true in 2015][23]

That afternoon Brigitta made two significant choices.

First, at 5.8 miles from the Pelican Valley Trailhead, past the Astringent Creek Bridge, she chose to hike on alone.

Second, she stopped for the night at a backcountry campsite that was *not* the campsite she had registered for, but one that was nearer. Brigitta had registered for Campsite 5B1 at Broad Creek, but 5B1 was an additional 3.5 miles (described alternatively in the Case Incident Record as 4.5 miles) beyond where she ended up camping (White Lake campsite 5W1). Did she stop short of her assigned campsite because she felt anxious about proceeding farther into the backcountry? In the Case Incident Record, Ranger Blank noted that Brigitta "expressed a concern about meeting animals and about getting back on time. [She] decided to change [her] itinerary and return to the Pelican Trailhead most likely by the Pelican Creek Trail; [she] also told [her brother and sister-in-law] that [she] might not make it all the way to 5B1."

━ ━

A tampon was later found inside Brigitta's pack.

In his 2009 information paper "Bears and Menstruating Women," Yellowstone bear management specialist Kerry A. Gunther stated that a study by Cushing (1983) suggested "polar bears are attracted to odors associated with menstrual blood." Gunther added that "Herrero (1985) analyzed the circumstances of hundreds of grizzly bear attacks on humans, including the attacks on the two women in GNP [Glacier National Park], and concluded that there was no evidence linking menstruation to any of the attacks. The responses of grizzly bears to menstrual odors have not been studied experimentally." As for black bears, Gunther cited Rogers et al. (1991) that "Menstrual odors were essentially ignored by black bears of all sex and age classes." Gunther's paper ended with the following:

> The question whether menstruating women attract bears has not been completely answered (Byrd 1988). There is no evidence that grizzlies are overly attracted to menstrual odors more than any other odor and there is no statistical evidence that known bear attacks have been related to menstruation (Byrd 1988). However, park visitors have been injured and killed by bears (Gunther and Hoekstra 1996). If you are uncomfortable hiking and camping in bear country for any reason, you should probably choose another area for your recreational activities.[24]

Brigitta was later found to have carried a thirty-tablet supply of Micoren tablets (crotonyl-butyric acid), "an agent that arouses organic activity, strengthens the action of the heart, increases vitality, and promotes a sense of well-being" (see fifa.com/fifa/handbook/doping). This stimulant was banned in 2000 by FIFA, the soccer organization. In the backcountry packet Brigitta had received was a brochure entitled "Where Did The Energy Go?" Was she a bit intimidated by her proposed backpacking, and took along Micoren for energy "insurance"?

Whatever was going through Brigitta's mind, she continued on while her brother and sister-in-law returned to the Pelican Valley Trailhead.

Evidence later indicated that Brigitta hiked north up the Astringent Creek–Broad Creek Trail. She took photographs chronicling her trip as she approached campsite 5W1.

Then, among the meadows and the lodgepole-pine forest with spruce understory, Brigitta must have seen an orange placard indicating the campsite. Brigitta did not know the history of White Lake Campsite 5W1. In 1982, from July 19 through July 26, the site received "Strong Bear Warnings" for reported heavy bear activity, as did all of Pelican Valley. From July 26 through August 2, 1982, "Strong Bear Warnings" were issued for Campsite 5W1 alone. But in 1983, no warnings were issued.

Now, on July 30, 1984, standing by herself at Campsite 5W1, Brigitta photographed the arm of White Lake on her right, the center of the shot showing a lone sapling. Perhaps she already knew how the lake received its name. "This small lake at the head of Broad Creek on the Mirror Plateau," wrote Yellowstone historian Lee H. Whittlesey in his book *Yellowstone Place Names*, "was named in 1885 by members of the Hague parties of the USGS [United States Geological Survey]. They named it White Lake because of the white-colored areas of thermal activity in the vicinity."[25]

Perhaps Brigitta looked at campsite 5W1 and decided that she was too tired, or had had enough, or was feeling too lonely to go on to her assigned campsite. For reasons known only to herself, she chose to stay the night at 5W1.

In another twist of fate, Brigitta should not have been alone at 5W1. A party of three hikers had registered for the campsite that night, but they didn't start hiking until 6:00 p.m., too late to reach 5W1, so they camped in lower Pelican Valley instead.

Brigitta's next-to-last photograph was described by a ranger as "Looking from meadow SSW of tent. Campfire ring left center of photo." It showed the path leading directly to 5W1, where among the evergreens Brigitta later planted her green-domed tent.

Brigitta's final photograph showed her cookstove set up in the fire ring fifty feet from her tent. The shadows in the photo suggested she took this frame at approximately 5:30 p.m. (plus or minus an hour). She heated and ate her dinner (perhaps ham, since five slices were later found) and then drank tea while the sun slipped behind the treetops. Clouds began rolling in, suggesting rain later in the night.

To cache her food from animals, Brigitta located two old lodgepole pines with low broken limbs eighty-five feet east of her campsite. She climbed the ladder-like limbs to a height of twelve feet and suspended parachute cord between the two trees, from which she hung her food, cook kit, and stove. By then the evening light was nearly gone.

She probably felt physically tired, but with the tiredness came the hiked-out calm that is one of the rewards of backpacking. Her legs tingled, even ached, and she pulled her red mummy-shaped sleeping bag from its stuff sack, fluffed it up, then laid it inside her tent, headfirst toward the tent door. She put on garments to sleep in, and wrapped the clothes she had hiked in and probably cooked in within a plastic bag folded inside her poncho. On her right side she set her flashlight, and on her left side, her cassette-tape music player. She probably sat on top of her sleeping bag, legs crossed, to write in her journal. Among other notes about the day, she wrote: "I have taken all precautions."

Finally she crawled into her sleeping bag, her feet toward the rear of the tent, her head near the front with its zippered door: her only exit. She wore blue cotton pajamas, socks, and a sweater. It may have taken awhile, in the backcountry of Yellowstone far from home, but presumably she fell asleep.

During the night a lightning-laced thunderstorm moved in. Perhaps Brigitta briefly awakened. But she had stretched a waterproof rain-fly tightly above her tent and remained dry inside her personal cocoon. The only sounds she could probably hear were the thunderclaps overhead and the rain hitting her tent. Listening to the rain, she probably fell asleep again.

At some point in the night, a grizzly bear approached the front of the tent, ripped the side of the rain-fly, and made a single, neat twenty-seven-inch tear in the tent to the right of the door. The bear seized Brigitta by the top of her head (or alternatively the left side of the neck, breaking her jawbone). The bear pulled, and she slipped like a baby being born out of her tent and then her sleeping bag.

———

On Tuesday, July 31, at the Pelican Valley Trailhead, Brigitta's brother and sister-in-law expected to see her hiking toward them, a smile on her face. It was 3:30 p.m., the agreed upon time. Brigitta, normally a punctual person, did not appear. After half an hour, anxiety set in. An hour passed. Then another. Now their fear was sharp.

Around 6:00 p.m. Brigitta's brother hurried to the Fishing Bridge Visitor Center to report Brigitta overdue. Park Naturalist Lori Qualman called Ranger Marschall. "I asked [the brother] to return to the trailhead and continue waiting for his sister for another hour," Marschall stated in his park report:

> I attempted to contact by radio Ranger Bill Berg who was in Pelican Springs Patrol Cabin that evening. I was called to a fire alarm at the Lake Lodge before I could reach him. When I returned to the Ranger

Station, at about [8:00 p.m.], [the brother] was there and told me his sister had still not returned to the trailhead. I continued to try and contact Ranger Berg via radio while I asked [the brother] questions about his sister and her trip.

Using the brother's information, Ranger Marschall wrote an "Attempt to Locate" and contacted the Yellowstone Communications Center to have it read over the park's internal radio frequency. The operator's urgent voice, "Missing Hiker in Pelican Valley: Name Brigitta Fredenhagen," was heard by Park Service personnel across both Yellowstone's developed area and backcountry. As it turned out, Brigitta was not the only missing person that day. A search party headed by Incident Commander Randy King was moving south from Specimen Ridge toward Broad Creek (where Brigitta was registered to camp), looking for another missing hiker. Brigitta's "Attempt to Locate" was transmitted to this search party as well.

At 8:00 p.m. Brigitta's brother and sister-in-law met with Lake District ranger David Spirtes at Lake Ranger Station, telling him "that Brigitta, who was very responsible and punctual, was now 4½ hours overdue."

"I finally contacted Bill Berg [by radio] at approximately [8:14 p.m.]," Ranger Marschall wrote. Ranger Berg was known to be staying at the Pelican Springs Patrol Cabin in Pelican Valley that evening. Marschall then alerted Berg to the missing Brigitta:

I gave him a description of Brigitta and asked Berg to go out into the valley and see if he could see any sign of her. I told Berg not to search after dark. Berg checked back in at approximately [9:30 p.m.] and said he had seen no sign of hikers.

From approximately [8:30 to 9:30 p.m.] the Pelican [Valley] trailhead was monitored by either [name withheld] or [the brother and sister-in-law, who] decided to go back to Norris and camp for the evening. I had them leave a note for Brigitta at the trailhead register telling her to call our emergency phone number if she arrived late. I had Ranger Steve Harrel check the trailhead hourly from [10:00 p.m.–3:00 a.m.] that night.

Brigitta did not return to the trailhead that night.

On Wednesday, August 1, Brigitta was still missing, perhaps lying injured in the remote backcountry. Her brother and sister-in-law were "extremely concerned." Writing in his later report, Lake District ranger David Spirtes noted the following:

At approximately [9:00 a.m.] on August 1, [her brother and sister-in-law] returned from Norris Campground to the Lake Ranger Station. I advised them that a ranger was on the way in to Brigitta's campsite and the best thing that they could do was to wait at the trailhead and to let us know immediately if she returned. I assured them that we would contact them at the trailhead as soon as we had any news.

Following Ranger Spirtes' advice, Brigitta's brother and sister-in-law went back to the trailhead and waited. They strained to see movement coming toward them, movement of any kind that might indicate Brigitta coming home.

Early that morning, looking for Brigitta, Ranger Marschall rode on horseback toward campsite 5B1 on Broad Creek, the campsite she had registered for. His report detailed his efforts to find her:

I checked the area downstream from Pelican Bridge and the area north of Astringent Creek Junction but otherwise I rode up the Astringent Creek–Broad Creek trail headed for Brigitta's proposed campsite of 5B1. At approximately [8:30 a.m.] I talked with hiker [name withheld] near the Astringent Creek Junction. He reported seeing a large grizzly bear approximately 15 minutes earlier coming from the Astringent Creek trail area and headed south into Pelican Valley.

At approximately [11:20 a.m.] I arrived at campsite 5W1 on the edge of White Lake. I saw a green dome tent standing and a sleeping bag laid out in front of the tent. As I rode towards the tent, my horse spooked and would approach no closer than 20 yards. I walked to the tent and saw rip marks in the tent fly near the door. I looked into the tent and saw a sleeping pad, parka, and gear all apparently undisturbed. When I looked around outside the tent I noticed a piece of scalp and hair and a piece of what was apparently muscle tissue.

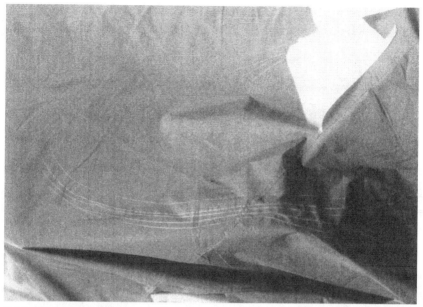

Brigitta Fredenhagen's ripped tent

I immediately called Lake Ranger Station on the radio and notified Area Ranger David Spirtes [now the operations chief and primary
investigator] and District Ranger Tim Blank [now the incident com-
mander] of what I had found. While they arranged for a helicopter
transport to the scene, I checked the woods to the east of the campsite
looking for Brigitta. I found Brigitta's food cache lying on the ground
where it had apparently been ripped apart by a bear. I looked for Brigitta
for about 20 minutes, but could not locate her.

Possible human tissue had been found outside of Brigitta's tent. The
Park Service response was immediate. "District Ranger Tim Blank and I
got two shotguns, a high-powered rifle, emergency medical technician kit,
compass, maps, ammunition, 35mm camera, binoculars, and other emergency equipment and proceeded to the Fishing Bridge helispot," reported
Operations Chief Spirtes. He described what he saw:

At [11:58 a.m.] we lifted off en route to White Lake. From the air we observed a green dome tent with Ranger Marschall standing in a meadow, waving his arms, and indicating a landing spot. At [12:06 p.m.], the helicopter touched down. Rangers Marschall and Blank loaded shotguns while I carried the rifle. We began a hasty search of the area. The dome tent looked normal except for the fresh tear next to the front flap. Six feet away was a zipped-up sleeping bag, appearing as if it had been laid out in the sun.

Several feet from the sleeping bag was a piece of lip, and nearby a piece of scalp with hair attached.

Marschall showed us the area, 30 yards to the east, where a bear had apparently gotten her food cache from between two trees. Over the past two days, there had been numerous localized severe thunderstorms pass through the park. Since no trail was discernible, we began a hasty search of the nearby woods . . .

From the sleeping bag, a trail of tissue led in a northerly direction, including a small piece of scalp, lip, more scalp, a small piece of fat globule, and some shreds of blue cloth. Approximately 22 feet northwest of the tent was an oblong 18-inch by 37-inch patch of discolored grass. Small blue-cloth fibers and tissue could be seen there. In subsequent days the patch smelled, felt greasy, and became more noticeable. It appeared that substantial bleeding took place at this location. This, coupled with the tissue spread around the area, would probably indicate the site where the victim died.

From there a barely discernible trail that went to the east of the fire ring crossed the trail, and went uphill toward the wood in a northeasterly direction was followed. Roughly halfway between the fire ring and final resting place of the body, a bloody sweater with numerous rips and tears was left behind. Thirty feet from where the body was found was a discolored cotton pullover shirt.

The body was lying approximately 250 feet from the tent. It was stretched out prone with the left arm bent at the elbow and pinned under the body. The right arm was extended over the head. Her right foot was detached at the ankle, but laying adjacent to it. Next to her left foot was her stretched-out blue pajama bottoms . . . The skin on the arms was peeled back as if cased; a characteristic suggestive of the way a grizzly often feeds on a carcass. The body was not eviscerated, although most of the muscle, flesh, and skin was gone from the arms, legs, buttocks, and upper torso . . .

It was not possible to determine the time of death . . . The average person after hiking 8.5 miles would eat dinner after arriving at their campsite . . . The victim's stomach was empty at the autopsy; since it takes approximately 6 hours for food to clear the stomach, this would place the time of death after [10:30 p.m.] if she ate dinner . . .

The rain destroyed much evidence. There was not a single bear hair stuck in the bark or sap of the lodgepole pine that the bear had climbed. The lack of even coagulated globules of blood suggest that it rained during or soon after the victim started bleeding. One had to get down on hands and knees to follow the path where the body had been dragged. There were only four bear tracks discovered near the site . . .

One scat was discovered at the site and another 1 mile south of the site that contained large pieces of undigested human tissue. Since a bear would normally pass feces from between 12 [and] 48 hours after the time of ingestion of food, it appears that the bear stayed in or returned to the area for at least 12 hours. Two other scats with human remains, one on the trail by the Broad-Pelican Trail Cutoff and a second found on a small pond north of the Mud Kettles, indicate that the bear moved several miles north and several miles east in the day following the killing. A scat with human remains on top of fresh bear tracks that measured 5½ by 4¾ inches for the front pad and 4¾ by 8 inches for the rear, was dropped on the afternoon or evening of August 2 or the morning of August 3. This scat was nearly 10% human and contained a large quantity of hair. Given the normal digestive time for a bear, this suggests that the bear returned to feed on the second day, July 31. The one measurable track found at 5W1 was on top of fresh rained-on ground and would seem to verify this. These scats with human remains also contained elk hair and no maggot casings, which in the end of July indicate a successful predatory bear.

Teeth marks that seemed to correspond to a matching set of canine teeth were measured on Fredenhagen's left hand at 5.5 cm and on the left shoulder at 5.3 cm. These correspond to the measurement of teeth marks recovered from an aluminum cookpot. The dental impression left in the cooking pot remains the best piece of evidence to identify the individual bear . . .

At approximately [5:50 p.m.], Fredenhagen's body and belongings were flown back to Fishing Bridge.

———

Incident Commander Timothy Blank wrote that "After the body was found, [names withheld] went to the trailhead and informed the brother and sister-in-law and provided support." Blank detailed the Park Service's concern for the relatives:

They took [brother and sister-in-law] to their house and stayed with them for the afternoon and arranged for lodging and meals at Lake. At [6:00 p.m.], Ranger Blank met with them and told them what had happened, arranged for medication for the sister-in-law and assisted the brother in contacting his father in Switzerland and making arrangements for them to fly to Switzerland. Arrangements were made with the mortuary and the hospital for the body and the coroner's report.

On August 2, Ranger Blank spent most of the day with the brother and sister-in-law, making arrangements for airline flights, car rental return, cremation of Brigitta's remains, and security arrangements with airport personnel. Brigitta's belongings were sorted and packed by her brother and sister-in-law.

As Incident Commander Blank reported, "On August 3, the brother and sister-in-law drove to Billings, and on August 4, they flew from Billings to Switzerland with the deceased's ashes."

———

Grizzly bear tracks, bite marks, and biological samples can provide forensic proof in investigations of bear attacks. To determine which bear was responsible, on Wednesday, August 1, rangers began field investigation patrols, including night-long patrols, to locate all bears in the area, and trap or tranquilize them. Culvert-pipe bear traps and tracking by both humans and scent dogs were used in an attempt to capture and identify the responsible grizzly.

On Thursday, August 2, rangers spotted Bear #1, a grizzly. In days to come they sighted three more grizzlies (one with a cub), which Marschall noted on his page entitled "Bear Descriptions."

*"Bear #1 Description:* 400 lbs, dark wide head, blonde white muzzle, dark rump. Silver tipping on neck and ribs—lightest towards front and gets darker towards rear.

*"Bear #3[sic] Description:* Sub-adult grizzly, 150-200 lbs., blonde face, blonde fore-shoulders, blonde ribs. Dark rump and hump.

*"Bear #4 Description:* Sub-adult grizzly. Darker and larger than #3. 200-250 lbs. Silver tipping on ribs, and fore-shoulders, and outside of eyes and on muzzle. Diagonal, elliptical patch of silver tipped fur just behind right shoulder. Visible only in bright light.

*"Sow and Cub Description:* (Sow)—450 lb. grizzly with blonde or silver tipped patch of fur between eyes and nose. Very prominent dark hump and dark rump. Overall appearance dark. Ear tags in both ears. *Description: (Cub)*—50 lb. grizzly with blonde ribs and collar. Light overall appearance."

Culvert bear traps were flown in by helicopter, baited and set (with rangers safely monitoring them from inside an extra culvert trap through the night). But for the moment all the bears eluded capture.

On Friday, August 3, Marschall noted among other items that "Tracks C followed in towards Pelican TH from about 1 mile out. Tracks were probably made the night of 8/2/84. Scat #8 picked up on tracks. Scat later tested out positive."

For ten more days, to Monday, August 13, trapping and patrolling continued. Suddenly on August 13 there was a possible suspect. Marschall noted that park personnel "Discovered bear-caused damage in Fishing Bridge campground from approximately 11:00 p.m. the night before. Three (3) traps set in Fishing Bridge campground. All night patrols continue. From Monday, August 13, through Saturday, August 18, Pelican Valley was monitored by rangers to enforce closures and monitor bear activity."

Finally, success? On Saturday, August 18, a grizzly was caught in one of the Fishing Bridge traps. Could this be the bear that had killed Brigitta? Marschall's entry for this date noted, "Tagged bear #88 trapped in Fishing Bridge campground around 2:00 a.m. Bear #88 weighed approximately 350 lbs., had a large, black bear-like head and dark brown coat. Pad measurements were similar to those of tracks C."

It should be noted that scat positive for human remains had already been found on *top* of tracks C.

"Evidence including hairs, scat, tracks and teethmarks [measured on Brigitta and on her cooking pot] was gathered," Operations Chief Spirtes wrote. He provided the Park Service conclusion:

> Identification of the species [grizzly] was made from hair recovered from Fredenhagen's body and clothing [at autopsy] and from associated tracks. The hair was medium brown and the measurements of the canine teeth [marks] suggest a sub-adult under 3 years of age.

But Bear #88 was not a sub-adult and its hair was not medium brown. And by August 18, nearly three weeks had elapsed since Brigitta died. If there were evidence, would it still be present? Apparently none was. Bear #88, noted for "problem behavior" at the Fishing Bridge campground, became an unremarked-upon "management kill."

Operations Chief Spirtes reported that three bears were captured and tranquilized after Bear #88, but their measurements did not match the bear that had killed Fredenhagen.

"The bear involved [in Brigitta's death] was never identified or captured despite major efforts," Stephen Herrero wrote one year later in 1985's *Bear Attacks: Their Causes and Avoidance.*[26] "Dr. Meagher [Yellowstone research biologist Mary] used available evidence to conclude that

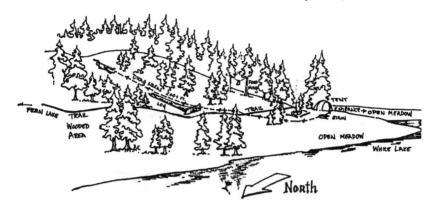

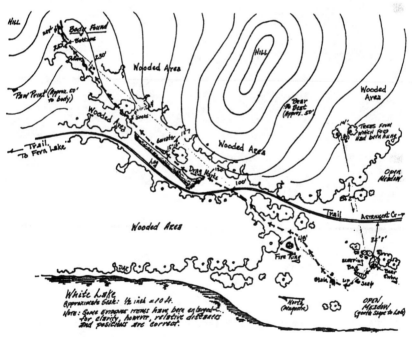

Drawings made to accompany Brigitta Fredenhagen investigation, 1984,
Case Incident #84-2913, YNP

the bear was probably a sub-adult grizzly (young grizzlies are more likely to climb trees), probably male, and apparently 'not a naïve bear relative to developed areas and human activities.'"

———

On August 23, 1984, in the Superintendent's Conference Room at Mammoth Hot Springs, the Board of Inquiry reviewed the facts of Brigitta's death. It reached the following conclusions:

> Based on all available information, the Board found that Brigitta Fredenhagen died as a result of hemorrhage and shock due to multiple wounds inflicted by a single subadult (2-3 years of age) grizzly bear [determined as most probable by Park Biologist Mary Meagher, based upon data including the size of paw tracks and the size and span of toothmarks].
>
> Ms. Fredenhagen had apparently received and followed all safety recommendations.

As this author can attest, it is natural that women want to participate in the natural world—to hike, to camp, to be free. And it is an entirely different experience to hike companionably with others than to do so by yourself. At its best, experiencing nature when you are alone can be a spiritual, even transcendent human experience. Perhaps Brigitta was hoping to have that kind of experience.

Brigitta was found to have done nothing wrong.

Being a bear, the grizzly did nothing wrong, either. When bears reach the sub-adult stage, they must leave their mothers and strike out on their own, foraging for a new area to live that is not already dominated by another adult bear. Sub-adults are often inexperienced, hungry, and on the move, and can be very dangerous to humans.

———

Even if the controversial notion that women's menstrual blood may attract some bears is considered, men may also attract some bears by odors such as their own (or with a partner's) sexual fluids.

In the previously mentioned "Bears and Menstruating Women" information paper from 2009, the following precautions are suggested:

### *Precautions*

Although there is no evidence that grizzly and black bears are overly attracted to menstrual odors more than any other odor, certain precautions should be taken to reduce the risks of attack.

The following precautions are recommended:

1. Use pre-moistened, unscented cleaning towelettes.

2. Use internal tampons instead of external pads.

3. Do not bury tampons or pads (pack it in—pack it out). A bear may smell buried tampons or pads and dig them up. By providing bears a small food "reward," this action may attract bears to other menstruating women.

4. Place all used tampons, pads, and towelettes in double zip-loc baggies and store them unavailable to bears, just as you would store food. This means hung at least 10 feet above the ground and 4 feet from the tree trunk.

5. Tampons can be burned in a campfire, but remember that it takes a very hot fire and considerable time to completely burn them. Any charred remains must be removed from the fire pit and stored with your other garbage. Also, burning of any garbage is odorous and may attract bears to your campsite.

6. Many feminine products are heavily scented. Use only unscented or lightly scented items. Cosmetics, perfumes, and deodorants are unnecessary and may act as an attractant to bears . . . .

---

Brigitta was from Switzerland, where the last brown bear was killed in 1904. On July 27, 2005, UPI picked up a BBC report:

Brown bears may have returned to Switzerland . . . Eyewitnesses report seeing a bear high in the Alps near eastern Switzerland's border with Italy, where there is already an established population. Officials say they are still looking for evidence such as bear droppings, hair or tracks to confirm the sighting. While conservationists would welcome the bears' return, some Swiss shepherds fear for the safety of their flocks.

# 7

# BLOOD ON THE LENS: WILLIAM TESINSKY

*Grizzly bears were to be Bill's next wildlife project . . . since he had never photographed one.*

—Bill Tesinsky's brother

## FATALITY—1986

*National Park Service—Yellowstone*

*Case Incident Record Number: 863976*

*Location: Hayden Valley (near Otter Creek)*

*Date/Time Discovered: Tuesday, October 7, 1986, 7:45 a.m.*

October 3, 1986, was a cold and blustering Friday. On the next day, a Saturday, William Tesinsky—known by the name engraved on his belt buckle: "Bill"—went missing somewhere in the great Hayden Valley where grizzlies once foraged among garbage dumps, growing larger and heavier than those seen since the dumps were closed.

Bill was a wildlife photographer scanning Hayden Valley for subjects, before descending onto its expanse. But Bill's desire to capture an image of a Hayden Valley grizzly would result in blood on the lens.

Bill's initial plan for that Friday, as he told his girlfriend, took him nowhere near Yellowstone Park. He was planning to meet with a rancher in Clyde Park, Montana, to try to sell some of his photographs. He was a wildlife and nature photographer, whose work was displayed in galleries in Great Falls, Montana. Bill had a family and friends he loved. His home was in the nearby small town of Stockett, and he was thirty-eight years old. Perhaps Bill felt what draws many to his chosen profession. "For me the greatest pleasure in wildlife photography comes from being able to visit unusual and beautiful natural areas in pursuit of my subjects," Ken Preston-Mafham wrote in *Practical Wildlife Photography*. "The supporters of studio 'wild' life photography ignore the importance of the thrill of achievement which can only come after successfully pitting your wits against a wild creature in its natural habitat."[27] Bill valued what he could see, not taking sight for granted. He was almost blind in his right eye in daylight, and could see nothing at all out of that eye at night. Yet he seldom took anyone with him on his hunting or photography trips, fearing that they would not be able to keep up with him.

According to his girlfriend, he planned after meeting a prospective photograph buyer to head into the mountains around Clyde Park (the Bridger Range or the Crazy Mountains), and search for elk to photograph. Bill was expected back soon. Tomorrow, Saturday, he looked forward to seeing his girlfriend as well as his daughter and her husband. Bill had planned dinner for all four of them in Great Falls.

Maybe the elk around Clyde Park were hard to find. Bill changed his plan. He decided to drive to Yellowstone to try his photographic luck there.

Grizzly bears were to be Bill's next wildlife project, his brother later told investigators, since Bill had never photographed one. It was also true that Bill was suffering some financial difficulties, and hoped to sell what he carved by camera from the wild. Photos of megafauna, especially grizzlies, sometimes produced the megabucks.

Bill drove his Chevy seventy-three miles south to Mammoth, Yellowstone Park's administrative headquarters and "company town," within sight of the famous terraced hot springs. Perhaps he slept that night in his car.

Saturday, October 4, dawned overcast and foggy. Very early that morning, while animals were about (and people generally not), Bill drove from Mammoth thirty-three miles south. He continued driving past Canyon Junction to Hayden Valley, looking for wildlife to photograph.

Perhaps Bill stopped at Grizzly Overlook above Otter Creek, as Chief Ranger Dan R. Sholly did later while trying to find him. As Sholly did, so Bill too may have looked down into the "edge effect" surrounding Otter Creek. Stands of lodgepole pine "edge" and separate gently rolling sagebrush meadows.

"Most animals prefer this 'edge effect' where forest and open land meet," Orville E. Bach Jr. wrote in 1979's *Hiking the Yellowstone Backcountry*:

Hayden Valley is prime grizzly bear country . . . Estimates of the grizzly population in Yellowstone range from 175 to 250. This amounts to only 1 bear per 14 sq. mi. throughout the park, but before you rule out the possibility of encountering one, you should realize that the grizzly often gathers in higher numbers in suitable habitats—such as Hayden Valley . . . [28]

On Saturday October 4 at about 7:00 a.m., Area Ranger Richard Divine "observed an early model Chevy Impala, MT 2-1546 later identified belonging to William J. Tesinsky." Divine's Case Incident Record report includes the last known sighting of Bill:

[The car was] parked westbound in the Cascade Trailhead Pullout, in Cascade meadows. I observed the rear window to be for the most part covered with apparent frost. The remaining windows were apparently covered with water and somewhat fogged over. I observed one individual behind the steering wheel, looking away from myself into the meadows with binoculars. The individual had a medium size jacket, dark hair and beard. Weather was overcast and foggy. Elk were in the meadow.

These meadows, looking much as they did in 1877 when Yellowstone's second superintendent, Philetus W. Norris, took office, were described by Norris as "my refuge." Bill did not enjoy the sight for long. After Ranger Divine spotted Bill's car, noted the circumstances and drove on, Bill left the Cascade Pullout and turned his Chevy south. The movement of bison caught his eye. From Bill's camera, frames nineteen and twenty of film developed later showed that he took two photos of the big brown animals, three to four miles south of Otter Creek.

Then, heading north again, Bill suddenly braked his car three-tenths of a mile south of Otter Creek and swerved over into the Otter Creek Picnic Area Pullout. He parked hastily, his breath coming fast. Five hundred sixty-eight yards away (measured later by investigators), Bill spotted a grizzly digging yampa and elk thistle—vegetation that, this late in the year, was dried out and no longer very nutritious. But there were lots of pocket gophers to interest a bear.

Bill got out of his car, pulling on his gloves. Against the gray mid-morning light, sprinkled with snow, his silhouette showed a man with dark hair and a beard, standing between 5'6" and 5'7" and weighing about 160 pounds. He put on his brimmed camouflage-printed hat and zipped up his insulated camouflage sweatshirt.

He grabbed his camera, whose 80mm-200mm zoom lens also wore camouflage. He left the lens cap in his car, and took his tripod. When he stepped out with all of his equipment, he felt the grass's wetness seep into the toes of his size 7½ high-top tennis shoes. As protection against the damp, he wore green-and-tan waterproof gaiters over his jeans.

Perhaps Bill's gloved fingers brushed the ground, gathered a handful of duff, and let the moist air carry it. The bits of dirt and leaf-meal would have moved toward him, indicating his scent was also directed away from, and therefore wouldn't alert, the bear.

It is legal to photograph wildlife in Yellowstone, but for bears one must keep a one-hundred-yard distance. Bill adjusted the photographic gear that hung heavily around his neck. Also around his neck he wore a triangular black rayon scarf knotted "John Wayne" style, and an elk-bugle call (illegal to use in Yellowstone) hanging on its cord. He picked up the camera tripod and moved quietly, gingerly toward the bear, ready to practice his art.

Bill prepared to take photographs. He was right-handed and so removed his right glove and tucked it inside his sweatshirt pocket. He set his camera securely atop the tripod, and bent over to look through the viewfinder, aiming the viewfinder center over the grizzly. He pressed the shutter button halfway, and the camera focused the grizzly. "It is only too easy to become dominated by the viewfinder," Preston-Mafham warned, "so that the wonderful world of living things is seen solely through a rectangular hole a few centimetres square."[29] Perhaps, overtaken by concern with camera technology, Bill let his caution drop.

Bill's camera showed this to be his twenty-first and final exposure. When he was finally found, and his camera with him, its loaded film was sent to the Kodak Laboratory in Palo Alto, California, for processing. Bill's camera focus was set on infinity. Forensic experts could not tell when Bill took his last photo. It showed only a blur: a dark surface, and at the bottom, a flare of light.

Bill's movements were tracked in the search team report and sketch. Where was the bear he wanted to photograph? Where was he? How did both of them subsequently come together? (See diagram on page 92.)

Just before noon on October 4 it was snowing, and visibility was limited. A second ranger on patrol noticed Bill's car in a parking area, but not, this time, at Cascade Meadows. Now at Otter Creek Pullout and Picnic Area, Bill's car looked haphazardly parked, as if he had seen something of interest and swerved over quickly, eager to exit his car. This sparked the ranger's concern.

"In my experience this parking area has been utilized mainly by people either picnicking or fishing," reported Canyon Sub-District park ranger S. Thomas Olliff. His concern grew:

> [S]ince it is not the terminus of a maintained backcountry trail. Since no people appeared to be picnicking on this snowy, overcast day, I stopped to check the bank of the Yellowstone river, but was unable to locate the occupant of the vehicle. I then checked for tracks on a non-maintained path that follows an unnamed drainage west to the Mary Mountain trail, but found nothing significant. Peering through the window of the vehicle in an attempt to gain information on the whereabouts and identity of the occupant, I noticed a business card that read:
> Bill Tesinsky
> Wildlife Photography
> Great Falls, MT 59405
> [phone numbers]

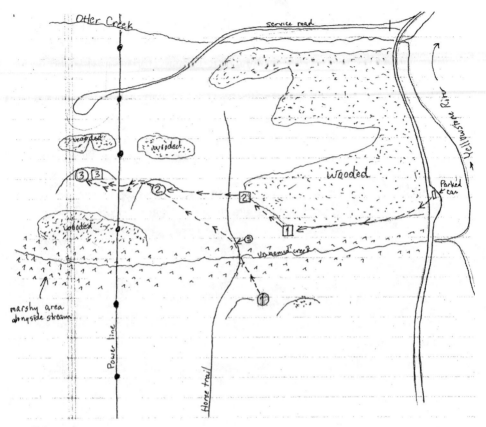

Diagram key:

1 = bear  2 = feeding site  3 = site with shoe track

1 = human  S = scat

**1** "Feeding site 38 x 30 meters, 193 digs, 250 meters from road, clearly visible from road."

1 "Human victim's likely vantage point while [bear] #59 fed at site 1 and moved to site **2**. A scat was found at S. Distance from 1 and 1 is 135 meters."

2 "Feeding site 40 x 60 meters, 51 digs, 200 meters from site 1 on the top of knoll."

**2** "Human victim's likely vantage point while #59 fed at site 2: 95 meters away."

3 "Feeding site 50 x 60 meters, 150 digs, 105 meters from site 2. The human victim then had to leave the security of the trees and enter the open meadow to maintain visual contact with #59 at site 3. A small tennis shoe track was found."

Circled numbers indicate the bear's movements: circled 1, 2 and 3.

Squared numbers indicate the victim's movements: squared 1, 2, and 3.

Circled 3 and squared 3 come together where bear attacked victim.

Probable path taken by Tesinsky with numbers representing bear's feeding sites and human victim's vantage points  Measured and drawn by (name withheld), on October 8, 1986, in Case Incident Record #863976

That evening in Great Falls, waiting for him at the dinner table, Bill's girlfriend, daughter, and son-in-law were looking forward to seeing him. When he failed to arrive they felt some concern. But they knew Bill had an independent spirit, and hoped he was just caught up in pursuing some unique opportunity to photograph wildlife. They could always count on seeing him tomorrow.

At 10:30 a.m. on Sunday, October 5, Ranger Olliff saw Bill's Chevy waiting unattended in the same spot. Olliff's report described what he saw:

[I] noted the vehicle had apparently not been moved. A registration check revealed the vehicle was owned by Bill Tesinsky of Stockett, Montana . . . I followed District Ranger John Lounsbury to the Canyon horse corral at approximately [11:30 a.m.], mentioned the vehicle, and expressed my concerns that an individual was possibly lost. Ranger Lounsbury agreed to check the area before returning to Lake. At approximately [4:00 p.m.], Area Ranger Dick Divine [who had also noticed the Chevy] and I compared notes on the vehicle . . .

We drove down to check the area, but again found nothing to indicate the whereabouts of the occupant or his reason for abandoning the vehicle. I agreed to attempt to reach both phone numbers from the business card, and we discussed organizing a search if nothing turned up on the occupant. I then followed the unnamed drainage to the Mary Mountain trail, and walked south along the trail until [I] entered a wooded area approximately ½ mile from the vehicle. During this walk, I found no tracks which would indicate the occupant of the vehicle had followed the same route.

At approximately [7:00 p.m.], I returned to find the vehicle apparently unmoved. Between [7:00 and 7:30 p.m.] I tried the phone numbers from the business card five times each, but was unable to get through.

Around [9:30 p.m.] I talked to . . . a wildlife photographer who resides at Canyon and films bears for the Yellowstone Research Department. He denies any knowledge of Mr. Tesinsky or his work as a photographer. I explained the situation and expressed concerns that Mr. Tesinsky has become lost.

At this time, we also discussed the whereabouts of the bear known as 59, and agreed it was odd that she hadn't been seen around the Canyon area since late afternoon on 10/03/86 . . .

Eventually Bill and Bear #59 were found, but in the last way any park ranger wants them to be: together.

❦

On the morning of Monday, October 6, Bill's Chevy had been sitting for two days, haphazardly parked in the same pullout area. Ranger Olliff, unable to reach Bill on his business card's phone numbers, was now very concerned for him. He checked the vehicle again and around 9:00 a.m. contacted rangers John Lounsbury and Alice Siebecker, and all agreed to organize a search. Olliff set out on horseback while a fixed-wing aircraft circled the area.

At 3:30 p.m., someone finally answered one of Bill's telephone numbers. "The connection was very poor but I thought I was talking to a young child," reported Ranger Siebecker:

> I explained who I was and why I was calling. The voice said that the telephone number that I had called belonged to Tesinsky's girlfriend's house. I asked the party if he knew where Bill Tesinsky was—the party said, "He's at work." I asked where that was, and the reply was some sort of Motors. The connection being so poor made many parts of the conversation unintelligible. The name sounded something like Biddy or Libby Motors . . .
>
> I came up with City Motors sounding the nearest. I contacted City Motors at approximately [3:45 p.m.] [listed alternatively as 4:45 p.m. in the report titled *Chain of Events*], and talked to a receptionist. She said Tesinsky worked there and was at work presently. I said I needed to talk to Tesinsky, and that it was very important. The receptionist put me on hold and then came back and said that Tesinsky didn't come to work that day (Monday, Oct. 6) and that he was reported missing to the Clyde Park Sheriff's deputies . . . A woman was put onto the phone and told me that Tesinsky was reported missing to the Clyde Park deputies. I asked her

if she was Tesinsky's boss—she said, "No, I go out with him." [She] said that Tesinsky called her Friday evening between 6-7:00 to say he was leaving for Clyde Park to show some wildlife prints to somebody there in hopes of selling them. [She] said she did not know who it was. She also said that Tesinsky was good about communicating with her. I informed her that Tesinsky's car was in Yellowstone National Park and we were trying to find out why it was here. She was quite surprised to find out that Tesinsky's car was here—it took a bit to explain to her where it was located in the park. She said that Tesinsky made no mention of coming down to Yellowstone, and had probably not been there before. Although he had hunted for wildlife in the Bozeman area.

I interviewed [her] as to the particulars of what he might have had with him, shoe size, brand of shoes, weapons, clothing worn and also mental condition. She was not sure about the equipment that he might have taken—but didn't think he had any handguns with him, possibly an animal skin to sleep on and probably no tent. She described him as a "real rustic."

I informed [her] that she was to call Yellowstone National Park with any additional information as soon as possible and contact John Lounsbury as we would probably be starting a search.

—◆—

To help them better understand the unfolding events, rangers prepared the report below about their search for Bill, attempting to reconstruct events (including his girlfriend's actions) in chronological order:

*9:00 a.m.* Tesinsky's girlfriend contacts Cascade County S.O. [supervising officer] to report Tesinsky missing. S.O. denies receiving report.

*9:05 a.m.* Girlfriend contacts her father, a Montana Highway Patrolman, and presents situation to him; asks his advice on who to contact. He advises to contact Park County S.O.

*3:15 p.m.* Girlfriend contacts Park County S.O. with report of missing person—William John Tesinsky—narrative reads: Tesinsky was to meet with rancher in Clyde Park on Saturday to try and sell photos to rancher. Tesinsky was then going into the mountains around Clyde Park to photograph elk . . .

*1:45 p.m.* [Ranger] Siebecker contacts [girlfriend] and determines that Tesinsky is missing.

*5:00 p.m.* [Ranger] Lounsbury begins organizing for search on 10/7/86 involving 2 two-person dog teams, 7 people on horseback, 4 people on foot, and either a helicopter or fixed wing aircraft.

*6:30 p.m.* [Ranger] Olliff returns to corral, no sign of Tesinsky. Olliff also learns from [name withheld] that bear #59's radio signal has hung pretty tight in the Otter Creek area close to the road for last few days.

At daylight on Tuesday, October 7, Bill still had not been found, and ranger concern grew sharp. A radio-collared grizzly bear appeared to be near the search area. "I left the Lake area with District Ranger Lounsbury at approx. [6:00 a.m.]," Ranger Mona Divine wrote, "en route to search area, located near Otter Creek." Her report detailed what happened next:

We drove to a picnic area located just south of Otter Creek, where Bill Tesinsky's vehicle was parked. This was to be a staging area for some of the search activities. We had received information the previous night that indicated the possibility of a bear near the search area. This was reported to be bear #59, which had a transmitting collar and was known to be in the Canyon area on Friday . . . One of the decisions and plans for the search involved locating #59 in order to avoid any encounters between searchers, dogs, and the bear.

We stopped at the picnic area and attempted to receive 59's signal from the location of Tesinsky's vehicle. We were unable to detect any signal. We then proceeded a short distance to the entrance of Otter Creek service road. We were unable to detect any signal there. Ranger Lounsbury and I then proceeded to the Concessions Horse operation and [name withheld] residence, where a very weak signal was detected.

The direction indicated was from the south. We proceeded back south, stopping at the Montana Power sub-station, but continuing from there after we discussed possible interference from the transmission lines. Next, we drove to the government horse barn, where a stronger signal was picked up from a south direction, which was where the old group campsite at Otter Creek was located. We drove to the parking area at the old campground and located a stronger signal from the direction of Tesinsky's vehicle.

At approx. [7:35 a.m.], Ranger Lounsbury and I walked up a slope from the pickup truck toward the picnic area and the power line. Using the receiver, we proceeded in the direction of the signal. We walked through an open area towards the crest of the slope and into a wooded section. As we approached the crest of the slope, the signal was much stronger and I observed two ravens fly off of nearby trees. Lounsbury was a few steps in front of me with receiver in hand. As I was suggesting contacting additional personnel for safety precautions, Lounsbury stated there she is, right there . . .

We could see a grizzly bear, which was at first digging something and slightly rolling something over. The position of the bear and the ravens gave me the impression of a bear on a carcass. I told Lounsbury that I would climb a nearby tree in an attempt to get a better visual on what the bear was working on. I thought that I had seen a human leg, but was unsure. I climbed a nearby lodgepole pine. We discussed the situation and it was decided that Lounsbury would return to the truck for binoculars, rifle, and more personnel. I remained up the tree for better visual and safety. While Lounsbury was going back to the parking area, I attempted to move up higher to see the location of the bear.

As I did, I observed what appeared to be two human legs with shoes plainly visible flip over as the bear dragged it a few feet further away. I radioed my observation to Lounsbury that the bear was dragging a human body.

While waiting for Lounsbury and additional personnel, I lost sight of the bear as it had dragged the body a few feet out of my vision, which was then blocked by another tree and its branches. At one point, I heard the bear snort and woof. I could also hear what appeared to be movement closer to my location. Then for a few moments I heard nothing. The next sounds appeared to be that of bones snapping and ripping sounds.

I waited in my location until Rangers Lounsbury, Fowler, D. Divine and Henry had passed under me. I then came down and took a position just to the rear of Fowler and D. Divine. We observed the bear feeding on the human form and asked for independent observation from the others that had arrived. Through rifle scopes and binoculars, we confirmed that it did appear to be a human form.

Lounsbury gave Fowler the order to take the initial shots and the others to shoot only if it became necessary. During this time the bear had become more agitated and looked up in our locations several times . . .

After Fowler took the shot the bear appeared to flip backwards away from the human form and was shot a second time by Henry. We approached the bear and observed some rib movement for a minute and then no apparent movement.

We secured the scene with flagging after Lounsbury approached the [human] body and confirmed that there was no hope of life. There was only a lower torso of a human person . . .

See diagram of scene . . . for further information.

Ranger Lounsbury's report details what he and others discovered:

Besides different parts of the victim's body there was his camera and tripod, some film containers, an elk calling device, some articles of clothing, some areas of soil that appeared to be blood soaked, and two trails that looked like some object like a body had been dragged. Also there were two areas where the bear had covered the body with grass and soil and where several body parts were found. The camera tripod had been knocked over and one of the legs bent. The elk bugling tube was torn with what appeared to be blood soaked into it and a carrying cord.

The victim's lower torso was intact from approximately the waist down. In the burial piles an arm and hand, skull, jaw, arm bone, and

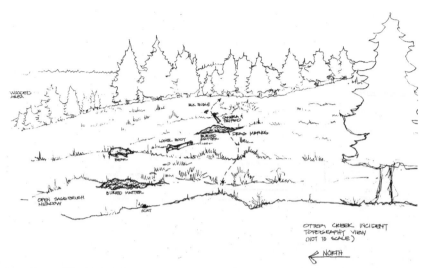

Locations of Tesinsky's body and dead bear at Otter Creek in Case Incident
Record #863976

The ridge from where bear was shot, from Case Incident Record #863976

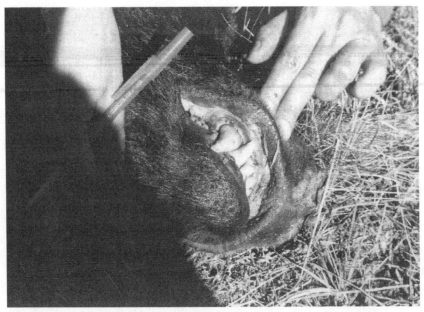

Condition of bear's teeth and gums, from Case Incident Record #863976

other bone fragments were found. Several articles of clothing were found including an undershirt, a cotton long-sleeved cowboy type shirt, a camouflage colored sweatshirt, and two gloves. These showed blood stains and teeth marks . . .

It appears that William Tesinsky was at Cascade Meadows early in the morning on October 4, 1986 and later that morning parked his vehicle [at Otter Creek]. He apparently left his vehicle and walked to the west into a large meadow with his camera and tripod. The time of this cannot be determined but based on observations of the vehicle is felt to be mid-morning on Sat. Oct. 4. The events between this and when his body was discovered shortly after [8:00 a.m.] on October 7 are unknown. Bear-59 was observed eating the remains of the lower torso of Tesinsky's body that morning. The evidence in the accident scene would indicate that much of Tesinsky's body had been consumed by a bear.

Details described in a report titled "The Conflict" were added to the draft copy of the Board of Review's report:

> The camera was covered with dried blood and smeared with dirt and grass consistent with Tesinsky's body being dragged across it. Bear hair was found on two of the tripod legs. Dirt was jammed into the hot shoe on the camera as though it had been thrust or forcefully pushed into the ground . . .
>
> The focus of the lens was set on infinity, but the focus of the camera could easily have been changed to this setting, particularly if the lens was struck from the front. Scuff marks, imbedded dirt on the front of the lens, and a loosened or wobbly lens body all appear to indicate the lens was struck from the front.

Field investigators included Park Ranger Jeff Henry, aided by his specially trained dog. "I assisted in the investigation," Henry wrote, " . . . and I was asked by Incident Commander John Lounsbury to use my search and rescue trained German Shepherd dog, Hoss, to comb the area peripheral to the scene of Tesinsky's death." Henry's report describes what he and his dog found:

> Soon after we began searching, Hoss found two fresh bone fragments, possibly fragments of a human humerus, about 40' southwest of the probable scene of Tesinsky's death; these bone fragments were small, about the size of quarters, and presumably had been moved to the point where found by bear #59, or perhaps by other scavengers (earlier in the day—when we first discovered Tesinsky's remains—I had seen one coyote and two ravens in the area where the body was found).
>
> After marking the site of the bone fragments, Hoss and I continued our sweep in a generally southeasterly direction; Ranger Brian O'Dea accompanied me and my dog. Near a grove of trees approximately 200 yards southeast of the site where Tesinsky's remains were found, Hoss began to exhibit the excited behavior that indicates he has scented the trail of a missing person (I earlier had offered to Hoss as a scent article a

camouflage shirt belonging to Mr. Tesinsky and procured for that purpose by me from Mr. Tesinksky's car).

I allowed Hoss to work, and Brian and I followed as the dog led us through the small patch of timber immediately adjacent to Mr. Tesinsky's car. Based on my experience with Hoss and his behavior when following a scent trail, I'm next to certain that he was retracing the path Mr. Tesinsky had used when he left his car; this judgment is somewhat corroborated by the fact that Ranger O'Dea and I were able to spot three or four human footprints along that path that Hoss was following; although the shoe tread pattern in these prints was not discernible, the outline of the shoe was, and we judged the tracks to be in the range of man's shoe size 7–9 . . .

The scent trail followed by Hoss seemed to be a path taken by someone who might have been trying to take advantage of available cover and concealment; Ranger O'Dea and I both agreed on this point. We made this judgment because the path outlined by my dog's workings often did not follow the way of least resistance—the path often left clear game trails that seemed to offer easy passage and instead passed over and through fallen trees and other seemingly avoidable obstacles. The apparent attempt to maintain cover seemed to have been plotted relative to the open drainage immediately south of the two groves of trees through which my dog Hoss followed the trail.

— ◦ —

After the discovery of Tesinsky's body, rangers gathered important information about Bear #59, and her two missing cubs. In the days before the Tesinsky tragedy, and after ranger attempts to relocate her to the backcountry, she was again spotted grazing in the Canyon area softball field, to the joy of visitors and photographers.

"The family history and origins of this bear are not known," stated Chief Ranger Sholly in his paper "Bear No. 59."

She was first captured in 1980, in the Canyon area, in a trapping operation for another bear. She was 2 years old at the time. The bear was relocated 31.5 miles to High Lake, but returned to the Canyon area . . . She was captured on 8/11/81 and relocated 25 miles to Saddle Mountain, but returned to the Canyon vicinity in 5 days.

In 1984, she was trapped twice in the Antelope Creek area during IGBST [Interagency Grizzly Bear Study Team] research efforts. The bear was monitored through '81, '82, '83, '84, and '85 as part of regular research monitoring . . .

Early in 1986 she was seen with two cubs of the year. She was frequenting the Canyon area in July and August 1986, and the Antelope Creek area prior to this time. She was photographed preying on elk calves in the Antelope Creek area in June with her cubs. By late July she was reported to be using a bison carcass in the Canyon area. In August she was verified in the Canyon area, grazing in the softball field, and walking near the campground. At this time, she was attracting crowds of people on a regular basis. On many occasions during this time, Bear #59 was observed and photographed, and displayed no aggression or even acknowledgement of people.

It is noteworthy that the bear was approached by two rangers when she had possession of Tesinsky's remains. The distance was 75-80 yards and the bear's response was to observe the rangers and move the remains 12 feet away from the rangers. She was heard to woof twice, after they backed off, but displayed no aggression again prior to being shot. However, she did show signs of becoming increasingly agitated with the rangers' presence immediately prior to being shot.

A bear thought to be #59 was seeking "people" food on several occasions in the Canyon area during 1986. On the evening of August 22, the bear attempted to enter an electric freezer illegally placed outside a trailer in the Canyon employees' residence area. The bear was sprayed with a fire extinguisher and scared away from the site (the distance from the bear to the person scaring it away was approximately 6 feet). No food was obtained. It is noteworthy that even at this close range, at night, the bear displayed no aggression toward the human . . .

On 9/04/86, Bear #59 was captured with her two cubs and moved 22 miles to Cub Creek. By 9/19 she had returned to the Canyon area and was without her cubs. She apparently left her cubs on her return to the Canyon area . . .

In summary, Bear #59 was a bear that frequented the Canyon area for 7 years. She was familiar with the area and had many years of experience with people and human use in the area. Bear #59 would, on occasion, feed fairly close to large groups of people and would allow people to approach fairly close to her. She did attempt to obtain human foods on several occasions, but was not dependent upon them. The evidence indicates she obtained few, if any, food rewards despite living in the area for 7 years. There is no evidence that the capture history or research encounters were related to the behavior of the bear. Available data on the feeding behavior and food habits of the bear indicate the bear was behaving normally. Although she was frequently in close proximity to large groups of people over an extended period of time there are no confirmed reports that she ever approached people in an aggressive or abnormal manner.

The specifics of the incident suggest a bear feeding on natural foods that was closely approached by a human. The bear possibly exhibited normal defensive behavior to an apparent close approach by the victim. She was a bear that was familiar with people, but despite numerous encounters, displayed no aggression toward humans until she killed Tesinsky . . .

There is no indication or evidence that the bear's physical condition, its history of handling, drugging, and monitoring, or the low levels of the whitebark pine nut crop in the Yellowstone ecosystem were directly related to the incident.

The Board found that Yellowstone National Park officials acted appropriately in destroying Bear #59, in accord with procedures outlined in the Interagency Grizzly Bear Management Guidelines.

Despite the Board's findings, above, there was some public controversy about whether Bear #59 should have been destroyed. Journalists and others noted that officials at Yellowstone had ordered Bear #59 killed, while those at Glacier National Park spared a female grizzly with cubs which killed a photographer, Charles Gibbs, who was also stalking it for a photograph. Bear #59 was also a mother with two cubs of the year, still dependent on her to survive. Where were her cubs, which had not been seen with her for some time?

To clarify Yellowstone's decision, officials at the park issued the statement below:

> In response to concerns as to why the bear that killed photographer William Tesinsky was destroyed while Glacier National Park is presently taking no action with the bear that killed photographer Charles Gibbs, we offer the following:
>
> The Glacier incident involved a sow with cubs—defense of young while the Yellowstone incident involved a single bear in a predation situation.
>
> The Glacier incident involved a dog which likely aggravated the conflict.
>
> The bear involved in the Yellowstone incident was at the scene protecting and consuming the remains of the body while the bears involved in the Glacier incident were not at hand and positive identification may have been impossible. Also, the bear did not consume the body.

D. C. Lehfeldt, MD, of Physicians' Laboratory Service, Inc. performed the Tesinsky autopsy:

> No evidence of foul play was found either on x-rays taken prior to my examination or during the course of my examination. As stated in my report, a large portion of the body was devoured and was unavailable for examination in the usual sense. However, a large portion of skin remained attached to the remains of the body. Within the skin, in the region corresponding to the back, there were many puncture wounds. Extravasation of blood into the skin was present in some of these wounds and I believe that this is evidence that the man was alive when first encountered by the bear. Hemorrhage into the connective tissue around puncture wounds of the left calf is also present.
>
> In examination of the clothes, which I have sent to the State Crime Laboratory in Cheyenne, Wyoming, the greatest degree of impregnation with blood and body fluid appears to be around the region of the collars of both the camouflaged jacket and woolen shirt. It seems to

be most likely that the initial opening of the body, by the bear, is most likely the region of the neck.

A month before Bill's death, Bear #59 was captured with two cubs—born during that winter's hibernation—doing nothing aggressive but being considered too close to humans. On September 4, 1986, she was relocated with the cubs to an area called Cub Creek, twenty-two miles away.

But by September 19, 1986, she had returned to the Canyon area. The two cubs were not sighted with her. Perhaps they had been traumatically killed in an attack by a male bear. Perhaps she had abandoned them in her urgency to return to Canyon.

On September 30, 1986, she may have been the bear seen at the following "bear jam." The estimated weight was the same. Lake Fire Protection Inspector Arthur W. McIntyre wrote the following account:

I was en route from Canyon to Lake. About ½ mile south of Otter Creek, I came upon a traffic jam of about 8 to 10 cars. The attention of the occupants of the cars was directed toward a 175–200 lb. grizzly bear, which was in a meadow area about 150 to 200 yards west of the roadway. About 50 to 100 feet from the bear, towards the road, were four people with cameras taking pictures of the bear. At about [2:58 p.m.], I contacted Canyon Area Ranger Mark McCutcheon by radio, informing him of the situation. I told him I was concerned about the four people who were closest to the bear. Mark said he would send a ranger to handle the situation. He directed me to request the four people closest to the bear to return to the roadway. At this time, I walked a short distance toward the four people, and called for them to return to the roadway. They complied with my request. After the four people returned to the road, all of the people who were viewing the bear were doing so from the roadway. At about [3:10 p.m.] I returned to my car and continued en route to the lake area.

This was probably the next-to-last sighting of Bear #59 before the incident involving Bill. Bear #59 was last reported seen on October 3, 1986, again without her two cubs. What happened to them is unknown.

———

The Board of Inquiry met at Park Headquarters in Mammoth on October 15 and 16, 1986, and reached the following conclusions:

> The grizzly/human conflict of October 4, 1986, resulting in the death of both, occurred apparently because of two primary factors:
>
> 1. William Tesinsky was motivated to travel approximately 550 yards from his car to the bear's location to photograph the bear, and;
>
> 2. The bear, when pursued and approached at close range was disposed to attack and kill Tesinsky . . .
>
> We can speculate, based on information about Mr. Tesinsky's character, that when attacked, he fought the bear and thus precipitated further attack. There is, however, no physical evidence to support this view. After Mr. Tesinsky's death, apparently resulting from a defensive action by bear #59, the bear consumed part of the body. The circumstances do not suggest that the bear attacked and killed Mr. Tesinsky with the intent of preying on him. Rather, the circumstances suggest that Mr. Tesinsky approached and provoked the bear to attack . . .
>
> There is no indication or evidence that the bear's physical condition, its history of handling, drugging, and monitoring, or the low levels of the whitebark pine nut crop in the Yellowstone ecosystem were directly related to the incident.

In the interest of pursuing his art—wildlife photography—Bill Tesinsky approached Bear #59. The end result was the death of one human, and as many as three bears (the two cubs were probably too young to survive without their mother). For those who blame Tesinsky for getting too close to the bear, this question may also be asked. Hunters sometimes take chances to obtain their targets, just as photographers sometimes do.

Why is hunting widely respected in Montana, Wyoming, and Idaho (in which lies Yellowstone Park), and wildlife photography not? Hunting, like photography, occasionally results in the deaths of people, after which the responsible bears are killed.

# 8

# IN THE DARKNESS OF THE NIGHT: HARRY WALKER

*Bear, bear. It's got my friend!*

—Phillip Bradberry

## FATALITY—1972

*National Park Service—Yellowstone*

*Report No. 1419 [prior to park use of Case Incident Record]*

*Supervisor's Report of Accident/Incident, Form DI-134*

*Animal Incident Report, YEL 371*

*Location: Old Faithful: forested thermal area near Grand Geyser*

*Date/Time: Sunday, June 25, 1972, 1:00 a.m.*

About 12:30 a.m. on June 25, 1972, while walking back to their tent camp in the dark, Harry Walker was attacked by a large animal. To summon help Walker's friend Phillip Bradberry ran down off the hill where they'd been camping, only half a mile from Old Faithful Village. Later that day, Bradberry told Park Ranger M. Scott Connelly why the two had traveled to Yellowstone in the first place. An acquaintance "was telling us about Yellowstone—how good it was, how beautiful it was and everything. So I think that's the main reason why we wound up in Yellowstone."

Concerning Yellowstone's famous bears, both young men from Alabama believed that "as long as you don't bother the animals, they won't bother you," Phillip told Ranger Connelly. But now the two friends' adventure—their camping and hitchhiking trip discovering America—had led them to Yellowstone, where their path crossed that of a grizzly bear.

Phillip's friend Harry was twenty-five. Back home in Alabama he had most recently worked as a Rural Federal Delivery mail carrier, and he had a mother, father, and sisters whom he loved. He and Phillip, whom he called "Crow," had been close friends since the seventh grade. While stopping at the Dairy Queen in Livingston, Montana, about fifty-five miles north of Yellowstone, Harry saw an attractive young lady and introduced himself, and she offered them both a ride to Old Faithful.

The young lady worked for the summer as a maid at Old Faithful Inn. When she looked at Harry, she saw a tall, slim young man at just over six feet and weighing 135 pounds. He had hazel eyes and dark hair. In his backpack Harry carried a first-aid manual, a book on yoga, and his Bible. He had experienced something of life, currently serving in the National Guard and having been divorced for a year.

"We just wandered up there," Phillip told Ranger Connelly about the decision to camp where they did: the thickly forested hillside north of Grand Geyser. It wasn't a public campground—that cost money—but Harry had found a place out of sight where it seemed to him their campsite wouldn't bother anyone. By Saturday, June 24, they had been camped there for two days. That afternoon Harry visited again with the young lady, inviting her to come to Alabama to see the farm where he grew up and to meet his beloved horse, Comanche. Then he and Phillip went back to their campsite and cooked dinner, afterwards returning to relax in the rustic lobby of Old Faithful Inn.

The evening grew late. At about 12:30 a.m.—"in the darkness of the night" as Park Ranger James M. Brady later described it to Yellowstone's Board of Review—Harry and Phillip walked from the inn back toward their camping spot. To help find their secret camp, they had made a marker out of crossed sticks to indicate where their campsite was just up the hillside in the trees.

Phillip later told Ranger Connelly in his interview: "We went through the hot springs again, across the bridge as usual, and we got to the place where we usually go up where we had our marker and we couldn't find it." The interview continued:

> **Connelly:** What kind of a marker was it?
>
> **Bradberry:** It was two pieces of wood, crossed. So we couldn't find the marker so we just estimated that where we'd go would be right so we went up and there were some bones there—looked like elk bones. So we went up there and finally—sort of just wandering our way—finally I noticed we were at a little path over a rock that I particularly remembered Harry and I going over the night before . . . We were approaching the camp area so we were on the side of the hill. We were standing right beside each other and we stopped—we had a light—and we stopped.
>
> **Connelly:** Were you talking on the way up?
>
> **Bradberry:** Yeh, we were talking. All the way up we talked. We stopped and I heard something in front of us. Moved rather rapidly. Harry shined the light. Just as he shined the light could see what looked like a bear, coming at us. Approximately 5 feet away. And I immediately dove to my left and sorta rolled down the embankment. I got back on my feet and was running and then I stopped and paused for a second and I could hear a lot of commotion and I heard Harry hollering, "Help me, Crow, help me." And I hollered back, "Is there a bear there?" And that's all—he didn't respond anymore.
>
> And then I heard more ruffling and it sounded like the bear was coming towards me. So I continued to run and I ran down off the hill and I don't remember where I came off the hill but I think it was back on—off the side where we came off—sorta on the front side and I finally ran into the boardwalks. From there I ran to the Inn.

The first person to see Phillip was an Old Faithful Inn kitchen employee. "I was standing in front of the fireplace at Old Faithful Inn," he reported. "Phil Bradberry came crashing through the front door of Old Faithful Inn." The employee described what happened next:

He [Phillip Bradberry] fell down and started yelling "Bear, bear. It's got my friend. Help him."

[Name withheld] and Ranger Ken Reardon and I approached Bradberry, helped him to his feet and escorted him to the ranger's car. We cruised down towards Castle Geyser. Upon arriving at the geyser we got out of the car and starting walking the boardwalk. About three/fourths of the way there Ranger Reardon asked me to run back to his car and get his .38 revolver. Ran back to car—ran back to Reardon and [name withheld] who were waiting at the location where Bradberry's book was lying (at Grand Geyser).

When I arrived we started asking Bradberry what happened, where it happened, the friend's name as well as his name. We waited till Nurse [name withheld] and two other rangers arrived with lights and arms.

We then continued up the hill yelling for his friend whose name was Harry. We searched the area for approximately 30 minutes and came back down where Bradberry and the nurse were.

According to Park Ranger Kenneth B. Reardon's account, "Old Faithful units were called. Mr. Bradberry and two other employees at the Old Faithful Inn accompanied me in a patrol car to Castle Geyser where we parked and walked to the supposed scene about 200 yards north of Grand Geyser." The search in the dark began. "At this point (1:30 a.m.) we received help from Rangers [Thomas A.] Cherry and [David G.] Trickett. At 1:40 a.m. a preliminary search of the woods back of Grand Geyser was begun with flashlights, rifle, shotgun and one pistol.

"The search lasted approximately 30 minutes until approximately 2:15 a.m."

Old Faithful sub-district ranger James M. Brady testified in the park's Board of Review conducted on November 6, 1972. "The problem was that it was a dark night and it's a wonder it didn't rain. We didn't have a very good location description, although Bradberry was able to identify where he ran out of the woods on account of the boardwalk." Brady described the desperate search:

He [Phillip Bradberry] had left a marker [a book] and he remembered a skull and bones in that area . . .

While he was being checked over by the nurse, I sent a team of three men armed with a light, one shotgun man and one backup man to the hill that Bradberry had come off. We sent the team of three men up to initially scout out the area and see if the campsite could be located. They were unable to locate the campsite and they did not hear any noises that would indicate where the campsite might be. At that time, we regrouped and pulled the search party out of the woods. We then brought Bradberry over to the scene to retrace his steps to immediately find, or as-quickly-as-possible find, Walker and the campsite. [Ranger] Lynn Williamson arrived, some additional help came and we regrouped into a major search party about 3:30 in the morning.

We began up the hill, as nearly as Bradberry could tell, where he had come out. It wasn't a good footprint area because of the nature of the terrain; it was rocky, grassy, very heavily forested and swampy. At 3:30 a.m. until about 5:30 a.m., we searched and circled above and behind Grand Geyser for about half a mile. We were able to locate the campsite just before 5:30 a.m. We were able to locate the campsite with Bradberry's help. I think when he moved into the scene, he knew that he was very close to the area. He became a little emotionally disturbed and excited at that time, as you might expect.

We went into the campsite and some distance down the hill, approximately 150 feet over a little rocky knoll, we located the body of Walker, as indicated in this report. The body was found very close to 5:30 a.m. At that point, Bradberry was escorted back to the Ranger Station where he could receive more medical care and attention. We proceeded with the search party. [Rangers] Jerry Tays, Lynn Williamson and myself examined the scene to try to piece together a story of what might have happened.

Briefly the evidence at the site seemed to clearly indicate the spot where Walker had been knocked down. Bradberry indicated that Walker had been carrying the flashlight. We found the flashlight in several pieces just a short distance over a small knoll and south of the campsite. We are talking about maybe 10 or 12 yards from the campsite. Then from that point on there was physical evidence on the ground where the individual had been drug some 100 feet to the victim's final position when it was mauled by the bear. En route to this final position was a wallet, [and] things of this nature, which had fallen out of the victim's possession presumably when he was dragged or carried by the bear, we are not sure which.

At the final site of the mauling, there was no indication of prints of any type. There weren't many indications of prints around the campsite, giving us any clue as to whether the bear was a black or a grizzly. In fact, the findings were not certain that it was a bear, presumably it was, but no footprints were readily available at the immediate site.

Walker was photographed and this evidence categorized, diagrammed, and examined. Then he was prepared for transport and subsequently taken off the hill to the Old Faithful Ranger Station.

About 7:00 a.m., we were still at the site of the disaster when we heard someone shout "bear" from down below us.

Around 7:20 a.m. two Old Faithful kitchen employees on the boardwalk told Old Faithful sub-district ranger Chester O. Cantrell: "We saw a bear!" In his statement Cantrell noted that "Both said that about [7:15 a.m.] they were on the boardwalk near Grand Geyser looking towards site of where search party was searching. They said they saw a big brown bear at edge of woods. They stated the bear stood up and seemed to climb a tree. They said they yelled 'Bear! Bear!' and ran."

But, Ranger Cantrell noted, by the time rangers got to the area, the bear the two Old Faithful Inn kitchen employees saw had disappeared.

—◦—

Ranger Connelly's interview with Bradberry continued later that same afternoon at Old Faithful Ranger Station. "What brought your attention as to where to camp initially?" Connelly asked Phillip. Phillip replied as fully as he could:

> *Bradberry:* It was just sorta nonchalant like. We just wandered up there.
>
> *Connelly:* Kind of a first place landing?

*Bradberry:* Yeh, we just walked till—the mosquitoes were pretty bad when we first walked in so we walked to that campsite where we were at and put our gear down . . . and went back down and got some mosquito repellent. And then went back up . . .

*Connelly:* Prior to entering Yellowstone, how familiar were you with Yellowstone and this type area?

*Bradberry:* Nothing, actually nothing.

*Connelly:* How about Harry?

*Bradberry:* He knew nothing of it . . . we have national parks back home and you can camp in them anytime you want. I knew nothing about permits.

*Connelly:* Have you camped out a lot before? . . .

*Bradberry:* Back home in Alabama . . .

*Connelly:* Did you mention that some kind of animal had been in your camp?

*Bradberry:* Yeah. We heard an animal the night before . . . Harry or I neither one thought it was a bear. We thought it might have been an elk cause there was some pilings right close to the tent that weren't there before prior the night before . . .

*Connelly:* Small, round droppings or just . . .

*Bradberry:* No, just sort of large.

*Connelly:* Like stool type?

*Bradberry:* Stool type, right.

*Connelly:* Did you have any idea what kind of stool that might be?

*Bradberry:* No, I figured it might be elk stool maybe. I don't know much about wild things . . . we had seen elk down and all around—down at Mammoth Hot Springs and all, out in the fields.

*Connelly:* Are you aware of the different type bears that live in Yellowstone?

*Bradberry:* No. I had read, like I said, this article.

*Connelly:* You did see the bear jam. [Traffic jam where tourists got out of cars to watch bears near the road. Bradberry had earlier stated "Harry and I both felt that it was wrong for such actions to be going, ya know like feeding the bears and stuff like that. Where I'm from in Alabama we let the animals stay in their place and we stay in our place."]

Did you know then that as a result of the discussion that bears were wild and not tame?

*Bradberry:* Oh yes, yes

*Connelly:* You knew that bears were dangerous animals?

*Bradberry:* No, I didn't know that.

*Connelly:* Did you know they are wild and not tame? Do you know if animals are wild and not tame that they are dangerous?

*Bradberry:* Well, it's just like back home. Animals are wild and dangerous back home if you provoke them, you know if you mess with them, but to the best of my knowledge the way I have always looked at it was as long as you don't bother the animals, they won't bother you. That's the way I have always looked at it and that's the way Harry looked at it . . .

After three questions about bear jams, national parks, and camping, the interview continued:

*Connelly:* Would it seem to make sense that in a place where there was a lot of wildlife that campers should be in designated campsites?

*Bradberry:* No, not necessarily. Not to me. If I wanted to go camping with a bunch of people, I could just go down on the river bank in Alabama . . .

*Connelly:* What were your plans, you and Harry? What were you planning to do while you were here in Yellowstone? You say you were going to continue hiking and camping?

*Bradberry:* We hadn't really decided, actually. We were either going to go deeper into the woods, you know, a lot deeper into the woods or leave Yellowstone entirely and go to Canada . . .

*Connelly:* What were you going to do in Canada?

*Bradberry:* Same thing. Get back in the mountains in Canada . . .

*Connelly:* Okay. Do you have any idea of the conditions that might have led up to the bear incident? Why it happened and what contributed to it?

*Bradberry:* None whatsoever. Yes, I have these strange feelings. I even got them before we went up the hill there that night. Harry knew that something was going to happen. I can't explain it to you. Harry and I are close enough that I got those kind of vibes from him . . .

*Connelly:* This strange feeling. How would you describe that?

*Bradberry:* The only way I could explain it would be to tell you that Harry and I are close enough that I received vibes from him—maybe you are not familiar with vibes. But these vibes that I received from him were very strange prior to the incident and even before, all along the road, he has been singing a song, it still hits me right now—the vibes. He was singing a song about Davy Crockett met a bear and got a great big hug. And he was singing this song all along the whole time on the trip. A lot more especially on the road when we were out together by ourselves and for some reason somehow they seem to me, they seem to fit in and, like I said, the strange vibes prior to the incident . . .

*Connelly:* Had you had any arguments of any kind with Harry?

*Bradberry:* No. He had told me prior that if anything had happened to him while we were in the woods to leave him there—not to contact any officials or anything. Except that if anything happened while he was in the woods, he would want to be left in the woods.

*Connelly:* Do you know why he would want that? Do you have any idea why?

*Bradberry:* Yes. It probably goes back to sort of like a religious thing between he and I and a lot of other people we know.

*Connelly:* What kind of a religious thing?

*Bradberry:* Well, that we are here now and that when we die, we die. It's meant to be and that funerals and all this is something that is really not necessary in our views . . . Like, I wish it could have been me, myself personally, I do, but it was meant to be—the way I feel, you know. But as far as anything provoking the bear, even having any contact with the bear prior or anything—nothing whatsoever . . .

*Connelly:* Did you have any food at your campsite?

*Bradberry:* Yes, yes. We had cooked a meal prior.

*Connelly:* Was there any food left out in the open?

*Bradberry:* Yes. I had a pot of rice and carrots and stuff hanging in a tree and I had left it up to maybe keep any kind of animals from getting into it . . .

*Connelly:* Did you remember seeing campgrounds?

*Bradberry:* Signs pointing to campgrounds. Yeah, coming up to . . . yeah.

*Connelly:* Did you ever consider camping out in one of these?

*Bradberry:* No, because, like I said, we didn't want to camp with tourists. We just wanted to get as far away from it as we could.

———

Volney W. Steele, MD, a pathologist from Bozeman, Montana, had the task of performing Walker's autopsy. "The body is that of a badly mauled, scratched, traumatized male, appearing about the recorded age of twenty-five," he noted. The rest of Steele's findings shed some light on what happened to Walker:

On external examination the entire skin surface of the face shows multiple small lacerations and puncture wounds. The soft tissue of the nose has been avulsed exposing the nasal bones and nasal passages. There is no obvious elevation or depression of the skull. Some of the wounds appear to be claw marks and extensive hemorrhage and hematoma formation, and claw marks are noted in the neck anteriorly. The neck is bowed posteriorly. Similar wounds are noted over both shoulders and upper arms . . .

Similar changes are noted in the skin of the abdomen to a lesser degree than that noted in the face and head. The lower abdomen for about an inch below the umbilicus is completely absent and all of the peritoneal tissue[s] . . . have been eaten away. In addition to this, there is a large defect extending into the upper thigh anteriorly including the quadriceps muscle in this area. The entire small and large bowel from the ligament of Trites to the anus is absent. Little or no blood is noted in the abdominal cavity at this point.

Pathologist Steele wrote in his "Final Anatomical Diagnosis," "The most outstanding pathological changes are reflected in the lungs and the trachea." He detailed the probable means of death:

The trachea has been extremely traumatized with multiple fractures and evidence of hemorrhage and edema. The lungs show marked degree of emphysematous change with rupturing of alveolar walls and interstitial hemorrhage. These changes would suggest that suffocation played a great part in the terminal event of this unfortunate patient . . .

After the autopsy was completed, Coroner Harold J. Estey and Pathologist Steele concluded that Harry's death was due to: "Injuries, multiple and extreme, consistent with mauling by grissly [sic] bear."

Park personnel conducting the Board of Review asked Ranger James M. Brady, "What was done to find the bear?" The exhaustive efforts are detailed below:

Ranger Brady: Management activity separate from that [precautions taken for visitors' protection] would be that Mary Meagher, Doug Houston and myself went up to the site that afternoon of the incident. The tent, food and other materials and all other evidence had been removed from the site. We set three wire metal bear snares which are tripped by a lever in a small can. Two in the campsite and one at the exact position of the victim. We spent about an hour and a half setting the snares in that area. The following morning early about 6:30 or 7:00 a.m., we returned to the site.

We observed a female grizzly around 400 pounds in the upper snare at the tent campsite. The lower snare where the victim had been mauled had been tripped, but there was no bear in it. Still we were unable to locate prints except for right around the area where she had been snared and had been digging for several hours. She had darn near dug out the lodgepole pine which are shallow-rooted. We picked a very large one, but if we had picked the one next to it, without a question, she would have gotten out of it.

When we first observed her, she was fairly quiet. It was interesting to note that there was some noise in the woods behind her at the time. I don't know for certain, but it could have well been another bear [*or her cub? Author's emphasis*]. As it turned out, she was still in the breeding season. As I understand it, [she] had just stopped lactating and at the time there is a possibility there was another bear in the woods behind her. I don't know for sure, but there is a possibility and very likely this time of year, especially since the female was in heat. If the bear in the snare had been young and a black bear or one we thought might [not] have been responsible, we might have drugged the bear, examined and released it.

But this particular bear, I recognized. I could only remember two digits of her tag #. I had trapped her two years ago in the evening behind Camper Cabins. While she was growling and snarling, we could see that she did not have much in the way of teeth. The decision was made at that time to kill the bear and send her in for an autopsy and further professional examination.

Grizzly Bear #1792, a twenty-year-old female, was euthanized. On June 26, 1972, Wildlife Lab Supervisor Kenneth R. Greer of the Montana Department of Fish and Game gave Resources Management Specialist Edmund J. (Ted) Bucknall some additional information about the bear:

> The sow had only recently ceased lactating, which would indicate she had either lost a cub of the year or was weaning a yearling. The scat which was collected at the camp site contained hair and broken teeth of an elk, probably a post-natal individual. [So she had eaten prior to the attack on Harry Walker, if this same bear left this scat.]

To help determine which bear attacked, Harry's body had been "examined carefully for tooth marks in an effort to measure spacing between canine tooth punctures," Specialist Bucknall wrote in a letter to Yellowstone superintendent Jack Anderson. "Very few puncture wounds were found, however, and none appeared to have been caused by large canine teeth. Most of the injuries seemed to have been caused by claws . . ."

In Bozeman, the "Wildlife Lab received a female grizzly bear (No. 176789) from Yellowstone National Park on June 26, 1972," wrote Lab

Supervisor Greer in his "Report of Necropsy." His document details his findings:

> *Cause of Death:* Captured in snare and shot with powder cartridge.
>
> *Pertinent Circumstances for Necropsy:* A bear consumed portions of a human between [1:00 and 4:00 a.m.] on June 25, 1972.
>
> At site of attack, a bear was snared and shot at [7:45 a.m.] on June 26, 1972.
>
> *Special Request for Necropsy:* Any evidence of human tissues present in the bear submitted.
>
> *Findings:* . . . Descending Colon = about 100 cc fecal material was removed when dressing out the bear. This was composed of grasses and included a few large pieces of tinfoil. This material was carefully disentangled while washing in a screen container. I personally found from 50 to 80 short, curly, black hairs. External features of these hairs resembled those of human genital hairs. Many hairs were in and around the sharp edges and creases in the tin foil. It is possible that without this tinfoil that the large amount of hair would not have been accumulated in as small an area . . .
>
> *Further Examination:* The unknown hairs, known human hairs, and animal hairs were examined microscopically for internal and external features. These materials were also viewed by Dr. C. Anderson of the Vet Research Laboratory in Bozeman.
>
> Our independent examinations revealed that the unknown hair samples found in this bear were genital hairs [human].

Lab Supervisor Greer's report of the bear's necropsy noted that this was a very old bear, notable for its very worn-down teeth:

> All canine teeth were broken and worn smooth to the level of the worn incisor teeth. The cheek teeth had considerable use and were smoothly cupped.
>
> The ossification of all but one skull suture is indicative of about 20 years of age . . .

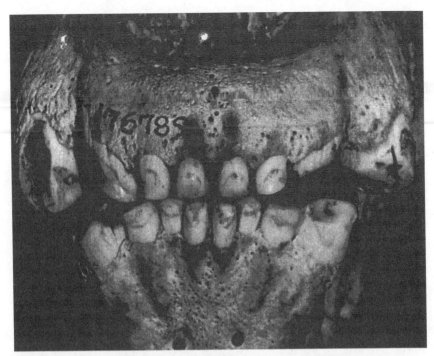

The bear's worn-down teeth

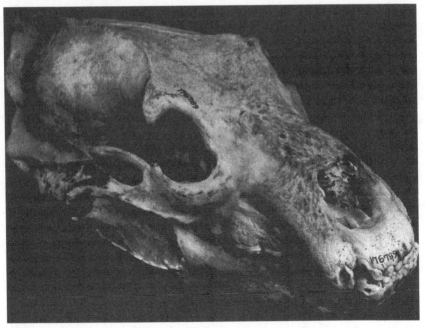

The bear's skull

A method used for assessing physical condition of game animals is the kidney fat index. This bear had an index of 29, which was similar to other bears at the same time of the year.

Generally, this female was a very old individual of average size [and] weight and at the time of death its physical condition was normal.

———

On November 6, 1972, the Board of Review met at park headquarters at Mammoth to sort out the facts of what happened to Harry Walker. Board members determined that he was a very young man who lost his life to a "very old bear," yet one whose "physical condition was normal," and which had a cub of the year, or was weaning a yearling.

A Board of Review member asked Old Faithful park ranger Gerald W. "Jerry" Tays about the cleanliness of the campsite, as well as the cleanliness of the two campers:

> *Question:* You indicated that some of the cans were crushed. Were there any indications that the bear got into any food?
>
> *Tays:* Oh, yes. There was considerable food left open in the campsite to begin with. We found a pot of rice and other already cooked food hanging in a tree. Also, on the ground near the tent was the remainder of freshly cooked food that had been the evening's supper. There had been to the best of my remembrance, a jar of jelly which had been broken open, a flour material spread from one area to the other which the bear had gotten into. I can't recall exactly what the other items were, but much of the food items the bear had gotten into . . .
>
> *Question:* Was Mr. Walker carrying anything?
>
> *Tays:* In the area where he was dragged to his final resting place, we found a tube of toothpaste and a toothbrush—nothing other than that which would have attracted attention. But that was the first thing that we noticed not far from where his body lay.

A Board of Review member posed the following questions to Rangers Brady and Tays:

*Question:* Have you had any bear in this area [where Harry died] during the spring or early summer?

*Old Faithful Sub-district Ranger James M. Brady:* I would comment that the area in the past has been frequented by bears and there are bear signs all along the ridge, just above the geyser basin. If you notice back behind, there is a long ridge that actually ties in with the Rabbit Creek area [where the Rabbit Creek Dump, three miles north, had been closed two years earlier]. It's heavily traveled by black and grizzly bears. You could find signs up there right now. . . .

*Question:* How did you determine that this [Bear #1792, euthanized] was the bear?

*Ranger Brady:* . . . none of the food items and none of the marks on Walker's body seemed to indicate that it was caused by a sharp or normal bear type mouth. So we were probably looking for a bear with worn dentures. When this bear yelled and bawled at us in the snare, it was apparent that she did not have much in the way of teeth. Secondly, she had a tag [#1792] in her lower left ear and I knew her and basically how old she was. I had trapped her once and Lake had trapped her once. I knew she was a former Craighead [Frank C. Jr. and John J. grizzly researchers] garbage bear and she was at Rabbit Creek dump and probably lived in this area a good # of years. At least four or five years that we know about.

*Question:* She was in poor condition too, wasn't she?

*Ranger Brady:* Well, no, not too bad. She was just a large female grizzly bear.

*Comment:* The guy that did the autopsy on the bear said that for her age she was in good shape.

*Ranger Brady:* That was the primary reason-ability behind it and particularly since she had been snared right there at the site. Those factors added together made a good decision on taking the bear. Had it been a non-tagged bear, a black bear or one that I had a feeling [about] . . .This is just a feeling, and I am talking in generalities now, I would have let it go.

*Old Faithful Park Ranger Gerald W. Tays:* From the indications on the body, we were not quite sure at that time what had attacked him

[Walker]. We thought, of course, it was a bear and naturally assuming that from the impressions we gathered from Mr. Bradberry [Walker's friend] of seeing this form in the night and the type of incident that it was a bear. Other than the wound in the lower abdomen, there seemed to be nothing on the body that would indicate sharp instruments such as teeth had been working on the body. On the neck for instance, the front was almost black and yet very little in terms of scratches or scars were present to indicate that teeth had done any work on the individual. The same thing applied for the upper torso. The lack of scars for such a mauling. Then in reviewing the material left in the campsite, it became evident that the cans had been crushed, but not punctured—almost as if something had stepped on them.

─ ⌒ ─

National Guard member Harry Walker—although not left in the woods should he die there as he once requested—"was given a full military burial," according to his estate's lawyer, "with full military honors." Harry's grieving family later brought suit, suggesting that in 1970 Bear #1792 might have killed another man. This lawsuit is discussed in the following chapter, "The Scalp on the Blanket."

Phillip Bradberry was charged with violating two federal laws, establishing a camp at a location other than a designated site and leaving food out in the open without suspending it properly from a tree. He pled guilty and received a suspended sentence.

─ ⌒ ─

Based on the official reports, the following is what may have occurred the night Harry died.

An old sow bear, having lost its (still nursing) cub, or having weaned its yearling, was foraging along the ridge above Harry's campsite. Its age and proximity to the closed Rabbit Creek Dump might indicate that earlier in its life the bear habitually fed on garbage at the dump, thus learning to associate the area, and human beings, with easily obtainable food.

The bear scented food at Harry's campsite, where food supplies on canvas were covered with an aluminum-like material, and a pot of rice and carrots hung from a tree. The bear tore apart the campsite, eating the food. It then encountered Harry and his friend, attacked, and treated Harry as prey. Alternatively, the bear killed Harry first and then ransacked the campsite for more food.

Phillip reported that he and Harry, walking side by side, were talking steadily as they climbed the hill to the campsite, and Harry was shining a flashlight ahead. Given the sound of their talking and the flashlight, surprising the bear may not have been a factor in its charge. If not, why did it attack? Did it have a cub nearby? Was it attacking for food? We do not know. We only know that the bear charged Harry and suffocated him, using her worn-down teeth and her claws to crush his windpipe. She then proceeded to maul and feed upon his body.

Four factors may have played a role in the mauling, and avoiding them, the men might have had a different, better outcome. The factors were:

- They were not camped in a designated campground.
- They camped in an area heavily used by bears.
- Their food was accessible to a bear.
- The victim and his companion were hiking at night.

Of these four factors, the first two seem, to this author, less critical than the latter two factors. Even in designated campgrounds people have been killed by bears, and even when camping in areas frequently used by bears, people have not been attacked. But accessible food always seems to lead to trouble, and hiking at night—the period when bears are most active—is never recommended. Was the attack caused by one of these things, by all of them, by the simple scent of a man being interpreted as prey, or by something else? We will never know.

# 9

# THE SCALP ON THE BLANKET (1970)

*David Hamilton, Old Faithful, reports that visitors at the upper*
*Firehole Bridge are gazing at a scalp on a blanket.*
                              —OLD FAITHFUL RANGER STATION LOG

## PROBABLE FATALITY—1970

*National Park Service*

*Prior to park use of Case Incident Record*

*The Firehole River Incident: Old Faithful area, upper Firehole River*
*Bridge*

*Location: The Firehole River Camp: ½ mile south of upper Firehole*
*River Bridge*

*Date/Time: August 23, 1970, 4:51 p.m., day of week not known; Sep-*
*tember 16, 1970, time and day of week not known*

Reported at 4:51 p.m. on August 23, 1970, the Firehole River Incident, a
probable fatality, actually took place a number of days earlier—the time it
takes for flies to lay their eggs, and for the maggots to hatch.

A person—unidentified, who may have been male or female—placed
his blanket on the riverbank very near the upper Firehole River Bridge.
He settled down on the blanket, perhaps to enjoy the sunshine, time
alone, or a chance to fish. Despite the hot springs running into the Firehole River, the water there was cold and contained trout.

The Firehole River was so named, according to the *Haynes Guide,
Handbook of Yellowstone National Park*, for the following reason:

> [It] was named very early, not from the fact that hot springs and geysers
> adorn its banks for many miles and pour their hot waters into the stream
> but because the trappers who frequented this region found a burnt-over,
> heavily forested "hole" or valley through which the river coursed, and
> from the name "burnt hole" developed the present name of the stream.[30]

There in the heavily visited and developed area of the Upper Geyser
Basin—which had the world's largest concentration of geysers (including Old Faithful)—the unidentified person felt perfectly safe. After all,
he was sitting almost directly beneath the road bridge that crossed the
Firehole River, part of the Grand Loop Road through Yellowstone. West
of him, a short distance away, was the car turnoff and parking area for visitors to Biscuit Basin, who followed the boardwalk past the bright colors
of Sapphire Pool, Mustard Spring, and Jewel Geyser.

No fishing was allowed east of the upper Firehole River Bridge, in the
direction of Old Faithful. So perhaps the person went fishing just west
of the bridge, between the river and the highway, landed one (without
hooking a passing car on his back cast), and was now packing up to return
with his catch.

Then something happened.

And days later the person's blanket, without the person, was found.

⸺

The first known (to this author) published account describing what this
author is calling the Firehole River Incident appeared in Frank C. Craighead
Jr.'s 1982 book, *Track of the Grizzly*. Frank and his brother John pioneered
the scientific field study of hundreds of grizzlies in Yellowstone National
Park and its ecosystem, spanning three states, from 1959 through 1971.

"There is some evidence," Frank Craighead reported, "to link the bear
that killed Harry Walker with another possible, though unpublicized,
fatality in 1970. The Old Faithful Bear Log for August 23, 1970, contains
the following chilling entries."

[Time] 1651 – David Hamilton, Old Faithful, reports that visitors at the upper Firehole Bridge are gazing at a scalp on a blanket.

1736 – Re: 1651 – It is a scalp with pieces of flesh and maggots, pictures taken and pieces collected and [placed] under rear of building.[31]

Two years after the above reported scalp on a blanket, the same bear responsible may have also killed Harry Walker (see Chapter 8).

A copy of the typed Old Faithful Bear Log for 1970, obtained from the Yellowstone Bear Management Office in November 2007, contained no reference to the entries quoted above concerning a scalp on a blanket. Could Craighead (now deceased) have meant to reference instead the Old Faithful Ranger Station Daily Log Book for 1970?

The Yellowstone park archivist as well as the research librarian reported, in November 2007, that no 1970 Old Faithful Ranger Station Daily Log Book could be found. The archives contained Old Faithful Ranger Station Daily Log Books for 1968–1969, and for 1972–1973. In 1975 when Harry Walker's estate's lawsuit against the US government (charging the government with negligence in the bear attack) went to trial, the missing 1970–1971 Old Faithful log books may have been sent as an exhibit and never returned.[32]

The civil court in Los Angeles, where the Estate of Harry Walker lawsuit was brought, currently does not have this or any of the Walker trial exhibits. According to Supervisor Dawn Bullock, Records Department, Civil Court, on November 29, 2007, "We would keep exhibits only until the final appeal is heard. Then the attorneys are notified that they have thirty days to pick up the exhibits or they would be destroyed. That far back, we have no records as to whether the attorneys picked them up or they were destroyed."

But the transcript of the Walker trial does refer to exhibits, as noted below, and corroborates the Firehole River Incident.

On February 19, 1975, Yellowstone park ranger James M. Brady appeared as the defendant's (the government's) trial witness in *Estate of Harry Walker v. United States of America.* Judge Hauk for the Court asked the following:

*The Court [Judge Hauk]:* Then as I read this—wait a minute. Once again, [Exhibit] EE seems to indicate that on August 23rd, 1970, there was discovered a piece of scalp that looked like a piece of scalp with some hair on a blanket in the Fire Hole Bridge area?

*Ranger Brady:* Yes, sir.

*The Court:* And that was sent back to the FBI for analysis?

*Ranger Brady:* Yes, sir.

*The Court:* That is EE.

*Ranger Brady:* Right . . .

*The Court:* Nor was any camper or even bear tied in to the August 23rd incident?

*Ranger Brady:* That is correct.[33]

Resuming testimony a bit later that same day, Stephen I. Zetterberg (Zetterberg & Zetterberg), attorney for the Estate of Harry Walker, clarified as follows:

*Mr. Zetterberg:* What is this attached to the back of EE here? It looks to me like some kind of a log.

*Ranger Brady:* That represents or is in fact a page out of the Old Faithful—

*Mr. Zetterberg:* In other words, this is actually an original page out of the log?

*Ranger Brady:* Yes, it looks like the original . . . That is a page out of the Old Faithful Ranger Station log.

*Mr. Zetterberg:* Now, it says here: "1651, 23 August 1970, David Hamilton, OFL." What is that?

*Ranger Brady:* Old Faithful Log, apparently.

*Mr. Zetterberg:* Old Faithful. It reports, "The visitors at the upper Fire Hole Bridge are gazing . . . and it looks like "are gazing at a scalp on a blanket."

That message just came in some way. Could you tell us how this came in?

*Ranger Brady:* I might be able to. Let me take a look at it.

[Court recesses] . . .

*The Court:* All right, Plaintiff's 62 for identification at this time, that's the logbook, Park Service, the Old Faithful subdistrict, right?

(Plaintiff's Exhibit 62 was marked for identification.)[34]

In the transcript, Judge Hauk and trial participants at times appeared confused as to which records pertained to the Firehole River Incident (the scalp on the blanket), and which pertained to another episode entitled "The Firehole River Camp" (of which, more below).

Regarding Exhibit EE, on February 19, 1975, Judge Hauk and the attorney for the government, William B. Spivak Jr., *attempted* to clarify:

*The Court:* EE is a microscopic and chemical analysis of September 23, 1970, of—
*Mr. Spivak:* Of some hair.
*The Court:* Certain specimens of what though?
*Mr. Spivak:* Of a blanket and some hair.
*The Court:* Black hair on a blanket. . . .

Then Ranger Brady continued his testimony:

*Ranger Brady:* The other bit of information is another report occurring with regard to an incident in August of 1970, as I recall, in which some hair was found on a blanket. The hair was subsequently analyzed as indicated there, and found to be nonhuman . . .
*The Court:* Well, that was August 31, 1970?
*Ranger Brady:* Yes, sir, as far as I can recall.[35]

There was, then, legally acknowledged evidence of a scalp with hair, resting incongruously if it was nonhuman on a blanket close to a road bridge over the Firehole River. The evidence in the trial transcript was unclear (to this author) as to whether the scalp with hair found on the blanket on August 23 was sent to the FBI to be tested, or if a "tuft of hair" found at the site of a bear-destroyed camp three weeks later was tested to see if it was human or nonhuman (results in the missing Exhibit EE).

If anyone reading this book knows what happened on this blanket, by the banks of the Firehole River, on or before August 23, 1970, please contact the author in care of the publisher.

Frank Craighead, in his book *Track of the Grizzly*, appeared to believe that the scalp (see below) belonged not to an animal but to a very human individual. And as the British say of those missing, "he was not since heard of."

—◦—

Three weeks after the Firehole River Incident, discussed above, a visitor discovered a deserted campsite by the Firehole River that had been ransacked by a bear.

Nothing, even today, is known about who set up and then abandoned, or went missing from what came to be known by the Park Service as "The Firehole River Camp."

In 1982, Craighead's *Track of the Grizzly* reported the following:

On September 16, 1970, Dan Bean of Eugene, Oregon, reported to rangers at the Old Faithful Station that an abandoned camp on the Firehole River a half mile south of the new highway bridge had been ransacked by a bear. It appeared that the bear might have been old and toothless, cans of food having been mouthed but not broken open. An official Park document stated that the camp was damaged by a bear—no sign of occupant. Apparently, no other evidence was found. The camper never showed up, and the camp was removed by rangers. Rangers Herbster, Cherry, Connelly, Argill, and Williamson inspected the site on September 16 and took all items to the Old Faithful Ranger Station. They estimated the camp had been there at least 5 days to one week. Seventeen items were found, including a tent with accessories, clothing, a fish net, a swimming face mask, and fins—and a duffel bag which bore the name Herbert Muller and the #37790176. Was this the name of the camper who had disappeared? . . . I found no evidence that any warnings were issued to the public that there had been a man-grizzly incident perhaps resulting in a fatality.[36]

This author's research, in 2009, shows that Herbert Muller, whose Army service number from World War II is #37790176, was honorably discharged on November 6, 1946, and later died of cancer in his hometown of Gackle, North Dakota, at age seventy-four. According to his nephew, who was very fond of him, he did not do much if any fishing, and had never gone missing from Yellowstone or any other place.

But someone *was* missing, or had abandoned a camp and left behind valuable equipment, for some reason. Apparently that person had bought a used duffel bag, bearing the name and number of veteran Muller at an Army surplus store.

For those who may question the existence of the unknown Firehole River Camp occupant, the Harry Walker trial testimony corroborates that the *camp and its camper did in fact once exist.* On January 17, 1975, Judge Hauk questioned Yellowstone park superintendent Jack K. Anderson as to whether, in 1970, a camper was presumed to have disappeared:

> ***The Court:*** Now, I suppose it came to your attention that it [Bear #1792] was in the Old Faithful area and in a potentially dangerous position?
>
> ***Supt. Anderson:*** Yes, but this would have been, what I would consider, a routine transplant the first time around.
>
> ***The Court:*** Even though there was this, I suppose, rumble or rumor around Yellowstone that the previous month or so the campsite had been rummaged and somebody had apparently disappeared.
>
> ***Supt. Anderson:*** Yes, sir. But I had no evidence that—there is a number of bear in the area. There is nothing to indicate this bear from the reports that I received.[37]

A short time later the same day, when questioned by US Attorney Spivak, Park Ranger Brady confirmed that the Firehole River Camp underwent a thorough "grid" search:

> ***Mr. Spivak:*** You stated in your written statement that you made a grid search of the abandoned campsite?
>
> ***Ranger Brady:*** Yes.

*Mr. Spivak:* Will you explain what that means?

*Ranger Brady:* In this particular case eight or ten rangers and Fire Control personnel, searched the area in a grid-like fashion, beginning at the campsite and moving in all points of the compass or all directions about a half a mile in every direction from the campsite.[38]

Questions about the scalp on the blanket were posed on Thursday, February 20, 1975, to Ranger Brady by Attorney Zetterberg for the plaintiff:

*Mr. Zetterberg:* Your Honor, may I point out that the item, the specimen was Q-1 blanket; and may I point out that 1736, the message entry by a person that might or might not have been [Ranger] Steve [Stu] Orgill:

"Re: 1651," that is three entries up, "It is a scalp with pieces of flesh maggots. Pictures taken and pieces collected under the rear of the building."

And the records of the FBI show that what was sent was a blanket; and the report from the blanket, the report refers to hair taken from the blanket. There is no reference to the scalp.

Now, where is the scalp? [author's emphasis]

*Ranger Brady:* Is the question for me?

*Mr. Zetterberg:* That's right.

*Ranger Brady:* Well, Mr. Zetterberg, I would think—

*Mr. Zetterberg:* I don't want your philosophy, Mr. Brady. I want to know if you know where that scalp is.

*The Court:* Let's let him answer. He is trying to answer.

*Ranger Brady:* I believe it is in Mammoth.

*Mr. Zetterberg:* On what basis do you base that belief?

*Ranger Brady:* This would have been returned. It was sent from the law enforcement office in Mammoth, which is a central area for handling evidence, taken from any area of the park. In other words, we process our evidence through the law enforcement office and it is sent to the FBI from there and returned to them.

*Mr. Zetterberg:* Wait, just a moment. You said it was sent to the FBI, but the report there does not say it was sent to the FBI. The report says, "Blanket Q-1 sent to FBI," and there is no reference there to any maggots and there is no reference there to scalp; and you have got a weekend in between. And what can maggots do to a scalp in a week?

*Ranger Brady:* I see. Well, to the best of my knowledge, Mr. Zetterberg, the blanket and the scalp, which were kind of stuck together were sent.

*Mr. Zetterberg:* . . . let me read the report exactly, so I don't make a mistake. All right. It says: "No blood was identified on specimen Q-1. No blood identified on the blanket. No tissue was on Q-1."

When it went in, there was tissue from the report to the ranger station, and tissue from the report logged into the book; and there was no tissue reported by the FBI, so somewhere in between the tissue [of the scalp] disappeared.[39]

First there was the scalp on the blanket, and then the discovery of the torn-up camp destroyed by an old, partially toothless grizzly.

Was an offending grizzly found? Frank Craighead's *Track of the Grizzly* continued:

A month after the torn-up camp was located in 1970, an old partially toothless bear was trapped near the Camper Cabins Café at Old Faithful, less than a mile from the camp, and tagged with National Park Service tag #1792. The bear had been seen in this developed area four or five times before it was trapped but apparently no association between the presence in the area of this old bear and the destruction of the nearby camp and disappearance of its occupant was considered. Bear #1792 was transplanted only 18 miles away, a distance easily traveled by a bear in a single day.[40]

At the Walker trial on January 17, 1975, Judge Hauk questioned Brady about all three: the Firehole River Incident, the Firehole River Camp, and Bear #1792:

*The Court:* Did you find any evidence to connect Bear No. 1792 with the incident described in Exhibit DD, namely the unknown bear and the unknown camper campsite torn up, reported on September 16, 1970?

*Ranger Brady:* No, sir, I did not find any evidence.

*The Court:* All right. Or any evidence to connect it with the August 23, 1970, episode of the scalp with some hair on it found in the Fire Hole area?

*Ranger Brady:* No, sir, not to our information.[41]

The tragedy of the missing camper, if he/she did die after being attacked by a grizzly, reverberated nearly two years later when Harry Walker was attacked a few miles from the grizzly-destroyed Firehole River Camp. Walker died near his tent, on a wooded hillside above Grand Geyser (near the Old Faithful Village developed area).

The bear that killed Walker—an old female with worn teeth—was identified as the same bear suspected two years earlier in tearing up the Firehole River Camp, and relocated for that presumed action: Bear #1792. Unfortunately for Walker, Bear #1792, after being transported elsewhere, returned to the Old Faithful area.

It should be noted that from 1970 through 1972, when the garbage dumps were available to bears, many bears had worn teeth from munching on, among other things, tin cans. However, the Craighead brothers in their research were well aware of this fact, and still drew the inference that Walker's bear was the same bear that could have left behind a human scalp on a blanket, and also destroyed a missing camper's fishing camp.

Further, if the August 23, 1970, scalp on the blanket did not belong to the missing camper but to another person, *and* if on September 16, 1970, the missing camper was dragged off from his ransacked campsite and killed by a bear—all "ifs"—could Bear #1792 have been responsible for *three* bear attacks?

You the reader decide.

—⁓—

The following is a guess as to what may have occurred in the Firehole River Incident, the day the scalp was found on the blanket.

A fisherman's catch smelled inviting to a foraging grizzly bear, which may have investigated the source of the scent. The fisherman was on his blanket, possibly asleep. The grizzly bear wandered up, ate the fish, then attacked the fisherman, and as grizzlies are wont to do, went for the head first, scalping it. The grizzly then made off with the person into a thickly wooded area, in order to eat undisturbed.

The scalp remained behind, on the blanket, where it was discovered by park visitors almost a week later. The human corpse by then was long gone.

Next is a guess as to what may have happened at the Firehole River Camp, which contained swim fans and mask and a fishing net, and was ransacked by a bear. No person to whom the camp belonged was ever found. It may be that the camper had been killed by a grizzly bear when he took his blanket and fishing pole, walked half a mile north, and sat down on a blanket by the Firehole River Bridge.

Alternatively, the person on the blanket may have died a natural death, and only then been found by the old sow with worn teeth, Bear #1792, who scalped the victim, leaving the scalp behind, and then opportunistically dragged away and devoured his body.

The following are hypothetical ways in which the owner of the scalp (presumed to be human) could have met another, better outcome. First, the owner of the scalp could have camped at a public campground. But if he/she wished to set up camp away from the public (two years before backcountry campsite registering was instituted), he/she may have thought it legal to do so without checking first with a ranger. Second, the person fishing could have contained such odorous items as freshly caught fish in a sealed, airtight container.

On the other hand, in 1970 there were all too many bear/human incidents. Two fishermen were charged by a grizzly sow with two cubs on June 26, 1970, and the next day twenty-five-year-old park visitor James Freeman was mauled by a bear. Freeman survived.

# 10

# WEAKEST PREY IN THE FOREST (1 MILE FROM PARK): ROGER MAY

*I asked Roger if he was still alive and he said "Yes" but he "wasn't doing too good."*

—ROGER MAY'S FRIEND

## FATALITY—1983

*National Park Service—Yellowstone*

*US Fish and Wildlife Service*

*Gallatin National Forest*

*State of Montana Department of Fish, Wildlife and Parks*

*Yellowstone Park "Bear #15 Incident" Case File*

*Location: Rainbow Point Campground (Loop A, Unit 17)*

*1 mile west of Yellowstone Park*

*Gallatin National Forest Hebgen Lake Ranger District*

*Date/Time: Saturday, June 25, 1983, 2:30 a.m.*

*Country Journal's* Terry Chilcoat and Michael Petron wrote about the joys of camping. "Something wakes you, and you lie listening to the gentle flap of tent walls and the last scattered patter of retreating rain, until you begin to sink into sleep again."

Then you may realize it's the middle of the night and you're in grizzly country.

Roger May woke suddenly that night of June 25, 1983. Something was tearing a hole in the roof of the tent. His friend was still sleeping beside him, surrounded by the seeming security of many others in the car campground, one mile outside Yellowstone Park's western border.

Where Roger's death occurred—Rainbow Point Campground— certainly looked like a very civilized place. The roads, looping between campsites, were identified with alphabetical signs. The campsites, known as "units," were helpfully numbered. Cars, recreational vehicles, kids, plus electric lights, flush toilets, and showers made this a microcosm of a city in the woods. It was thought to be safer, without the dangers of city nights. The campground was located just north and a little west of Yellowstone's gateway town, West Yellowstone, on a headland above Hebgen Lake— where in 1959 an earthquake killed campers, drowned roads, and tore down an entire mountain. To the south of the campground was Targhee National Forest, where loggers' clear cutting of timber can be seen from outer space.

On the afternoon before—at 5:46 p.m. on June 24, a Friday—two campground collections officers checked in with the police dispatcher at the town of West Yellowstone. Then the two collections officers began their car patrol down the campground roads to Loop A, Loop B, Loop C, and Loop D. Their report is included in Yellowstone Park's Bear #15 Incident Case File. The "campsites appeared to be clean," one officer wrote, and added the following:

> [W]e did not see any violations of the Food Restriction order in which ice chests and other food containers must be locked in a vehicle . . . there were no unattended food items that we noticed. [At Loop D] there were no campers in the loop, so after we drove through the loop we closed the gate behind us, leaving only loops A, B, and C open.
>
> We checked out with the police dispatcher at 6:09 p.m. and left the campground.

At about 8:00 p.m. that same Friday evening, June 24, Roger steered his car into the Rainbow Point Campground. He and his friend had driven there from Sturgeon Bay, Wisconsin. The collections officers had left, and the two men chose to camp in one of the three remaining loops, Loop A, and deposited the fee envelope into its vault. They chose the unoccupied Unit 17, where Roger and his friend set up their tent and prepared for a relaxing evening.

Unit 17 was located just off the paved road, in a clearing bordered by a small grove of trees. It had a firebox for cooking, and twelve feet east of the firebox, a picnic table. Thirty-one feet east of the picnic table, Roger and his friend parked their car (with a grocery-filled cooler locked in the trunk). Twenty-one feet east of their car they set up their heavy-duty umbrella-type tent. Both Roger and his friend were careful campers, and officials later determined that the two "took all recommended measures for careful camping in bear country."

The two men had not so much as a candy bar inside the tent. Around 11:00 p.m. they settled in for the night in their down sleeping bags—safe and sound so they thought, in a public campground with others nearby.

Roger May's friend [name withheld] related what happened next when he was interviewed at the campground by George E. Hubbard, warden sergeant for Montana Fish, Wildlife and Parks, and Gary Brown, bear management specialist for Yellowstone National Park, as well as others. Ellipses indicate words removed for brevity:

> *Hubbard:* What I would like to have you do, is give me . . . just how this thing started last night, how you remember it . . .
>
> *Friend:* I woke up last night and the tent was shaking and it just felt like some—felt like almost a prank type of shaking—Boy Scouts or something like that. Then the tent collapsed and I started saying "Roger" and he said [deleted] and then all of a sudden he started screaming and the tent just sort of moved—pulled—and then Roger was really screaming and I started fighting my way out of the tent which was all the way down by now and when I got out of the tent I saw Roger with a bear standing over Roger about ten feet away from the tent and I started screaming and yelling and the bear seemed startled and grabbed Roger and dragged him off—oh, about another 20 or 30 feet and I charged the bear yelling and screaming with a tent pole in my hand and threw the

tent pole at him and chased the bear off into the woods and I asked Roger if he was still alive and he said "Yes" but he "wasn't doing too good" and so I ran back to the tent to try to find the keys to the car and my glasses, and uh, I couldn't find the entrance to the tent right away and by the time I got inside the tent all of a sudden I heard Roger screaming again and I heard the brush start r-r-rumbling like somebody was running through it. I located a flashlight and my glasses and I came out and tried to see anything and I was yelling for him and I didn't hear anything and then these other people came up and one guy helped me look and the other couple went and called the rangers and then the police came and we went out searching and found his corpse across the road over there.

*Hubbard:* . . . when you come out of the tent and saw the bear drag him, Roger, was he dragging him at that time?

*Friend:* Well, he was standing over him and I started—when I came out of the tent yelling and screaming it seemed to startle the bear a little bit and he ran off with him in his mouth.

*Meyer:* This is Ralph Meyer, District Ranger. Would you tell me again how big you thought the bear was when you first saw it.

*Friend:* I thought he stood just about three and a half feet at the shoulders standing on his all fours, and I don't know how long he was probably, about yea long or so.

*Meyer:* Looks about five-six feet long what you just showed us there . . .

*Hank Fabich:* Did you have anything in that tent that would attract a bear at all—anything you can think of?

*Friend:* We got everything out of the tent that we could—we didn't even carry any beer in there.

*Hubbard:* I know you cooked over here last night. Did you do all your eating at the picnic table or did you take any foodstuffs . . .

*Friend:* We ate at the picnic table.

*Hubbard:* You didn't eat anything during the evening in the tent at all?

*Friend:* No, no, we did our dishes over there too, right after we got done eating—disposed of the charcoal in the pit over there and poured some water on it.

*Fabich:* You didn't notice anything on that bear, any patches of hair missing, any crippling type of walk or . . .

*Friend:* No, it just seemed like a dark gray color to me.

*Hubbard:* You mentioned you threw that tent pole at him or did you run up to him and hit him with it—it's bent pretty severely right in the middle—do you recall?

*Friend:* It was bent when I picked it up.

*Brown:* The clothes that you had on cooking yourself, or the deceased, were those taken into the tent with you or placed—

*Friend:* Both were in the tent.

*Fabich:* When you started yelling at the bear or throwing that tent pole did he exhibit anything—aggressive behavior—growl, stand up—

*Friend:* Not toward me, no, he ran off. He was growling a little bit before that, Roger was screaming pretty heavily. He had a few RRRRRRRRs types of—but no hind legs stuff or anything like that.

*Brown:* At any time while camping with the tent that you weren't in what you might have considered bear country, did you cook or have food in the tent?

*Friend:* Uh—not that I remember.

*Hubbard:* When you mentioned you saw the bear dragging the victim could you describe to me how it had ahold, how the bear had ahold of the person . . .

*Friend:* The bear was—the bear was going forward. Seemed like to me and he grabbed, seemed to have ahold on his lower leg.

*Hubbard:* Was the victim struggling at that time do you recall?

*Friend:* Uh, he was screaming until the bear started dragging him and then he sorta stopped and then when the bear stopped he started screaming again. He moved—the bear moved real quick with him.

---

At noon on June 25, 1983, an investigation team met with Ken Gallik, deputy forest supervisor, as its coordinator. According to the investigation team's report, on the night of the bear attack Roger's friend ran to seek help from the people at the nearest occupied campsite. The people responded immediately:

These people called the Dispatcher in West Yellowstone, and Bob Pearson left for Rainbow Point at 3:08 a.m., and arrived at the scene in approximately 10 minutes. Bob said he did not see any drag marks across the road 20 or 30 minutes later. He said the bear apparently ate on the individual before he crossed the road. The bear dragged the victim across the road before the ambulance arrived, approximately 3:30 a.m. . . . The body was found at approximately 3:30 a.m. by Bob Pearson. The bear had left at that time. Bob was asked if he thought he could have scared the bear away, and he said, "Yes." He said there were five people helping him look, and they did a lot of yelling (calling Roger) as they were following the drag marks . . .

Ralph [last name not given] said the victim weighed 170 pounds, and there was approximately 100 pounds put in the bag . . .

Gary (Fish & Game) [last name not given] reported on the collared bears in the area. #92, #38 who has two yearlings, #60 with two cubs (seen at Fan Creek the first part of June), #97 seen at Tepee Creek the first part of June, and #71 whose collar is not working, but who is thought to be in this area. Number 15 is also in the area, but has thrown its collar . . .

Dick [Richard R.] Knight [National Park Service] arrived at 12:30 p.m. and was brought up to date on this incidence. Dick said he thinks Bear #15 is the one. He is big enough (as was described to him) . . . Dick showed the fellows on a map where he thought Bear #15 should be bedded down in swampy land. He said this was Bear #15's pattern to roam as was reported earlier.

Yellowstone Park's final report noted that the bear had collapsed the tent and made a hole in the roof of the tent. The report concluded:

The first bite apparently caught the victim in the upper part of the body because there was a large amount of blood in the upper portion of the sleeping bag and in the tent. The victim was apparently out of his sleeping bag by the time that [his friend] managed to escape from the tent and stand up, since the sleeping bag was found a distance of 6 feet from the tent . . .

The clothes in which they cooked their evening meal were in the tent, but there was no evidence that these clothes were in any way especially dirty or that they had spilled anything from dinner on their clothes . . .

## *Findings*

The victim and his camping partner had taken all recommended measures for careful camping in bear country . . .

The bear had been observed in normal breeding behavior within the previous month . . .

The bear displayed no aggression to the victim's companion when on two occasions, at close range, the victim's companion attempted to scare away the bear.

The bear displayed unusual persistence in remaining with, and consuming, the victim, while considerable human activity occurred within 200 feet, and with very little visual cover.

Thirteen traps were set; however, the only trap disturbed was within 10 feet of the site at which the victim was found. This was a garbage set. Two other traps near the body site were baited with meat (road-killed antelope).

## *Trapping Operation*

. . . During the first trap inspection at 12:20 a.m., on June 26, 1983, a large male grizzly bear (identified as bear #15) was found at the campground where the victim had been found . . .

The bear was tranquilized and material evidence was collected: scrapings from the claws and toes, hair and skin from the muzzle region, and fecal material from the trap site. This material was submitted to the State of Montana, Forensic Laboratory, Missoula, Montana.

The bear was held until the Forensic Laboratory results were received, providing evidence that the collected fecal material contained human head hairs matched with hair from the head of the victim.

The bear was destroyed and transported to the State of Montana, Department of Fish, Wildlife and Parks Laboratory in Bozeman for necropsy.

## *Conclusion*

The investigation team is unable to find any overt explanation for the attack on Roger May by Bear #15 . . .

———

Roger's friend returned to Wisconsin and was interviewed there on August 4, 1983, by Robert Thomas, special agent with the US Fish and Wildlife Service, who attempted to find an explanation for the bear's attack:

> *Thomas:* Well, possibly they'll have to sort through this stuff and compare it with maybe other grizzly attacks they've had in the past and see if they can come up with some kind of a common factor there.
>
> *Mr. May's friend:* To me it just sounds like the bear was hungry.

———

The history of Bear #15 was included in Yellowstone's report. Wrote Montana Fish, Wildlife and Parks lab supervisor Kenneth R. Greer, [The] "known history of bear #15 from lab field work during 1971–77, and continuing grizzly studies of the Interagency Study Team" were as follows:

> . . .[bear #15] was initially captured as a cub of year and marked in YNP [Yellowstone National Park] on August 9, 1971. *He was trapped a total of 19 times* [author's emphasis] at West Yellowstone dump and vicinities of Rainbow Point, Cougar Creek, Fir Ridge, Richard's Pond and Madison Fork. During this time he was relocated 4 times with one including release in Sunlight Basin of Wyoming.

———

The Yellowstone "Bear #15 Incident" Case File included the following letter and *Cody Enterprise* newspaper article, both sent on December 28, 1983, to Yellowstone's Superintendent Robert Barbee:

Dear Mr. Barbee:

I read the enclosed article and cried for Bear #15—and I felt sorry for Chris Servheen [Grizzly Bear Recovery Coordinator—US Fish and Wildlife Service] when he had to administer the fatal overdose—God forbid that we leave any natural habitat for the wild life—let us graze, drill and mine all available land!!—and the devil take the animals that live in the territory—

I really don't [know] why I'm writing—but I thought you'd like to read the article—

[name withheld]

In the article, titled "Local Bear Goes Bad," *Cody Enterprise*'s Carl Bechtold wrote "Some nights later, Bear No. 15 . . . came to camp to feed."

He found nothing else as he came to what was perhaps his last tent in the campground. He grabbed a camper, carried him off, ate about 70 pounds of him and left the remains for horrified campers and officials to find.

It was described as a classic case of predation. When the bear came back to feed again on his kill, as bears do, then Bear No. 15 was killed.

I have a friend who has a theory about bears in Glacier National Park, where a similar incident happened a few years back. He thinks there's a new super strain of grizzly developing. Because of the extended contact with man, this fellow theorizes the bears are losing their genetic, instinctive fear of people. When that happens, men become the weakest prey in the forest . . .[42]

*Cody Enterprise*'s Bechtold then quoted Grizzly Bear Recovery Coordinator Chris Servheen, who had recently told reporters: "The incredible thing is not that bear attacks happen. The incredible thing is that they don't happen more often."

❧

What happened the night Roger died? It would appear that Bear #15, a large male grizzly, had over the years become habituated to human beings by receiving food rewards, by being trapped, and by losing its sense of caution and fear. "He was trapped a total of 19 times at West Yellowstone dump and vicinities of Rainbow Point, Cougar Creek, Fir Ridge, Richard's Pond and Madison Fork." It would appear that Bear #15 not only came to associate human beings with food, but perhaps finally saw humans *as* food.

On the night of June 25, 1983, Bear #15 was foraging in the vicinity of the Rainbow Point Campground, where, despite the ongoing best efforts of its staff, it may have been attracted by smells of food. Alternatively, the bear may have been attracted by the scent, from inside their tent, of the two humans themselves as potential food.

Acting in a predacious manner, it tore open Roger's tent and carried him away. The bear "displayed unusual persistence in remaining with, and consuming, the victim, while considerable human activity occurred within 200 feet, and with very little visual cover." It was noted that of three traps, two baited with road-killed antelope, Bear #15 chose the trap with a garbage set.

What on that night caused that particular bear to behave in that predacious a manner will never be known. Although reference to the possible adverse effects of the drugs used in trapping and handling the bear so many times was not made in the Yellowstone report, persistent comments to this day have raised that possibility. For a time Sernylan—known to humans as "angel dust" or "PCP"—was used as a veterinary anesthetic. Known side effects in humans include rage, convulsions, excitation, and delusions. After being trapped and anesthetized so many times, could permanent damage have been done to Bear #15?

See also Chapter 4, "Final Expedition," for a discussion of this possibility related to the grizzly-caused death of Erwin Evert. The answer remains, so far, unknown.

# PART III— NIGHT SIDE OF NATURE: FOUR MORE FATALITIES, SEVEN MAULINGS

**11**

# FATALITY—JUMPED FROM THE REAR (1942): MARTHA HANSEN

*She has severe damage to the scalp and the muscles are torn loose in the back of her neck.*

—Livingston Enterprise article on Hansen attack,
August 24, 1942

*National Park Service—Yellowstone*

*Special Incident Report Case File (prior to park use of Case Incident Record)*

*Location: Cabin 381, Old Faithful Cabin Camp*

*Date/Time: Sunday, August 23, 1942, 1:45 a.m.*

August 22, 1942, was a tense time worldwide. Newspaper headlines in the United States read: "Nazi Subs Credited with Sinking 17 Merchant Ships."

That Saturday Martha Hansen arrived in Yellowstone Park with some friends, hoping to escape from worry about the war. Martha also needed a well-deserved respite from her duties as superintendent of nurses at Idaho's Twin Falls County General Hospital. She began that job four years previously, when she was forty-one, and her career in helping others had been long. Martha was a former supervisor at the Mary Lanning Hospital in Hastings, Nebraska, and a former surgical supervisor at the

Nebraska State Hospital for the Tubercular. She served for several years on the Nebraska State Board of Examiners for Nurses. Nursing excellence ran in her family. Ellen A. Hansen, her sister, was superintendent of the Masonic Hospital at Plattsmouth, Nebraska.

Yellowstone Park seemed far removed from stress. Martha was there to relax and enjoy traveling with her close friends: another woman, and a couple with their baby. Martha's party of five arrived in the Old Faithful area and checked into a rustic, no-frills, unfurnished cabin at Old Faithful Cabin Camp. All five were to share one space: Cabin 381. The outhouse-style restrooms were centrally located for all the cabins, and a short distance from where Martha would sleep.

It was still daylight, and Martha and her friends took a stroll. At that time, the Old Faithful area looked relatively undeveloped, with some hewn-in-half logs to serve as benches for those who waited for Old Faithful geyser to erupt. Yellow-bellied marmots peered from under the few boardwalks. The white of geyser sinter surrounded the cone of Old Faithful, as well as the lip of Morning Glory Pool. The Upper Geyser Basin, pale with sinter and rising steam, was darkly rimmed with evergreens.

Then it was night.

By 1:35 a.m. on Sunday, August 23, almost all of the tourists slept, as had Martha. But then she woke up in the cabin. Martha recognized what woke her: the need to visit the restroom, ordinarily an easy task. But here in Yellowstone it meant dressing with at least shoes and bathrobe, and venturing outside to find the outhouse. It must have been warm under her blankets and she hated to leave her cocoon. The cold night in Yellowstone, at this elevation, replaced so quickly the heat of the day. And the night was very dark.

Probably Martha tried at first to ignore the need to go. But then the bladder promptings could no longer be ignored. It was time to get up, find shoes, try not to wake her woman friend and the couple with their baby. But her woman friend woke up and asked where Martha was going. Martha whispered her reply and edged out the door.

Outside it was colder still, and the blackness of the sky looked primeval. Perhaps Martha felt small underneath the stars. She hurried toward the restroom door.

What happened next was recorded by the seasonal park ranger on duty, D. H. Bremer, and included in the Special Incident Report Case File:

According to [name withheld], at 1:45 a.m. Miss Hansen arose and left the cabin en route to the ladies' rest room when she was attacked by a large brown bear.

Miss Hansen told her rescuers that the bear jumped on her from the rear without warning as she passed the opening between the cabin they occupied and the one directly in the rear. Her screams brought [name withheld], who immediately retreated when the bear turned on her. [Name withheld] then came to the rescue and he also retreated. The bear was finally driven off by the consistent efforts of neighboring tourists having been aroused by Miss Hansen's screaming, who threw sticks of wood at the bear. Still conscious, but suffering a rapid loss of blood, Miss Hansen was carried back to their cabin, and [name withheld] left in his car to obtain aid.

Then on night duty, [I] first became aware of the injury about 1:50 a.m. when [I] stopped [name withheld]'s car in front of the ranger station as a routine check on persons driving at that hour. [Name withheld] said he was en route to Old Faithful Inn to obtain a doctor and told [me] of the accident. Since [name withheld] stated that his wife was a registered nurse, [I] sent him back with the first aid kit and then left immediately for the Inn and summoned Miss [name withheld], the [park] nurse, and drove her directly to Cabin 381. After a brief examination Nurse [name withheld] told [me] to obtain a doctor if possible and to call for an ambulance from Mammoth Hospital.

Returning to the Inn, [I] summoned a Dr. [name and address withheld], who was a registered guest there; called Mammoth Hospital for an ambulance (2:15 a.m.), and called Acting District Ranger Watson to inform him of the affair. Watson in turn notified the Chief Ranger's Office. Dr. [name withheld] was driven to Cabin 381 by [myself], arriving there at 2:21 a.m. The ambulance arrived at 4:20 a.m. and departed at 4:28 a.m. [Name withheld] and the remainder of his party followed the ambulance to Mammoth in their car, while [the doctor and nurse] returned to Old Faithful Inn.

According to [name withheld], the bear was a large brown and had been eating out of the garbage cans near their cabin during the day. [Name withheld], a tourist, although he did not actually see the accident, claimed that he saw the bear a short distance from the spot where Miss Hansen was attacked and that the bear was not a black but a grizzly; his statement has been attached to this report. However, [names withheld] reported to [me] that at 4 a.m. a large brown bear came prowling near Cabin 381, this bear being identified by [name withheld] as the same bear that caused the injury. As no grizzlies have been seen in Old Faithful Cabin Camp this season, the probability of it having been a grizzly is slight.

Several tourists in the area had been awakened by Miss Hansen's screams and having seen the accident were considerably alarmed and upset. For that reason Rangers Keller and Keck came on duty at 6 a.m. and patrolled the cabin area to reassure tourists regarding their personal safety.

Dr. [name withheld] described Miss Hansen's injury as follows: Incised wound 6" from top of scalp down over the back of neck; 2" incised wound directly over bridge of nose and extending over right eye; lacerated wound on face in front of ear; small wound over jaw; jagged wound on left side of face extending down into ear; severely lacerated wound on left side back of ear and extending down back of ear (believed to be a bite); superficial skin abrasions.

Ranger Bremer, citing the account of a person whose name was withheld, described the bear as follows. "The bear was a large brown, and had been eating out of the garbage cans near their cabin during the day . . ."

Other adjectives used to describe the bear that caused Martha's injuries, listed in the Individual Bear Injury Report include "Light brown," "Male?," "Mature," and "Fat." The bear was also described as a "poor-looking brown" as well as "gray" (see below).

Although he did not actually see the attack, a fellow tourist sighted a bear a short distance from the scene of the attack. His handwritten note in the Case File described the bear:

This bear in my estimation would weigh approximately 500 pounds and was gray not brown. It is indeed a grizzly bear. I am not misinforming you as to the identity of this beast as I study the animal life of North America, being a Scout Master at Idaho Falls, and teaching the characteristics of the especially more common animals, the grizzly bear being one of them. So therefore I am not mistaken in its identity.

The impression of its color as gray, to which the Scout Master referred, may in fact have reflected the silver-tipped hairs that give the grizzly bear its "grizzled" name.

———

Ranger Bremer noted that "[Name withheld] returned to Old Faithful on the morning of August 25th, for the purpose of collecting their personal belongings left in Cabin 381." Bremer wrote further about attempts to clarify how the attack happened:

> At that time he [Martha's friend] had a conference with [District Ranger] Bauman and Chief Ranger LaNoue, for the purpose of determining further the type of bear causing the injury to Miss Hansen and any other information that might throw more light on the incident. The following information was gained from the conference.
>
> Miss Hansen's account of how the injury occurred as related to [name withheld] at the hospital in Livingston is considerably different from [name withheld]'s statement recorded in paragraph two of the Special Incident Report dated August 23rd. This later statement shows much more probability than the one she made immediately after the accident. Miss Hansen now claims that she confronted the bear face to face suddenly as she came around the corner of the cabin (the bear did not jump on her from the rear), both stopped and were apparently startled. The bear reached for Miss Hansen as she tried to turn and run. Miss Hansen was unsuccessful in her attempt to escape. The bear then severely clawed Miss Hansen and dragged her several feet. [Names withheld] also state that the bear was a rather poor-looking brown.

[Name withheld] was assured that action would be taken towards exterminating the bear that caused the injury; that the rangers are here to protect the public and are doing all they can to discharge this duty successfully . . .

So, was the attacking bear "fat" or "poor-looking"? Was it male? Was it a black bear that was brown in color, a brown grizzly, or a silver-tipped gray-appearing grizzly?

In the days long before ear tagging, radio collaring, and DNA analysis of blood and hairs, how could it be known which individual this bear was, and whether in fact it had caused previous damage or injury?

There was no indication in Yellowstone's files that the responsible bear was ever found, identified, or (as cited above) "exterminated."

⁓

And what happened to Martha, who had been moved from Mammoth Hospital in Yellowstone Park to the hospital in Livingston, Montana? Page one of the *Livingston Enterprise* newspaper on Monday, August 24, 1942, read as follows (courtesy of Livingston-Park County Library, Montana):

### *Idaho Woman Hurt By Bear In Park Early Sunday Morn*

Miss Martha Hansen, 45, Twin Falls, Idaho, was in the Park hospital here today [Park County Hospital in Livingston] with serious lacerations inflicted by a black bear at Old Faithful early Sunday morning.

She was reported resting as easily as could be expected this afternoon after having been on the operating table for two hours and a half today.

Miss Hansen's face and head were reported to have been seriously lacerated by the bear, which attacked her when she left her cabin.

Dr. G.A. Windsor reported late this afternoon that Miss Hansen's condition was critical.

She has severe damage to the scalp and the muscles are torn loose in the back of her neck, he stated.

Miss Hansen was rescued only after her screams had attracted other members of her party.

By the next day, Tuesday, August 25, a front-page story reported the following:

### Woman Mauled By Bear Is In Critical Condition

The condition of Miss Martha Hansen, 45, of Twin Falls, Idaho, was described today at the Park hospital as "very critical."

Miss Hansen was mauled by a black bear early Sunday morning at Old Faithful.

She was brought here late Sunday and underwent an operation Monday afternoon. Her relatives are here.

The following day's page one story must have given Hansen's relatives a moment of hope:

### Martha Hansen Resting Easily
### Undergoes Tracheotomy to Relieve Breathing

Miss Martha Hansen, 45, superintendent of nurses at Twin Falls county general hospital, who was attacked and badly injured by a bear in Yellowstone park Sunday morning, underwent a tracheotomy this morning at the Park hospital and was reported resting easily this afternoon.

The operation was to relieve her breathing because the swelling from neck injuries had pinched her windpipe, physicians at the hospital reported.

"She is much more comfortable now, although her condition is still critical," hospital attaches stated.

On Friday, August 28, 1942, page one reported as follows:

### Victim Of Attack By Bear Dies At Park Hospital

Miss Martha Hansen, 45, supervisor of nurses at the Twin Falls, Idaho, county general hospital, died at the Park hospital in Livingston last night of injuries sustained when she was badly mauled by a bear in Yellowstone park last Sunday.

She had been in a critical condition since she was attacked by a black bear as she left a cabin at Old Faithful. Her head and neck were severely lacerated. Two operations were performed in a futile effort to save her life.

Funeral services will be conducted at Grand Island, Neb. The body will be sent to Grand Island today by the Franzen mortuary.

The Supplement to *Special Incident Report of Hansen Injury*, written by Ranger Bremer and submitted by District Ranger John Bauman, concluded as follows:

[I]n the case of the Hansen [Fatal] Injury the bear was startled and probably acted instinctively. There was no record of any previous injury or damages caused by this bear; the rangers therefore had no indication that a vicious bear was in camp and little could have been done to prevent such an accident under the present park policy.

◆~◆

Why did the bear attack Martha Hansen that night? Because of the probable color (brown), the size (large), and the ferocity of the attack, it may be guessed that the bear was a grizzly. It was reported to have been eating out of the garbage cans near Cabin 381 during the day. At night, it was continuing to forage, and had become habituated to human beings perhaps because of garbage-feeding "bear shows" tolerated by park personnel (at which visitors watched from bleachers), as well as the presence of unsecured human foods in visitor areas.

Unafraid, determined to find food, this bear encountered Martha as she moved between two cabins on her way to the centrally located restroom. If it attacked her from behind, it may have seen her as possible prey, or as a challenge to a food source: garbage cans. If it attacked her from the front, it may have been as surprised and frightened as she was, and reacted instinctively.

# 12

# EARLY ATTACKS: THREE FATALITIES, SEVEN MAULINGS (1870–1930s)

*Mauling 1870—Frederick Bottler, guide, area unknown (before establishment of Yellowstone National Park)*

*Mauling 1888—George R. Dow, miner or railroad worker, June, Cinnabar Basin*

*Mauling 1902—R. E. Southwick, married tourist, early September, near Lake Hotel*

*Fatality 1912—John Graham, trapper, May 4, Crevice Mountain near Jardine, Montana*

*Mauling 1916—Chub June, during summer, Sylvan Lake*

*Maulings 1916—Ned Frost Sr., hunting guide, and Ed Jones, cook, August 14, Indian Pond*

*Fatality 1916—Frank [Jack] Welch, married Fort Yellowstone engineering employee, September 7, Turbid Lake*

*Fatality 1922—Joseph B. "Frenchy" Duret, married rancher and trapper, June 12, Slough Creek*

*Mauling 1930s—Female tourist, unknown area of Yellowstone*

Besides bears, another large predatory species—human beings—has long been drawn to the Yellowstone region. In the early official records of Yellowstone Park, known bear-caused human fatalities were few. Of course, even before the world's first National Park was approved by Congress and signed into law by President Ulysses S. Grant on March 1, 1872, there were even earlier bear-caused human fatalities with Native American victims.

Joel C. Janetski, in *Indians of Yellowstone Park*, wrote that "[T]he tribes most frequently mentioned as being in the area are the Blackfeet, Crow, and most importantly, the Shoshone-Bannock."[43] To Frank Linderman, the Crow medicine woman Pretty-Shield described in 1931 what living among grizzlies was once like:

> The white bears [grizzlies] were bad. One of them once bit off a woman's nose. We girls often met the white bears in the berry patches. Sometimes women were killed by them. Our men killed but few of these big bears in my day. They were very powerful, those big white bears.[44]

The Shoshone-speaking Sheepeaters lived among the bears in Yellowstone. In his 1880 Yellowstone *Report of the Superintendent*, Philetus W. Norris described finding artifacts they left behind, including "skin covered lodges [and] circular upright brush-heaps called wickeups, decaying evidences of which are abundant near the Mammoth Hot springs, the various fire-hole basins, the shores of Yellowstone lake, the newly explored Hoodoo region, and in nearly all of the sheltered glens and valleys of the Park."

Presumably bear attacks were an unfortunate risk to life. The hunting and exploring guides, miners, park workers, ranchers, trappers, and tourists—whose encounters are described below—sometimes unknowingly accepted that risk.

## THE BERRY BEAR

*Frederick Bottler, guide to Philetus W. Norris in Yellowstone*

*Mauling, 1870—location unknown*

The weather finally turned mild in 1870, but it was not the best season for guiding in Yellowstone. Frederick Bottler, an experienced guide, knew "the timing was poor; the streams were in flood and [he] had not entirely recovered from a mauling received six months earlier while disputing the possession of a berry patch with a family of grizzly bears," as Aubrey L. Haines noted in 1977's *The Yellowstone Story*.[45]

Frederick operated a ranch with his two brothers, Phillip and Henry, across from Emigrant Gulch just north of the present park.

But Philetus W. Norris (who became Yellowstone's second super-intendent) could be very persuasive. Bearded, at times wearing fringed buckskins and moccasins, he hired Frederick to guide an exploratory trip into Yellowstone. In 1895's *The Yellowstone National Park*, Hiram Martin Chittenden wrote the following:

> Norris filled with varying capacity the roles of explorer, path-finder, poet, and historian in the Park . . . He was pre-eminently an explorer. He not only traveled repeatedly over all the known trails, but he penetrated the unknown sections of the Park in every direction. Though not the discoverer, he first made generally known the geyser basin that bears his name.[46]

Where was he requesting his guide to lead him? As he told Frederick, Norris wanted to "ascertain the possibility of an exploring party going through the upper canyon and the Lava, or ancient volcanic country beyond, so as to reach the wonders said to be around Yellowstone Lake."[47]

So Frederick agreed to guide this explorer and the two set forth. Norris recorded this trip in his 1885 *Meanderings of a Mountaineer* (summarized by Aubrey L. Haines), in the excerpt below:

> Descending from Electric Peak—probably by the north ridge between Mol Heron and Reese creeks—they were attempting to cross the

swollen Reese torrent when [Frederick was] swept off [his] feet, washed downstream, and nearly drowned. [Frederick's] painful bruises, and the loss of their only rifle, left them no choice but to retreat to the Bottler ranch.

Home again, Frederick resumed healing from his painful new bruises as well as those from the six-month-old bear mauling—which was possibly the first-published account of a bear attack against a white man in Yellowstone.

## THE CINNABAR BEAR

*George R. Dow, miner or railroad worker*

*Mauling, June 1888—Cinnabar Basin*

George Dow was working at Cinnabar Basin, just north of the park. George was perhaps a gold miner or railroad worker. The Basin was flanked by two creeks, the Dixon and the Cinnabar, and shadowed by Cinnabar Mountain at 7,176 feet. Jack Haynes in 1910's *Haynes Guide* described railroad work in the Cinnabar region as follows:

Track-laying from Livingston, Montana Territory, was started southward up the Yellowstone River toward the park in 1883 past Yellowstone City, a frontier mining camp in Emigrant Gulch, and through Yankee Jim Canyon to the pioneer hamlet of Cinnabar which it reached on August 31, 1883 . . . Cinnabar was named for the bright red stone in nearby Devil's Slide believed to be cinnabar (mercuric sulphide) ore, but in reality only colored stone.

Whatever George was doing, he encountered a female grizzly with two cubs. Bears were still numerous, even though vast numbers had been killed. In 1870, for example, "the Yellowstone Basin . . . was without doubt a country unsurpassed on this continent for big game," wrote William E. Strong in 1876. "Large herds of elk, mountain sheep, the black and white-tail deer, and the grizzly, cinnamon and black bears were numerous . . . During the first five years the large game has been slaughtered here by professional hunters by [the] thousands, and for their hides alone."[48]

The female grizzly with two cubs charged George, sending him running to the nearest tree. George started scrambling up. Unfortunately the grizzly clamped down on George's thrashing foot, and using its teeth and claws, tore George's leg up.[49]

# THE BEAR THAT DIDN'T WANT ITS CUB PETTED

*R. E. Southwick, tourist*

*Mauling, September 1902—near Lake Hotel*

The *Livingston Enterprise* newspaper reported on September 11, 1902, that a Yellowstone visitor was attacked by a bear. Mr. Southwick, "a tourist making the rounds of the park, was dangerously and perhaps fatally injured Saturday evening by being attacked by a bear. The party with whom Southwick was traveling had stopped for the night at the Lake hotel." The newspaper report continued:

> During the early part of the evening he and his wife walked down the road for an evening stroll.
>
> Not far from the hotel they met a cub bear and Southwick began petting it when he was attacked by the mother. He was thrown to the ground and the bear began tearing him to pieces.
>
> Had it not been for the prompt action of his wife he would have been killed. She seized a club and wielded it upon the bear with such force that the animal was driven off. Parties from the hotel came to the rescue and carried the injured man to his room where it was found that he had received very severe, if not fatal injuries. He was bitten several times and the flesh was torn from his breast. One rib was broken and it is feared that his right lung is seriously injured. Southwick is a prominent business resident of Hart, Michigan.[50]

On September 18, the *Enterprise* added the following:

> The reported death of R.E. Southwick in the Park, who was injured by a bear, was evidently an error, and we are informed that he was able to leave the Park this week for his home.[51]

# THE MAMMOTH-SIZED GRIZZLY

*John Graham, hunter and trapper*

*Fatality, May 4, 1912—Crevice Mountain near Jardine, Montana*

John Graham made his living by trapping just north of Yellowstone Park. Reports varied as to the details of his encounter with a bear, but the following account was contemporaneous with his death (courtesy of Livingston-Park County Library, Montana):

The *Livingston Enterprise* reported on May 6, 1912: "JOHN GRAHAM MEETS DEATH IN FIGHT WITH BEAR. Pioneer Park County hunter and trapper killed in a fight with mammoth grizzly near Gardiner—dies before help arrives." The newspaper account continued:

> John Graham was killed in an encounter with a mammoth grizzly bear on Crevasse Mountain Saturday. Graham met the bear while walking through the forest and did not observe it until he was only a short distance from it. He shot, but before he could fire again the bear was upon him. Adolph Hagaman heard Graham's cries for help and ran to his assistance. He discovered the bear on top of Graham and fired at the beast. The bear rolled over on top of the unconscious form of Graham, as the shot from Hagaman's gun did its work. According to the report of our Gardiner correspondent, whose message was received Saturday immediately after we had gone to press, Hagaman hurried to Gardiner after caring for the injured man as best he could, to secure a physician. When the physician and Hagaman reached the side of Graham he was dead. The mammoth bear broke Graham's jaw and chewed terrible gashes in his head and arms.
>
> Graham was a pioneer of the county and was unmarried. He was 52 years of age. He was well known throughout the Gardiner country and was always known as a good hunter and trapper.[52]

# THE BEARS OF SUMMER, 1916

*Bear 1: The Sylvan Lake Bear*

*Chub June, unknown employment*

*Mauling summer, 1916— Sylvan Lake*

J. A. McGuire wrote in *Outdoor Life*, December, 1916, about bear attacks in Yellowstone. "In the past few months there have been at least three distinct attacks made upon men in the Yellowstone Park by a grizzly bear. During the past summer Chub June was chewed up and badly lacerated by a grizzly near Sylvan Lake; Ned Frost and Ed Jones [see below] were terribly cut up by a grizzly near the Lake Hotel on August 14, while in September, Jack [Frank] Welch [see below], a freighter, was so badly torn up by a big grizzly at Ten-mile Spring, near Turbid Lake, that he died a few days later."[53]

*Bear 2: Fiery Little Green Balls of Eyes*

*Ned Frost Sr., hunting guide, and Ed Jones, cook*

*Maulings, August 14, 1916—Indian Pond near Yellowstone Lake*

Yellowstone Guide Ned Frost Sr. wrote in *Outdoor Life*, 1918 about his incident with a bear. "It was a clear moonlight night, but rather cool and cheerless, so I put an extra heavy canvas pack cover over my sleeping bag just before I turned in. This I have often thought since may have been the means of saving my life."

> . . . At about half an hour after midnight we were aroused by the most bloodcurdling yells I ever heard come from human kind. Raising myself in my sleeping bag, I saw there in the bright moonlight about fifteen feet away from me a huge grizzly. He had Jonesy by the back and was shaking him, bed and all, as a terrier shakes a rat. Yelling at the top of my voice, as Shorty was also doing, I threw my pillow. As the white mass landed just in front of him, the bear flung Jonesy to the ground and started back. His fiery little green balls of eyes caught sight of me as I sat up in bed waving my arms over my head in a vain attempt to scare him. Then he made a lunge for me . . .
>
> The covers were finally pulled from my head and the gleaming fangs and drooling jaws were within a foot and a half of my eyes. The hot breath of the old devil had a very repugnant odor, which seemed

almost to choke me, and I wondered just how it was going to feel when he would finally loose his hold on my legs and sink his great teeth into my exposed throat. I remember thinking it wouldn't be a very hard death, for if he would just get me by the neck everything would be over quickly.

That I am alive today I attribute to a lucky fluke. After shaking and carrying me along several times he finally got a mouthful of sleeping bag only and with a vicious shake threw me clear of the bag, like a potato out of a hole in the sack . . .

The bear was still busy looking for me in the bed. By this time Shorty had made a dash for his night horse which was staked nearby; Jonesy, still yelling, upset stove and table, with all the dishes in camp, and with all the racket and disturbance, the old boy finally shambled off into the timber . . . Jonesy had four places in his back stitched up; and his face was sort of smeared sidewise a bit where old Bruin had stepped on it. I had six wounds in my legs sewed up. In one the main artery, the size of a lead pencil, was exposed for two inches, but not ruptured. If it had been, I should have bled to death in ten minutes.

Did that old boy intend to get me? Two weeks later he proved it . . . and poor Jack [Frank] Welch died the next day.[54] [see below]

It was not recorded whether the couple who had traveled from Boston and were the clients on this trip, Mr. and Mrs. Frothingham, felt that they got their money's worth.

*Bear 3: Great Holes in His Stomach*

*Frank [Jack] Welch, Fort Yellowstone engineering employee*

*Fatality 1916, Ten-Mile Spring at Turbid Lake*

Frank Welch, a rancher, was also a highly valued employee in the engineering department at Fort Yellowstone (now Yellowstone Park). In remembrance of Frank's contributions, he lies buried in the Army Graveyard atop one of the "balds," a treeless hill at Mammoth, Yellowstone. Frank's gravesite is listed as #52.

Tuesday, September 7, 1916, was Welch's unlucky day. The *Livingston Enterprise* reported what happened (courtesy of Livingston-Park County Library, Montana):

### Yellowstone Park Bear Kills F. Welch Of Corwin

Frank Welch of Corwin died last night at the hospital, Fort Yellowstone, Mammoth Hot Springs, as the result of injuries sustained in Yellowstone Park Friday evening when a bear came upon him while he was sleeping and tore great holes in his stomach and almost tore his arms from his body. Welch was married and has a married daughter. He owns a ranch near Corwin, but was driving a freight outfit for the government.

### Bear Killed by Dynamite

Welch had two companions, but they were unable to frighten the bear away until it had nearly killed Welch and had inflicted the fatal wounds. Having no guns within the park, and being far from a soldier station, the drivers determined to have revenge for the awful work of the bear and so spread bacon about and surrounded the meat with dynamite. The dynamite was then connected by a fuse with an electric battery and when the bear commenced to eat the bacon, the drivers shot off the dynamite and killed the animal.

### Working for Government

Welch was hauling supplies for the government over the Sylvan Pass road. He had gone to sleep under his wagon when the bear attacked him. He was taken as quickly as possible to the hospital at Fort Yellowstone but his injuries were such that death was certain. The men with Welch frightened the bear away by throwing bales of hay at it but it returned and ate the hay after Welch had been carried to a place of safety. It is against the government regulations to carry arms in the Park, and as a result people are almost entirely at the mercy of the animals when attacked. Welch has resided at Corwin for many years and was well known through that section of the county.

# THE BIGGEST-FOOT BEAR

*Joseph B. "Frenchy" Duret, married rancher and trapper*

*Fatality June 12, 1922—Slough Creek, 3 miles north of present-day Silvertip Ranch*

It was true that Frenchy Duret married Miss Jennie McWilliams (who came to Frenchy via letters), sight unseen. But Frenchy and his wife may have been as happy together as any other couple. Frenchy was a rancher and trapper just north of Yellowstone at Slough Creek. His fine piece of land and the spot where he died, half a mile from his cabin, can still be visited today.

"If you continue upstream along Slough Creek, you come upon Silvertip Ranch, just north of the park boundary," Orville Bach wrote in *Exploring the Yellowstone Backcountry*. "During the early 1900s, Frenchy Duret, a man of French-Canadian descent lived here."

He maintained a small herd of cattle that he often illegally allowed to graze inside the park. Duret was also a noted poacher of park game, but although rangers tried to catch him in the act, he always managed to elude them. Rumor had it that he harbored a particular hatred for grizzlies, since his pet dogs had been killed by one. One summer's morning in 1922 Duret discovered a huge grizzly caught in one of his steel bear traps. He returned to his cabin, retrieved his rifle, and proceeded to shoot the bear. Apparently he did not strike a vital spot, for the bear lunged forward and broke free from the trap, falling on Duret and wounding him severely. The grizzly then left the scene. Duret, upon regaining consciousness, began a slow crawl back to his cabin, 0.75 mi. away. He made it to the edge of his property, then died under his own fence. Frenchy Duret was buried near his cabin. His gravestone, near the Silvertip Ranch, reads "Joseph Duret, Born in France 1858, Died 1922."

The bear, whose bloody trail led down Slough Creek, was never found. Newspaper clippings and a 1922 letter from Horace Albright—then the park's superintendent—that discuss the fruitless search for the grizzly, are posted in the lobby of Silvertip Ranch. According to Albright, it left behind the largest set of tracks he had ever seen in

Yellowstone. Presumably, offspring of this bear inhabit Yellowstone Park today. Frenchy's Meadow is 3.0 mi. north of Silvertip Ranch.[55]

Fortunately, Frenchy's wife was able to retain the rights to their cabin and the valuable property it was built on, after relatives tried to seize it. "Jury Holds Joseph Duret Will Valid," a clipping in the Yellowstone Archives stated.

Instead of being ousted from her home, Mrs. Jennie Duret could visit Frenchy's gravesite only half a mile from where he died.[56]

## THE "JACK THE RIPPER" BEAR

*Female tourist*

*Mauling 1930s, unknown part of Yellowstone*

Sometime during the decade of the 1930s (date uncertain), a woman traveling in Yellowstone, seeing the sights which included a bear—was moved to do what those before her and those after her sometimes do.

"She stood directly in front of the bear, facing him but offering no more candy," William Rush notes in *Wild Animals of the Rockies*. "'Go away now,' she ordered. 'No more candy for you today.'"

> She did not move, and as the bear dropped down on all fours he put out his front feet toward her, much as he would to a tree or any other convenient object, to ease his descent. The woman screamed as his paws touched her shoulders. His claws, sharp as knives, seeking support, ripped through her clothing and skin. They tore deep cuts a foot long across her breasts and blood spurted from them. The woman fainted. The bear backed away and disappeared in the pandemonium that ensued.[57]

A similar story to hers had been related by Superintendent Horace Albright in the 1920s as well, and variants on her "classic" but unfortunate experience abound, all involving above-waist disrobing.

"The Ripper" experience doesn't seem to happen to men.

# PART IV— NARROW ESCAPES: FIVE NEAR-DEATH MAULINGS

# 13

# EYE GONE—COULDN'T FIND (1977): BARRIE GILBERT

*I couldn't tell exactly what the noises were, but then they just didn't sound right.*
—Mr. Gilbert's research partner, Bruce Hastings

*National Park Service—Yellowstone*

*Case Incident Record Number: 770637*

*Location: Crowfoot Ridge, ½ mile west of Bighorn Pass,*

*Gallatin Mountains in NW Yellowstone*

*Date/Time: Wednesday, June 27, 1977, 10:50 a.m.*

Events began routinely enough on Tuesday, June 26, 1977—the day before the bear attack. Mr. Barrie Gilbert and Bruce Hastings were just doing their job: looking for grizzly bears to observe for scientific purposes.

Yellowstone's spring had changed to early summer, and with the change came blooming flowers, some of which signaled the presence of food to bears. "The white compound umbels of yampa . . . are now appearing as are the light blue tubular flowers of wild hyacinth," wrote Frank C. Craighead Jr. in his book about Yellowstone, *For Everything There Is a Season*:

Yampa has a small, sweet-potato shaped tuber with a parsnip flavor, while wild hyacinth has solid bulbs or corms. Blue camas is at peak of blooming and has edible bulbs, layered like the nodding or wild onion

. . . also now in bloom. All are excellent wild foods, both for man and wildlife, and are sought out by grizzly bears who routinely visit patches of these plant foods at the same time year after year. (It is this habit, when applied to food obtained in campgrounds and developed areas, that makes potentially dangerous, man-conditioned grizzlies).[58]

It was also the season—high up in northwestern Yellowstone near Bighorn Pass—for Gilbert and Hastings' grizzly bear behavioral study.

Park Ranger Richard T. Danforth wrote the following background information in the Case Incident Record. "On June 26, 1977, Barrie Gilbert and Bruce Hastings left their vehicle at the Indian Creek Campground. [They] hiked to Bighorn Pass (A) (refer to quad map) [page 173] and set up camp." The ranger described the men's project: the bear study:

> Mr. Gilbert is a professor of biology at Utah State University and Mr. Hastings is a graduate student at Utah State. The National Park Service contracted Utah State University to do a grizzly bear behavioral study, and the two above mentioned persons were assigned to this project. Mr. Gilbert is the senior member of the group and Mr. Hastings is a graduate student working on his Masters' Thesis.

Unfortunately the men endured a bear attack. The day after the bear attack Yellowstone Park biologist Mary Meagher interviewed Bruce Hastings (on June 28) and described the starting location of their grizzly bear observations. (Mr. Gilbert remained in the hospital.)

> Barrie Gilbert and Bruce Hastings parked their car (tan, Ford Torino, station wagon, [numbers withheld] plates) at the Bighorn Pass trailhead at Indian Cr., and backpacked to Bighorn Pass on 6/26. They pitched their tent maybe 50 yds off the saddle of the pass (N of trail says Tom Black) which provided a vantage point for glassing the area for grizzly bear activity. They saw a single bear that evening, below and slightly SW, about ½ mi away. (See sketched quad map on page 173.)

Park Ranger Mark C. Marschall described the rugged area where the bear attack occurred (and its bear attractants) in his hiking book *Yellowstone Trails*. Marschall wrote that Bighorn Pass is located in the Gallatin Mountains, a range which "runs south-north from Mt. Holmes to the north border of Yellowstone at Electric Peak. In this area, the Gallatins are a range of 10,000 foot high, somewhat rounded, mainly sedimentary peaks . . . The Gallatins are also the home of the grizzly and black bear. The grasses and forbs favored by the bears grow in the fertile glacial soil of the Gallatin's ridges and valleys."[59]

The day of the bear attack, Wednesday, June 27, dawned clear, bright and windy. At sunrise Gilbert and Hastings were up and using binoculars to look for bears in the Gallatin Mountains' alpine meadows. Referring to the US Geological Survey quadrangle map, the report described the bear-sighting locations indicated by initials on the map:

> On the morning of 6/27/77 Gilbert and Hastings observed a single grizzly bear in a meadow to the southwest (B) of Bighorn Pass on the east facing slope of Crowfoot Ridge and also a sow with three cubs (C) of the year almost due west of Bighorn Pass in a large alpine meadow also on the east slope of Crowfoot Ridge. Since the two researchers were on an area familiarization trip, they decided to circle around the bears to the north and get up on top of Crowfoot Ridge (D) proper to do any further observing of these bears.

The day after the attack, in her June 28 interview with Bruce Hastings, Biologist Meagher clarified Hastings' and Barrie Gilbert's whereabouts and activities just prior to the incident:

> Bruce and Barrie started on down (NW) on the Bighorn Pass trail for a mile or slightly more (presume leaving tent etc camp as is—not breaking camp—I didn't ask specifically). They then cut SW across the Gallatin River and began angling upslope, intending eventually to reach the SE knob of Crowfoot Ridge (elev. 9755), high above and ¾ to 1+ mi away from the general area of observed bear activity. To do so, at about

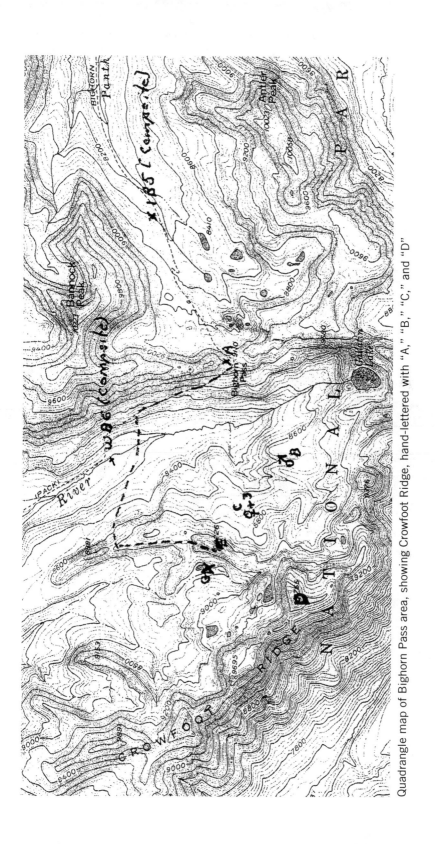

Quadrangle map of Bighorn Pass area, showing Crowfoot Ridge, hand-lettered with "A," "B," "C," and "D"

9100-9200 elev, they began to move along and slightly behind a small intermediate ridge. Bruce dropped his pack (an area of open trees) and stepped back some feet (a few yards?) to relieve himself. Barrie moved on ahead.

The attack occurred on Wednesday morning at approximately 10:50 a.m. at Crowfoot Ridge, near Bighorn Pass. Later the same day, Bruce Hastings told a park interviewer what happened next. In the report, because the interview was occasionally inaudible, there are blank spaces noted:

*Hastings:* We got up at sunset to glass the fields with binoculars and (interrupted) excuse me—sunrise this morning and we glassed the fields and saw one bear we felt was a boar—BLANK—There was the Gallatin Lake and the Bighorn Pass was here and it was in this white patch (referring to map at this time) and we also saw a sow with three cubs in this area, saw them with binoculars.

*Question:* You essentially sighted a total of five bears.

*Hastings:* Right.

*Question:* Were you sure they were grizzly bears?

*Hastings:* Yes, with binoculars we could see the humps. Both Barrie and I –BLANK.

*Question:* Okay, then what did you do?

*Hastings:* Okay, then we came down off Bighorn Pass, followed the trail to approximately here (referring to map), before the trail drops down to the creek shortly before, and crossed—Now this is pretty heavy timber right here. Some is pretty darn heavy here. . . . to my knowledge we went pretty much straight up to this section, and then I think we curved over here and got on the back side of this so that we would not be seen by bears. We . . .

*Question:* What do you mean, not seen by bears?

*Hastings:* . . . we wanted to stay on this side so that we wouldn't be disturbing the bears . . .

*Question:* Show me.

*Hastings:* Came up . . . ah . . . the back side of this and I told Barrie I had to use the restroom so I just stopped there and went back into the brush there five or six yards, and he said he was going to go on up here and I think he said he was going to glass . . . try to glass these fields . . . here . . . uh . . . and I heard something but the wind was blowing very, very hard so I couldn't be sure what it was and then I realized that something was wrong and pulled out my knife for whatever good that would do, and . . . ah . . . realized that something was wrong when I pulled . . .

*Question:* What made you think something was wrong?

*Hastings:* Noises that just . . . you know the wind was blowing hard and I couldn't tell exactly what the noises were, but then they just didn't sound right . . . uh . . . you know, I just been out in the woods a lot and some noises just don't sound right. So I went up into . . . to back where my pack was . . . I dropped my pack where I stopped and . . . ah . . . And then went a little further up and saw the grizzly. I could not see Barrie, but I could see the grizzly was mauling him, and uh . . . I wasn't quite sure what to do but I yelled, "Ha!" just at the top of my lungs and saw it bolt, but as it was bolting I went around one of these real brushy evergreens and by the time I got around to the other side, I could not see the grizzly; it was gone . . . Did not see the bear anymore, anymore. The only time I saw it was when I first saw it, yelled at it, saw it bolting like it was . . . it looked, it appeared like it was going to turn and go across the hill, opposite from me, but I got behind the tree . . . ran behind it to keep from being seen at that time and ran immediately to the other side of it to see [if] the bear was gone or if it was leaving . . . And . . . ah . . . it was gone.

*Question:* What did . . . what was Barrie's response as far as the bear . . . what . . . like when did he first see the bear . . . did he relate this?

*Hastings:* OK. I . . .ah . . . asked him about it when everything seemed stable . . . I believe he said that he sat down and [was] trying to glass those open areas where we'd seen the bear before . . . He said that he turned around saw the grizzly coming for him tried to run around . . . ah . . . an evergreen that was kind of bushed out there . . . BLANK . . . and said it was on top of him before he could hardly get anywhere. Now as best as I could tell from what he was saying, he said that it bit his legs first . . . then his stomach and then worked over his face . . . One single chocolate colored sow.

The "Details of Incident" report notes that "Mr. Gilbert indicated that Mr. Hastings should climb a tree in case the bear returned," then continues:

Mr. Hastings did not. He found Mr. Gilbert had severe facial lacerations. At this point Mr. Hastings called the Mammoth Communication Center at 10:50 a.m. with the emergency message that his fellow worker had been mauled by a bear approximately two miles west of Bighorn Pass. He indicated his co-worker had severe facial and head injuries.

The transcript of the call for help and the immediate response of the Park Service rangers, the rescue helicopter pilot, and medical personnel appear below:

[10:50 a.m.] (monitored) "Emergency, Emergency, we need a helicopter." (Got information from individual—his location is west of Big Horn Pass—one person has been injured by a grizzly bear. 120 Hastings talked to Tom Black on the radio—Is the bear still in the area?—They were not sure, they were in a wooded area—He could get to a ridge and signal the helicopter where to land. Tom assured him they were on their way. 120 Hastings told us the injured party's name is Barrie Gilbert. His scalp is torn—the face is ripped quite badly—the bleeding has mostly stopped—he was also bitten on the leg and stomach—120 Hastings requested first aid assistance. Dr. [name withheld] talked to him by radio. Told him to wash the wound thoroughly with soap and water. Is the bleeding stopped? Yes—breathing is normal and victim is awake and alert. Most of the bleeding has stopped.

[11:20] 120 Hastings—Gilbert is hurt badly—face is in bad shape—skull has been bitten. Ca. 1–2 miles NW Gallatin Lake; ½–1 mile west of Bighorn.

[11:27] Helicopter I—leaving for Big Horn Pass.

[11:41] (m) 211 weight and 126—If Gilbert is stable take to Lake, if he's lost a lot of blood and fluids take him to Mammoth.

[11:44] (m) Helicopter I spotted 120 Hastings and Gilbert.
[The Details of Incident report clarified: "At (11:44 a.m.) the helicopter located the victim. Because of strong winds in the area the helicopter was unable to land on the ridge where the victim was laying. The helicopter had to land approximately 300 yards from the victim on the northwest side of the spur ridge and approximately 400 vertical feet below the victim."]

[11:47] (m) 120 Hastings—be careful walking, a sow and three cubs . . .

[12:04 p.m.] (m) Helicopter I landed, they are getting Gilbert now . . .

[12:55] Helicopter I—request permission to start I.V. I talked to Dr. [name withheld]. He said start I.V. at 100 drops per/min. Gilbert's pulse 80, BP 115/80 . . .

[1:52] Phone Patch between Dr. [name withheld] and 126. Helicopter I taking patient to Lake [in covered Stokes litter carried outside the helicopter]. Patient has severely lacerated face, one ear missing . . .

[4:39 p.m.] (p) I called Lake Hospital to see if Gilbert was in the ambulance. They are taking him to West Yellowstone.

Attempting to determine what happened and why, Biologist Meagher continued her next day's interview of Bruce Hastings. "My Comments," Meagher wrote, "consider element of surprise—female with cubs had moved up ridge—moving west and Barrie [Gilbert] intercepted. Consider also female-male previously commented on interaction—if so female may have been well primed to hit anything." Meagher writes what happened next:

Bruce's subsequent impressions—

Efforts mainly to stop Barrie's bleeding, called Comm Center (1050 Mammoth Sub district radio log); Barrie urging him to save himself by climbing a tree, Bruce's refusal until Barrie pointed out that besides that way he could better attract the helicopter to the site—this some 10 min. before chopper found a place to land (see map). Barrie's probably unawareness of extent to injuries, concern for the bear, others. Bruce's relief—need for—the physical effort of helping to get the empty litter up the ridge—he and pilot. Tom Black with First Aid stuff working on Barrie. Barrie says eye gone—"couldn't find," torn out or mashed.

Two other parties, possibly in danger themselves, were reported to be in the same area. Ranger Danforth wrote of the effort to locate them, as well as to safeguard other backcountry users by means of trail closures. "At approximately 1500 [3:00 p.m.] contact was made with the West Yellowstone Sub-District and the Bighorn Pass and Fawn Pass trails were closed to all use." The report describes the helicopter search:

The helicopter searched the Bighorn Pass area for two hiking parties that had backcountry permits for that area, and was going to have them move out of that immediate area for the night and completely out of the area the next day. However, the helicopter could not find either party . . .

At approximately [8:00 p.m.] Park Ranger R.T. Danforth and Law Enforcement Officer Jerry Phillips interviewed Mr. Hastings, most of which is the above narrative. However, we did discuss the experience and awareness of grizzly bear behavior of the two biologists. Both were well-read on the subject of grizzly behavior. Mr. Gilbert had worked in the park previously on studies of animals in the park, both apparently were well aware of the hazards of working with grizzlies.

Mr. Hastings further stated that he had an American Red Cross First Aid Card at one time but that it had expired some time ago.

Mr. Hastings also had a conversation with Mr. Gilbert just after the incident happened, according to Gilbert, that he (Gilbert) after leaving Hastings had gone to the ridgetop and sat down and was looking the meadow over to the southeast side of the ridge with binoculars. When he heard a "woof" sound, he looked up to his right or northwest of him and he saw a grizzly bear. Gilbert got up and tried to get away from the bear by running around a little clump of trees. The bear got to Gilbert at that point and first bit Gilbert in the leg, then the abdomen and then his head and face.

After Mr. Hastings got to Mr. Gilbert he called in his emergency message.

<hr />

Barrie Gilbert suffered grievous wounds. Yellowstone Medical Services chief of staff M. H. Smith, MD, reported the following in the Case Incident Record:

> Mr. Gilbert was received at Lake Hospital, Yellowstone National Park, at [2:25 p.m.], by helicopter, following an attack by a bear. Immediate assessment revealed moderately severe shock, BP 80/60, P 120-130. Estimated blood loss was 2/5 of his total volume. 6000 ml. intravenous fluid were administered before an improved vascular condition existed.
>
> The injuries included multiple lacerations across the back of the scalp with avulsion of most of the scalp forward to the face. The left side of the face was destroyed, left eye missing, entire lateral aspect left mouth open, all salivary glands of left face destroyed, the left superior nasal and inferior orbit area open. In addition the right eye was compromised with decreased vision. Multiple lacerations were present on the chest, abdomen, and upper extremities. The right and left ears were partially avulsed and the left zygoma partially destroyed.
>
> Mr. Gilbert was transferred at [4:30 p.m.] to the airport and to Salt Lake City, Utah, where he underwent an 11 hour operation with a team of Plastic Surgeons and Ophthalmologists.

Throughout the Yellowstone community and elsewhere, concern continued for Barrie Gilbert. In the report "Bear Incident at Bighorn Pass for June 28, 1977," the Mammoth Communications Center radio log was included, below:

[1:20 p.m.] (p) called Salt Lake City concerning the bear mauling victim Barrie Gilbert. He was in surgery for 11 hours. He underwent plastic surgery. He had severe lacerations mainly on his face, but he is a strong patient. Don't know how successful the surgery was or how much additional surgery he will need.

Meanwhile at the Indian Creek Campground, Larry Hill, a seasonal ranger at Norris Ranger Station, helped to warn park visitors. In the report "Grizzly Mauling on Bighorn Pass" he wrote: "My regular work shift was [10:00 a.m. to 7:00 p.m.]." He wrote of his duties after the bear attack:

At the request of Mammoth Subdistrict Ranger Terry Danforth, I remained on duty at the Indian Creek Camp Ground, assisting with Bear Trap, covering the camp ground with information to all campers relating to bears in the area, checking the perimeter of the campground for sign of Grizzly Bear in the immediate Area.

The Case File indicates that no management action was taken against the chocolate-colored sow grizzly with three cubs, who was presumed to be defending her cubs against a sudden, perceived threat.

———

In 2010, Dr. Gilbert made available the following bio update, excerpted below.

"Dr. Barrie K. Gilbert is Senior Scientist (retired) from Utah State University. His specialty is behavioral and conservation ecology, especially the application of behavioral science to management of human-wildlife interactions. He began studying bears in 1974. For the last 15 years he directed studies of human-bear interactions along salmon streams in Katmai National Park, Alaska, and in Southeast Alaska."

# 14

# SUPER-BAD NIGHTMARE (1992): SARAH MULLER

*[She] made an off-hand comment to friends that she would see them on Wednesday if she didn't get mauled by a bear.*
—TOWER AREA RANGER COLETTE DAIGLE-BERG

*National Park Service—Yellowstone*

*Case Incident Record Number: 922604*

*Location: Buffalo Fork Trail, 2 miles from Lower Slough Creek*

*Date/Time: Wednesday, July 29, 1992, 10:58 a.m.*

That Wednesday, July 29, 1992, began no differently than had many other days—another warm summer morning near Yellowstone. But it was Sarah Muller's first substantial hike of the season. She started out at about 9:00 a.m., heading south on the Buffalo Fork Trail, knowing that if she got too hot she could take a dip in Slough Creek to cool off. An experienced outdoorswoman and formerly, for many years, a Yellowstone trail-crew employee, she chose to hike the six miles alone.

Then the unexpected occurred.

Tower Area Ranger Colette Daigle-Berg described what happened next in her "Report of Interview." "On 8/02/92 I interviewed Sarah Muller at the Eastern Idaho Regional Medical Center concerning events surrounding her mauling by a grizzly bear sow and cubs on 7/29/92."

Muller said she left work at [name withheld] on Sunday, July 26, 1992, and made an off-hand comment to friends that she would see them on Wednesday if she didn't get mauled by a bear. Muller drove to the Slough Creek Campground in the afternoon on 7/26/92. She parked her vehicle and forded Slough Creek at the crossing near campsite #5. She hiked up the old Soldier's Trail on the west side of Slough Creek, stopping briefly to speak with rangers Nancy Martinz [sic], Morris Bray and Andy Knight. (Martinz, Bray and Knight had just cleared the Buffalo Fork Trail.) Muller joined the Buffalo Fork Trail where the Soldier's Trail meets the Buffalo Fork Trail to the west of the first meadow up Slough Creek. She hiked to [name withheld] outfitter camp on the Buffalo Fork trail. Muller noticed no bear sign on the Buffalo Fork Trail on her hike in. Muller said that Sunday was the very tail end of her menstrual period.

Muller arrived at [the] outfitter camp in Grassy Meadow on USFS [US Forest Service] land about a mile outside the park in the evening on 7/26/92. She stayed at camp until Wednesday morning 7/29/92 visiting her friend [name withheld]. [The friend] told Muller he hadn't seen any bears yet on his trips into camp, but had noticed tracks.

On Monday, 7/27/92, Muller went on a long horseback ride into the national forest. On Tuesday, 7/28/72, Muller mostly stayed around camp helping with camp chores.

On Wednesday, 7/29/92, Muller estimates she left camp, on foot, at approximately 0945 hours [9:45 a.m.]. (Muller states she doesn't wear a watch.) She left camp about one-half hour before [her friend] and another [name withheld] employee. [They] were on horse and they estimated they'd all be to the trailhead at about the same time.

Prior to her leaving [name withheld] asked Muller if she wanted a leather strap to attach to her car key since the key was not on a key ring. Muller replied, saying something to the effect that "she wouldn't need one unless a bear started playing with her."

On the hike out that morning Muller was wearing a pair of Patagonia hiking shorts, clean underwear from the night before, a bra and tank top, socks and Merrel hiking boots. She had on a straw cowboy hat. Muller had washed the night before with Dr. Bronner's almond scented soap and had applied lotion the previous day after swimming. She had applied no perfume, no deodorant, no suntan lotion and no mosquito repellent the morning of her hike out.

Muller said she was carrying a water bottle and a small blue stuff sack containing some Muskol mosquito repellent, Camphorice Skin Balm, a small amount of trail mix and a small first aid kit.

Muller said she had just stopped to fill her water bottle in a creek and after resuming hiking was thinking about a dip in Slough Creek and possibly a soak in Boiling River [legal hot-potting area at Mammoth] when she got out. She said she was hiking quickly, occasionally looking up but mostly looking down at the trail in front of her. She said she wasn't deliberately making any noise. She felt that the wind was calm during that part of her hike.

Muller said she was about 20 feet away when she first saw a sow and two grizzly cubs in the trail in front of her. The sow was in the middle of the trail with her head down eating the tall grass. The cubs were slightly off trail, one on each side of the sow, also grazing. At first Muller thought they were black bears and then realized they were grizzlies due to the shape of the sow's nose.

Muller said that she stopped, quietly said "Oh shit," realized she was in trouble and started backing up to the nearest tree. Muller thinks she saw the bears a split second before they saw her and thinks the bears may have realized she was there when she said "Oh shit." As she was backing up, Muller said the sow stood up, looked at Muller, and dropped back to all four feet to settle down her cubs which were making a weird, "I'm scared" type noise. Muller thinks the sow may have been making a growling noise, but wasn't sure. The sow stood up once more and then dropped back down before charging Muller. Muller said that she was so close to the bears when she saw them that she had no time to play dead.

She said she threw her water bottle down as a possible diversion but that the sow continued charging. Muller had hoped it was bluff charge. She backed up to the tree, evaluated it, her tree-climbing abilities, the circumstances and decided the tree seemed too spindly for her to attempt to climb. Except for the split second it took to look at the tree, Muller thinks she had her eyes on the sow the entire time. She was standing up, facing the bear when the sow attacked. She thinks the sow was also standing up when she first attacked. Muller remembers thinking to herself that she should drop down to protect her vital areas but that she was so panic-stricken she yelled, "no, please don't." She thinks the sow knocked her down and started biting. She can't recall which area the bear bit first, possibly her face or arm, but thinks the bear chewed one part of her body first and then went on to the next. She described the biting as "vicious chomping and tearing, from side to side."

Muller said she did what came naturally, started fighting back, and yelling for [her friend]. When asked, she said she didn't swing her fists to try to strike the bear but fought back by pushing her stuff sack in front of her face and toward the sow's mouth. During the attack, which Muller estimates as lasting approximately four minutes, she tried to keep her stuff sack between her body and the bear. Muller said the bear either dragged or threw her just up the trail to the point where she was later found by [names withheld].

Muller said that the cubs were with the sow the entire time of the attack, trying to climb onto the sow. She thinks that the injury on her right hand may have been from a cub but isn't sure.

Muller said she had no clue as to why the bears eventually left. She thinks that it could possibly be that since she was now on the ground that she was no longer a threat to the sow. She isn't sure exactly where the bears went after the attack due to the blood in her eyes but said she felt that they had left and possibly headed up the hill in the direction of Cutoff Mountain.

Muller described the sow as relatively small in size for a grizzly, weighing approximately 175 to 200 pounds. She qualified her estimate by saying she had never seen a grizzly up that close before. She said the sow was a beautiful bear, mostly all one color, a light brown, with very little silver to her coat. (*Note:* This varies slightly from her initial report to [names withheld] that the bear was medium brown in color.) She said that the bear seemed young, approx. 3 years of age, and her fur had a young appearance. She said it had a "snout like a grizzly" and appeared to be 5'8" standing up.

Muller said the cubs were identical in appearance, small in size, definitely cubs of the year, and that their coats were slightly darker than the sow's.

Muller said she yelled for [her friend] once after the attack ended but then quit yelling and concentrated on conserving her energy, slowing down her breathing and administering first aid to herself. She tried to push herself up after the bear left to see what had happened but lay back down since her arm hurt too much. She tried to prop her head up with her stuff sack and used moleskin and Kleenex to try to stop the bleeding from her head. She couldn't see out of one eye and thought she was blind in that eye. She concentrated on not losing consciousness and doesn't remember ever passing out. She tried to move around enough to stay awake but not too much in order to prevent more bleeding. Her main fears were that the bears might return and that she would go into shock.

[Names withheld] rode up approximately 10 to 15 minutes after the attack. Muller remembers sticking her arm up in the air to indicate where she was so the horses wouldn't step on her lying in the tall grass, half-on and half-off of the trail.

Sarah Muller's friends on horseback, who had thought they would catch up with her at the trailhead, encountered her much earlier than that. One of the horses saw her first.

Park Ranger Daniel A. Krapf wrote in his report that "[Names withheld] left the [outfitter] camp on horseback with one pack animal at approximately [9:30 a.m.], one-half hour after Muller."

After riding a little over an hour [name withheld] horse shied and he looked down the trail to see Sarah Muller lying in the trail. Muller told him that she had been attacked about 15 minutes before (approx. [10:20 a.m.]) by a medium-sized, medium brown Grizzly sow with two cubs of the year. The bears were walking on the trail when Sarah came on them. Sarah stated that the sow Grizzly looked around, checked her cubs and then charged. The attack lasted just a few moments and the bears departed in which direction Ms. Muller did not know.

[Names withheld] decided that as he was the better rider, he would ride out for help. The time was approximately [10:40 a.m.] [Name withheld] was left with Sarah Muller and the two horses. [She] tried to splint Muller's arm with some towels and sticks. She also tried to stop the bleeding on her face and back with towels.

[Name withheld] arrived at the Slough Creek transfer (a distance from the scene of a little over three miles) at approximately [10:55 a.m.]. At the transfer he found USFS [US Forest Service] employees Larry Sears and Scot Shuler. Sears radioed the Yellowstone Park Comm. Center and notified them of the mauling.

The Comm. Center notified the Tower Area Ranger Colette Daigle-Berg, District Ranger Mona Divine, and the Fire Cache of the incident. The first broadcast of the incident was at [10:58 a.m.]. Immediately after his initial report USFS supervisor Larry Sears headed out on horseback with [name withheld] to return to the scene of the accident.

After the Yellowstone Communications Center notified Ranger Daigle-Berg, she wrote that "I requested a life-flight helicopter via the communications center." She added the following:

The park contract helicopter working in the Northeast corner of the park was reassigned to fly helitack crewman and EMT, Jim Sites, and me into the scene. We left the Slough Creek transfer barn at approx. [11:29 a.m.] and landed at the incident scene at approx. [11:31 a.m.].

Sarah Muller, victim of the mauling, was lying on her right side on the Buffalo Fork trail, being tended by [name withheld . . . who] had improvised splints and splinted Muller's left arm and left leg with sticks and clothing.

Muller was conscious and able to respond to questions concerning her condition, although she was in considerable pain. Primary assessment revealed that Muller had an open airway although she was bleeding slightly from her nose. Her breathing was somewhat labored . . .

Secondary assessment revealed numerous puncture wounds and lacerations to her face, left shoulder, torso, and legs . . .

Victim packaged for transport, EMS team attending. Photo taken on July 29, 1992 by Park Ranger Daniel A. Krapf, from Case Incident Record #922604

Air One had landed about 100 yards from Muller's location. Once loaded and securely packaged on the backboard, Muller was carried to the waiting helicopter and loaded. Air One departed the scene at approx. [1:11 p.m.] en route to Eastern Idaho Regional Medical Center . . .

On 7/30/92 [name withheld], director of nursing at Lake Hospital, advised that she had received a summary of Muller's injuries from [name withheld], M.D., from EIRMC. She advised that Muller had received more than 50 lacerations including a laceration above her left eye which had punctured her sinus cavity allowing outside air and contamination into her cranium. She had sustained six open rib fractures with resulting pneumo- and hemothoraxes. Her left arm had been fractured at the elbow and had been repaired with external fixatures. Although the lacerations on her left leg had exposed the bone, her left leg was not fractured. She had required approximately 11 hours of initial surgery.

Meanwhile, investigators were gathering at the scene of the mauling. "Shortly after the departure of the Lifeflight," Ranger Krapf wrote, "[Ranger] Brian Chan arrived on scene and subsequently [Bear Management Specialist] Kerry Gunther also arrived to assist Krapf in the investigation of the incident." The ranger described what happened next:

On his way into the scene Chan had posted the trail as closed at Lower Slough Creek meadow. Gunther's staff also posted the Buffalo Fork trail closed at various other locations at the direction of Ranger Daigle-Berg. As the Forest Service personnel were headed North up the Trail and past [the] camp, Krapf asked Sears to clear the trail of visitors and post it closed at the boundary. Krapf and Chan would also ride this trail later in the day and check with the one person left in [the] camp. The trail was closed to all parties until our investigation could determine the danger and reduce restrictions. Under normal circumstances this is not a heavily used trail. Much of the traffic that does use it is horse usage. Subsequently, we opened the trail to horse parties on the afternoon of the 30th. The trail remained closed to foot travel for one week . . .

Krapf, Chan and Gunther investigated the incident over the afternoon of the 29th and the morning of the 30th. The following is the results of their investigation:

### *Results Of Investigation*

The incident occurred on the Buffalo Fork Trail approximately three miles from the trailhead at the Slough Creek transfer. This trail follows a North-South axis and parallels Buffalo Creek from the Northern Park boundary to its confluence with Slough Creek. The trail is on the East side of the creek and upslope from the creek. The slope to the creek is generally gentle as the trail averages one-half to one mile from the creek. The trail to the north of the incident is primarily through the trees. Much of this area was burned in 1988, however the area immediately around the incident was not burned. The terrain where the incident occurred is open meadow with small groups of mainly spruce trees and aspens. Using Sarah Muller's statement as a guide we found that she had just come through a small group of trees approximately 100 feet from where she would first see the bears. This group of trees may have provided some screening contributing to the fact that neither Sarah nor the bear saw each other sooner. The bear was presumably headed north along the trail and would have just come up to the trail from a small intermittent stream. The bear would have been out in the open for over 100 meters after it crossed the stream. However the trail is coming to a gentle crest near the point where both parties first saw each other. Sarah had been hiking uphill from the group of trees that screened the trail to the north and the bears were coming upslope from the small intermittent stream. The grade in the immediate area is gentle in both directions and neither party was on a grade greater than 10 percent. The cresting of the trail at the point of the incident does limit the visibility for both parties. The maximum distance one could see a four foot high object from where Sarah came out of the trees into the open is approx. 150 feet. The fact that Sarah reported that she was within 25 to 30 feet when she first saw the bears is an indication that she was not looking down trail as far as possible.

The vegetation that the bear may have been grazing on in the area is primarily timothy, grasses, and yampa (although there is no sign of the bear having dug up any yampa).

Within 20 feet of where Sarah reported that she was when she first saw the bear there is a medium sized spruce tree that splits into three sections near the base and is over 40 foot tall. In subsequent interviews Sarah stated that she tried to use this tree for cover but did not feel it large enough to climb. (See the diagrams and photos of the scene.) Also, the wind at this location was out of the southwest and at the bear's back which did not help the bear to be aware of Sarah.

TRACKS—There were no tracks. Unfortunately, the activity required by the medical [personnel] obliterated any tracks of the bear which might have indicated the size of the adult bear and the presence of cubs. We did find a trail that left the scene on a course perpendicular to the trail and headed directly downslope towards Buffalo Creek. This

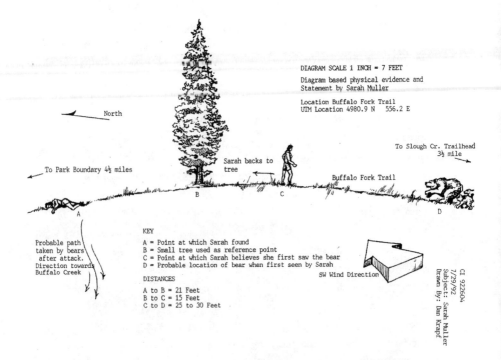

DIAGRAM SCALE 1 INCH = 7 FEET

Diagram based physical evidence and
Statement by Sarah Muller

Location Buffalo Fork Trail
UTM Location 4980.9 N    556.2 E

North

To Slough Cr. Trailhead
3½ mile

To Park Boundary 4½ miles

Sarah backs to
tree

Buffalo Fork Trail

B                    C

A

KEY

A = Point at which Sarah found
B = Small tree used as reference point
C = Point at which Sarah believes she first saw the bear
D = Probable location of bear when first seen by Sarah

Probable path
taken by bears
after attack.
Direction towards
Buffalo Creek

DISTANCES

A to B = 21 Feet
B to C = 15 Feet
C to D = 25 to 30 Feet

SW Wind Direction

D

CI 922604
7/29/92
Subject: Sarah Muller
Drawn By: Dan Krapf

Diagram based [on] physical evidence and statement by Sarah Muller. Drawn by Park Ranger Daniel A. Krapf, in Case Incident Record #922604

trail was through high grass and prints were not possible to find. This was a trail of more than one animal however and very recent. The duff under the grass had been pushed down slope in a manner that indicated a heavy animal running and probably not an ungulate. This trail went straight towards Buffalo Creek for approximately 200 meters and then turned North which is the direction Sarah reported that the bear was headed prior to the incident. We considered this trail from the scene to probably have been made by the bears although we found no hair or scat or other evidence along this trail.

SCAT—We found no scat. Not in the immediate area of the incident, nor in the direction from which the bear had come nor in the direction in which we thought the bear had fled the scene.

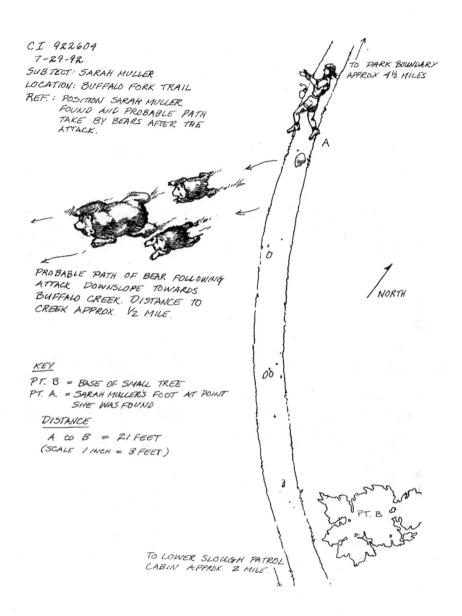

CI 922604
7-29-92
SUBJECT: SARAH MULLER
LOCATION: BUFFALO FORK TRAIL
REF.: POSITION SARAH MULLER
FOUND AND PROBABLE PATH
TAKE BY BEARS AFTER THE
ATTACK.

TO PARK BOUNDARY
APPROX 4½ MILES

A

PROBABLE PATH OF BEAR FOLLOWING
ATTACK. DOWNSLOPE TOWARDS
BUFFALO CREEK. DISTANCE TO
CREEK APPROX. ½ MILE.

NORTH

KEY
PT. B = BASE OF SMALL TREE
PT. A = SARAH MULLER'S FOOT AT POINT
SHE WAS FOUND

DISTANCE
A to B = 21 FEET
(SCALE 1 INCH = 3 FEET)

PT. B

TO LOWER SLOUGH PATROL
CABIN APPROX. 2 MILE

Position of Sarah Muller as she was found and probable path taken by bears
after the attack. Drawn by Park Ranger Daniel A. Krapf, in Case Incident Record
#922604]

SIGNS OF PRIOR BEAR ACTIVITY—We found very little indication that the bear had been spending very much time in the area. There was no sign that the bears had been digging the abundant yampa in the area. We saw one or two rocks which had been turned over some time ago by the stream that crosses the trail 100 meters from the incident but there was no digging or other signs of activity in that area. We searched the area extensively for signs of an animal carcass (either recent or winter kill) and found nothing. Sarah reported that the bears were grazing on grass when she first saw them.

HAIR—We found 30-40 bear hair samples at the point where Sarah's body was found. These were later identified at MSU [Montana State University] as being that of a Grizzly bear . . . Sarah's clothing was also sent to the lab for further collection of hair samples and evidence.

PHYSICAL EVIDENCE ON SARAH—In addition to any hair samples that may be found on Sarah's clothing, I saw at least two apparent bite marks made by a large canine tooth. One on her left thigh and one on her back.

This is the totality of the physical evidence that we have discovered at this time.

Ranger Daigle-Berg wrote in her report that "Muller was very introspective about the attack, and volunteered quite a few related comments which I will summarize here."

She felt it was ironic that she had worked in Yellowstone for six years on the trail crew and after resigning her position was attacked on her first hike of the season. She admitted that she hadn't done much hiking alone and that most of her hiking had been in groups while working on trail crew. She allowed how she felt rather carefree on her hike in to [the outfitter] camp in that she had no tools to carry and she was hiking for pleasure rather than for work. She said it felt kind of different being a "tourist."

She said that she carried "bear spray" while hiking during her first few years with the trail crew. Then she said she got slack and only had it available in her tent while camped. She said her biggest fear of bears was during her menstrual period. Although she had given some thought to buying and carrying "bear spray," she hadn't and was not carrying it the day of her attack. She thinks that using "bear spray" during her attack would have only made the sow angrier and would have had little positive effect. She attributes this comment to the fact that the attack happened amazingly fast and that the sow was solely intent on protecting her cubs.

Muller mused over whether she should have been making loud noises while hiking down the trail. She said she used to wear a "bear bell" while hiking in Glacier Park. She allowed that she maybe had too much over-confidence and that it was stupid not to make noise while hiking alone in bear country. Muller said [she] hadn't seen that many bears in Yellowstone's backcountry and that she had had only one other close encounter with a bear while hiking in Yellowstone.

Muller noted that as she approached the area where she was attacked she broke out of the woods and came into a small meadow with a tree on the left (the same tree she backed up to). She said that visibility was pretty good down the trail in front of her, if she had been looking up. She said that one lesson she learned was that when hiking in bear country you have to look up and be aware.

She said something to the effect of "who's to say if the attack could have been prevented?" She felt as if she would have been hurt worse if she had stayed in [the] trail and not backed up to the tree. She said it seemed like a super-bad nightmare and couldn't believe it had happened to her. Two of her strongest memories of the attack are how large the bear's mouth was, and how powerful the teeth were. She said she remembers Ranger Ann Marie Chytra telling her never to forget how powerful bears can be.

Muller reiterated during the interview what she had said at the scene regarding the sow protecting its young. She said she could accept the incident as "Mother Nature doing her thing."

In his report Ranger Krapf characterized the mauling of Muller as a "chance encounter and unlikely to be repeated." He continued:

> It is extremely unlikely that any bear will attack horse parties so we opened the trail to horse parties on the afternoon of July 30, 1992. We patrolled the entire trail on the 30th. Larry Sears of the USFS rode the trail on the 31st. NPS patrolled the trail on August 2 and 4. At no time was the bear sighted nor was there any physical evidence of the bear during this period. The trail was opened without restriction (but continued strong bear warnings) on August 4th.

As for the bear and her cubs, the Case Incident Record concluded: "Disposition of Animal: No action taken, or planned. Chance encounter."

~

One year after the attack, Sarah Muller displayed her courage by returning to the scene. She agreed to a newspaper interview about the mauling's long-term effects upon her (including more surgery still to come):

### *Wiser Mauling Victim Returns To Attack Site*

BOZEMAN (AP) –A woman mauled by a grizzly bear in Yellowstone National Park last year returned to the scene of the attack this month, whistling as she rode a horse.

Sarah Muller believes that if she had been making noise as she walked Yellowstone's Buffalo Fork Trail in 1992, she might not have surprised a grizzly sow.

"If I had been making noise, she might have heard me and taken her cubs and run off," said Muller, 35, who was with a dozen companions when she returned to the scene.

Muller, a former Yellowstone trail worker, who had taken an airport job in Belgrade, was hiking alone on July 29, 1992, and intended to meet two friends riding horses. She came upon a grizzly, with a cub on either side, feeding 40 yards away.

The hiker moved behind the only trees nearby—two spruces about 15 feet high. The cubs shrieked, and the sow charged . . .

Yellowstone medics administered emergency care, and physicians at the Eastern Idaho Regional Medical Center in Idaho Falls worked on Muller for 12 hours. Stitches numbered in the hundreds.

Muller continues to deal with her injuries, and is about to undergo surgery at Minnesota's Mayo Clinic. Unable to work, she lives off of savings and money from friends and acquaintances.[60]

Six years after the bear attack, an editorial writer [unnamed] for *Ladies Home Journal* interviewed Sarah Muller. Muller described what happened to her:

### *Summer Dangers – Wildlife Attacks*

Just as people are more active in the summer, so are many animals. In fact, of the seventeen bear attacks reported in Yellowstone National Park since 1980, thirteen have occurred between June and August.

One of those victims was forty-year-old Sarah Muller. On July 29, 1992, she was hiking on Yellowstone's Buffalo Fork Trail, in Wyoming, when she crested a hill to a sight every hiker fears: a mother grizzly with her two cubs. "I started slowly walking back, looking for a tree to climb, but there wasn't one," says Sarah, a ranch caretaker in Paradise Valley, Montana. "The mother bear came charging at me."

The bear bit though Sarah's rib cage, breaking seven ribs and collapsing her lung. "At one point, she had my whole head in her mouth," Sarah remembers. "She punctured my brain and bit through my sinus cavity, breaking my nose. One of her teeth even went right into the corner of my eye, popping it out of its socket. After a few minutes, the bear just walked away from me. I remember screaming my head off. I thought for sure I was going to die."

If there was anything lucky about Sarah's attack, it was that her boyfriend was following a short distance behind her on horseback. He tracked down a park ranger who called for help.

After nine hours of surgery, two and a half weeks in the hospital, and several plastic surgeries, Sarah still isn't totally healed today. "My broken ribs cause me pain, and there's a lot of nerve damage and scars," she says. "I have plates in my nose, and wiring that holds my eye in place."

Despite her ordeal, Sarah hasn't given up hiking, but she is smarter about safety strategies. "My big mistake? I didn't make noise on the trail," she says. "If that grizzly had heard me coming, she would have taken her cubs to safety."[61]

## 15

# BITING HIM ON THE HEAD
# (TWO MILES FROM PARK, 1992):
# HUNTERS MARK MATHENY AND FRED BAHNSON

*Matheny said he turned for a tree to climb but the bear was already upon him.*

—INVESTIGATOR KEVIN FREY OF MONTANA
FISH, WILDLIFE AND PARKS

*United States Forest Service*

*Gallatin National Forest*

*Montana Department of Fish, Wildlife and Parks*

*Location: Just northwest of Yellowstone Park*

*Eldridge Creek–Taylor's Fork Drainage*

*Gallatin National Forest*

*Date/Time: September 25, 1992, 12:15 p.m.*

Conflicts between hunters and bears (outside but close to the park) present important issues for all who use and love Yellowstone, and so are discussed through the example below.

The weather was clear and calm at 50 degrees that September 25, 1992. Shortly past noon the two bow-hunting partners, one mile from a rural road just northwest of Yellowstone, had taken a mule deer buck, left it for the time being, and were looking for elk. They were hiking through the Gallatin National Forest west of Highway 191 and the Gallatin River, in an area buttressed by two units of the Lee Metcalf Wilderness.

Clyde Ormond wrote in his *Outdoor Life Complete Book of Hunting* that "The real purpose of any big-game hunting trip is to have an enjoyable and rewarding experience in the great outdoors."

In addition, every hunter hopes to climax such an experience by taking a prized game animal. That is the unsurpassed thrill of any hunt . . .

### The Hunting Partner

Perhaps the most important [choice] is the wise choice of hunting partner . . . For short hunts, or hunts not involving wilderness country and pack trips, a party of two hunting companions is ideal. It is indicative of the importance of good hunting partners that in many instances the same two fellows hunt annually, over a period of many years. Often they are as varied in financial, social and occupational status as the poles. But as hunting companions their likes and interests are the same and they make a fine partnership.[62]

Bow-hunting partners Mark Matheny, thirty-nine, a Gallatin Gateway contractor, and Fred Bahnson, forty-nine, a doctor, were soon very glad indeed to have each other along.

By 2:30 p.m. that same day, Matheny and Bahnson found themselves being treated for extremely serious bear mauling injuries at a hospital in Bozeman, Montana. Investigator Kevin Frey of Montana Fish, Wildlife and Parks interviewed them and wrote that they "were hiking down the Eldridge Creek Trail, approximately 1 mile from [the] trailhead and main road." Frey's report described what happened next:

They were returning from the Eldridge Creek/Wapiti Creek Divide, where they had killed a mule deer buck. They had left the deer and were hunting elk back down. They were going to return 9/26/92 to retrieve the deer. Matheny and Bahnson had been talking quietly and slowly hunting down trail, through trees when they came upon a female grizzly with 3 cubs of the year that were day bedding or nursing on a slight rise approximately 40 yards ahead. Matheny was in the lead. He said the female looked at him and jumped up over [the] cubs and came running without a sound other than huffing. Bahnson said he saw a "herd" of bears coming and then realized it was a sow with cubs. ("Definitely a grizzly, dish-face, hump, gold color.")

Matheny said he turned for a tree to climb but the bear was already upon him. He faced the bear and held his bow out in front of him. The bear knocked the bow away and knocked Matheny down and began biting him on the head. He was yelling for Bahnson to get the bear repellent spray. Bahnson yelled, got the bear's attention and sprayed her. She then knocked Bahnson down. Matheny tried to get into a ball position—the bear returned to him. Bahnson got up, yelled, got the bear's attention again and at about 5 feet distance, sprayed till [the] can was empty. The bear then knocked him down, bit him on the back and ran off with cubs in a northwesterly direction.

*Notes:* Neither hunter was wearing scent or mask. Cubs stayed by female entire time. Friends of the hunters returned to site and found cow elk carcass approximately 30 yards from site. Bahnson stated all arrows were gone from quiver except one broken in half. Hunters were understanding of situation—felt glad they had spray.[63]

In the same report, Frey documented the injuries that Mark Matheny suffered as follows. "Severe cut left cheek to down under jaw, a horizontal cut on throat (center), cut on right eyebrow, tooth puncture wounds to scalp, top-front and right-front side."

Frey also documented the injuries to Matheny's hunting partner, Fred Bahnson, as follows. "Tooth puncture wounds (bite) to back, right side below shoulder blade."

Matheny felt so glad his hunting partner, Bahnson, had the pepper spray "Karate In A Can" (made for protection against humans), that he founded his own bear-spray company, UDAP Industries, Inc. Its website includes safety information for traveling and hunting in bear country.

Additionally Mark Matheny reenacted the attack, with information about how to avoid such an attack, in his video "Bear Attacks" by Stoney Wolf Productions.

The US Forest Service investigated the incident and concluded the following:

> Gallatin National Forest Ranger Alan Vandiver said Saturday the two men . . . surprised the bear and two [sic] cubs Friday on the Eldridge trail . . . The trail is in the Taylor Fork and Hebgen Lake area, home to at least 14 bears, he said. "Since the bear was defending her cubs, there are no plans to relocate or disturb them."[64]

———

There is an inherent competition for space between hunters and grizzly bears during the fall hunting season in the areas immediately adjacent to Yellowstone Park. The bears are in the late summer and fall "hyperphagia" period, during which they forage for and consume as much food as they can to prepare for winter hibernation. Thus they are on the move throughout areas legally open for hunting.

In addition, the bears are attracted to the hunter-killed carcasses (either those freshly killed or the gut piles remaining after butchering), as well as wounded game that have escaped. Some persons have posited that the sounds of gunshots may attract bears, which have learned that such noises can mean carcasses, or wounded and thus easily dispatched game to eat.

"It is estimated that an average of 75 pounds of edible material remains as entrails, hide, bones, and waste after a hunter kills an elk or a moose. Twenty-five pounds of material is estimated to remain after a hunter kills a deer," wrote the authors of *Report to the IGBC on the Availability of Foods for Grizzly Bears in the Yellowstone Ecosystem*, in December 1986. ("IGBC" is the Interagency Grizzly Bear Committee.) In considering the hunter harvest and wounding loss for elk alone, the following figures, which "originated in the respective game and fish departments of each state," were reported:

The elk harvest by sport hunters in occupied grizzly bear habitat outside Yellowstone National Park and its resultant contribution to food availability is as follows:

Wyoming sport harvest 1976-85 x = 4,893 x 75 lbs = 183.0 tons
Wyoming wounding loss 1976-85 x = 245 x 700 lbs each = 86.0 tons

Idaho sport harvest 1985 = 200 x 75 lbs = 7.5 tons
Idaho wounding loss 1985 = 10 x 700 lbs = 3.5 tons

Montana sport harvest 1985 = 1,588 x 75 lbs = 60.0 tons
Montana wounding loss 1985 = 80 x 700 lbs = 28.0 tons

The estimated elk remains available due to sport hunting each fall = 368.0 tons

In addition, the report stated, "the estimated moose remains available due to sport hunting each fall equaled 37 tons," and "the estimated deer remains available due to sport hunting each fall equaled 90.7 tons."[65]

While these remains supply grizzly bears with protein and calorie-rich food, the number of hunters trekking through the grizzly-occupied "hunting units" makes conflict inevitable. In addition, bow hunters, by the nature of their hunting technique using silent stalking or stationary ambush to get close enough to dispatch their targets, may be more likely to accidentally get too close to a bear.

# 16

# MULTIPLE WOUNDS, MULTIPLE BODY PARTS (1994): ROBERT O'CONNELL

*The bear did not move away during his first attempt to drive the bear away, but just kept chewing on O'Connell.*
—FROM REPORT OF CANYON SUB-DISTRICT
RANGER ROBERT W. LOVE

*National Park Service—Yellowstone*

*Case Incident Record Number: 942477*

*Location: Hayden Valley, Sulphur Mountain area*

*Date/Time: Sunday, July 17, 1994, 2:30 p.m.*

Except for the unusual heat, July 17, 1994, was a good Sunday for riding mules off trail in the Yellowstone backcountry. Two men accompanied by large riding stock would seem to make the odds of a bear attack unlikely.

The sky was cloudless that day at about 2:30 p.m. Robert O'Connell, thirty-two, and Brian Moore, thirty-one, both from Wyoming, were riding on the south side of a summer range preferred by many large animals: Hayden Valley. For the men, Hayden Valley had not even been their first choice for that day's ride.

Hayden Valley has long been known for wildlife spotting, the *Haynes Guide* reported, and was "named for Dr. Ferdinand Vandiveer Hayden

(1829–1887), leader of the famous expeditions of 1871, 1872, and 1878." The Yellowstone guidebook described the valley:

> This valley, once an arm of a vast prehistoric lake of which Yellowstone Lake is a remnant, has an area of about 50 square miles, and is traversed by the Yellowstone River and several tributaries. It is part of the summer range of big game animals and is a year-round range of bison of which individual specimens are seen frequently in view of the road.[66]

Wildlife spotting is so frequent in Hayden Valley that *Hiking Yellowstone National Park* author Bill Schneider in 1997 described a hiking trail here as one of "The Author's Favorites," "for wildlife."[67] His book adds a warning:

> The Hayden Valley is a mecca of wildlife watching, and an early start helps you see as many wild animals as possible.
> Along with the other wildlife comes the likelihood of seeing a grizzly bear on this trail. Because of the high population of bears in the area, the NPS prohibits off-trail travel along this trail and recommends parties of four or more hikers.[68]

A Yellowstone Park news release reported that O'Connell and Moore "were riding mules off-trail in the Sulphur Mountain area in Hayden Valley for the day, and had stopped for a short break."

After the break, "Moore thought the time was around 1630 hours [4:30 p.m.]," wrote Canyon Sub-District Ranger Robert W. Love in the Case Incident Record. The ranger described what happened next:

> Moore stated he mounted his mule, while O'Connell started to walk, leading his mule . . . they were moving along just inside the tree line, in order to avoid some Bison down in the flats. Moore said O'Connell was about 20 yards above him, inside the tree line, when he heard O'Connell yell, "bear, bear!"

When he heard O'Connell yell, Moore stated he saw a 200 pound plus, light blond, fairly long haired bear charge through the trees toward O'Connell. Moore stated the bear knocked O'Connell down, and that O'Connell's mule broke away . . . At this time his view of O'Connell was somewhat obstructed by a downed log, but he could see the bear jumping up and down on something, presumably O'Connell.

According to Moore, he charged the bear while riding his mule, in an attempt to drive the bear away . . . as he approached the bear, he could see that it was on top of O'Connell, who was in a fetal position . . . the bear did not move away during his first attempt to drive the bear away, but just kept chewing on O'Connell. Although his mule was bucking and side-stepping, Moore stated he eventually got his mule under control and tried a second charge of the bear.

This time as he charged the bear . . . he yelled at the bear too. According to Moore, after this attempt, the bear began to move away, slowly walking off . . . O'Connell got to his feet after the bear walked off, but he looked dazed and confused. Moore stated he rounded up O'Connell's mule, and began to walk O'Connell down the hill . . . O'Connell kept saying his head hurt . . . O'Connell told him he was able to ride, so they both began riding out toward the road. Moore stated it took them approximately 25 to 30 minutes at a fast trot to reach the road.

Once out on the road, Moore stated he flagged down a passing park visitor, and asked them if they could take O'Connell to Lake Hospital. The visitors agreed, and transported O'Connell, while Moore rode to their truck and loaded the mules. Moore stated he then drove to Lake Hospital.

The visitor, or visitors [names withheld] were later contacted by telephone. [They] essentially confirmed what Moore had previously told Ranger Youngblood. [They] added that O'Connell did not talk much while traveling to the hospital.

After a brief interview, Ranger Youngblood drove Moore back to Hayden Valley to pinpoint the location of the incident.

A ranger was dispatched to interview the wounded man. "On 7-18-94, Ranger Youngblood traveled to West Park Hospital in Cody, Wyoming, to interview O'Connell," the report noted, continuing below:

O'Connell had been transferred to West Park from [Yellowstone's] Lake Hospital the previous evening.

O'Connell stated that he and Moore had first arrived to Yellowstone on 7-16-94 at about [3:30 a.m.]. According to O'Connell, he and Moore set up camp just inside the park boundary, but before they got to the entrance station, at the park's northeast entrance. At about [6:30 a.m.], O'Connell stated they were contacted by Park Rangers about camping in an undesignated area . . . during that contact the rangers found loaded weapons in their vehicle, but only gave them a verbal warning.

At about [8:30 a.m.], O'Connell stated that he and Moore entered the park's northeast entrance, where they paid the park entry fee. At this time . . . they received the park's newspaper and other information relating to bear warning.

O'Connell stated he and Moore then did a day ride in the Blacktail Deer Creek area, returning to the trailhead at about [9:00 p.m.]. According to O'Connell, he and Moore exited the park's north entrance and camped about five miles north of Gardiner, at a Forest Service trailhead.

On 7-17-94, O'Connell stated he and Moore re-entered the park and proceeded to the Tower Ranger Station. O'Connell stated they tried unsuccessfully to obtain a backcountry permit, so instead headed for Hayden Valley for a day ride. At about [12:30 p.m.] . . . he and Moore began riding into Hayden Valley . . .

He and Moore had stopped to take a break and drink a cola. After the break, O'Connell stated he was leading his mule on foot because the mule had been "a pain in the rump." O'Connell also added he needed the exercise. According to O'Connell, he was walking just inside the tree line, attempting to avoid the heat and sun . . . Moore was to his right, riding his mule about 20 yards downhill. As he was walking along,

O'Connell stated his mule suddenly spotted something, and turned its head and laid its ears back.

O'Connell stated he looked in the direction the mule was looking, and saw a blond grizzly bear with long hair charging him. As his mule ran off . . . the bear started to attack him . . . he yelled, "bear, bear" to Moore.

O'Connell stated the bear first bit him on the left leg. According to O'Connell, he had some bear repellent made from pepper spray with him . . . he attempted to reach for the spray, but . . . the bear bit him on the head.

At this point, according to O'Connell, the bear paused, and he again attempted to reach for his bear spray. And again the bear began to bite O'Connell on the head. O'Connell stated that Moore was eventually able to drive the bear away, and that he and Moore rode out to the road. Once out to the road . . . they flagged down a passing motorist who took O'Connell to Lake Hospital.

O'Connell stated that before the attack, he and Moore had not seen any carcasses, nor any bear sign. O'Connell added that when the bear attacked him, he did not see any cubs.

During the incident, O'Connell sustained multiple lacerations, puncture wounds and avulsions [forcible separations] to multiple parts of his body.

At 4:07 p.m. the park announced that "all off-road activity on the south side of Hayden Valley is closed until further notice."

—◦—

Several rangers surveyed the area on horseback the next day:

During this patrol, no bears or carcasses were found, nor were rangers able to definitely locate the site of the incident. That same day, 7/18/94, the closure in Hayden Valley was lifted. It was determined that no management action would be taken against the bear. It was thought that the incident was probably a chance encounter, and the bear was possibly disturbed while it laid in its day bed.

On 7-25-94 Ranger John Lounsbury, Ranger Mary Taber and Brian Moore rode out into Hayden Valley. The purpose of the trip was to more accurately locate the site of the incident. During the ride Moore found a ball cap that he claimed belonged to O'Connell. The location was UTM: 4944.900Mn X 539.700mE.

According to the *Yellowstone Journal*, the attack on O'Connell was the third mauling of the season:

On June 15, National Park Service employee Glen Lacey was mauled [the bear punctured his shoulder with its teeth] near West Thumb Geyser Basin while hiking off-duty. And on June 20, TW Recreational Services employee Randy Ingersoll, of Gardiner, Mont., was mauled [by sow with two cubs, "breaking his shoulder, cutting his forehead and inflicting multiple puncture wounds"] while hiking off-duty on the Thunderer Cutoff Trail near the Park's northeast entrance.[69]

For reports on the season's two other mauling victims, see the sections on Glen Lacey and Randy Ingersoll in Chapter 19.

# 17

# HIS FACE WAS HANGING OFF—MAN'S SECOND MAULING IN SECOND NATIONAL PARK (2007): JIM COLE

*He said a "mother bear is point blank charging." He also saw one cub for a split second.*

—FROM YELLOWSTONE SPECIAL AGENTS' INTERVIEW WITH JIM COLE

*National Park Service*

*Case Incident Record Number: 071114*

*Location: Near Trout Creek in Hayden Valley, off trail*

*Date/Time: Wednesday, May 23, 2007, 11:00 a.m.*

Just after dawn that Wednesday, May 23, 2007, the air felt cold and damp when wildlife photographer Jim Cole parked beside Yellowstone's Hayden Valley. He stepped out of his 1990 green Chevrolet van, laced up his brown leather hiking boots, and put on black water-repellent gaiters over his boot tops and lower pant legs. Then he turned and surveyed the expanse of open valley, looking for animals to photograph. From the elevated rise of the roadside turnout, grizzlies could sometimes be spotted below, foraging on grasses and sedges beside the silver meanderings of Trout Creek.

Cole was alone.

Cole drew on gray wool fingerless gloves with thin black liners, enabling him to nimbly operate his camera equipment. As a photographer for and author of books about grizzlies in Montana, Wyoming, and Alaska, he had told a friend he was eager to try out his new digital camera with its removable media card. He screwed on the 70-200m zoom lens. The camera case itself was stocked with three more media cards and empty card cases. In his gray bag he put his binoculars, batteries, and another long-range lens with 1.4x magnification. To keep him supplied for a number of hours, his blue hip pack carried two fifteen-ounce bottles of orange juice, one roll of organic toilet paper, and four protein bars. And he had taken precautions: In black holsters attached to his belt hung two Counter Assault Grizzly Tough Pepper Spray canisters, each containing ten ounces of spray.

<hr />

Bear-repellent pepper spray had certainly helped Cole in the past. He had, unfortunately, gained direct knowledge of the power of a grizzly back in 1993, when he was mauled by one in Glacier National Park. Now fifty-seven, he was forty-three when he and his friend Tim Rubbert, day hiking in Glacier's Fifty Mountain area, surprised a 250–300 pound grizzly, which charged. "Cole was in the lead and Rubbert had paused to look through binoculars," reported the *Missoulian*'s Don Schwennesen in 1993, "when the men encountered the bear, about two miles into their 12-mile return hike." The newspaper described what the bear did next:

> The bear made a long hissing or exhaling sound, they told park rangers, then charged Cole from about 10 feet. Rubbert shouted a warning and Cole dropped into a fetal position as the bear hit him from behind.
>
> "The bear grabbed the back of his head with its mouth," [Glacier Park spokeswoman Amy] Vanderbilt said, then stood over him and bit his wrist when Cole raised his left hand.
>
> By then, Rubbert began approaching, spraying pepper spray but trying to avoid hitting Cole. When the bear turned and charged him, Rubbert sprayed it in the face. The bear stopped at about 5 feet and fled.[70]

Cole sustained a torn scalp and a broken wrist, and was admitted to Kalispell Regional Hospital. In the *Missoulian*'s follow-up story, "Cole said in retrospect he's amazed he was able to hike out of the area." Cole related what he did next:

> His adrenalin kept him going for the first five miles, but then he felt exhausted and wanted to lay [sic] down.
>
> After eating four power bars and drinking a lot of liquid, he was able to complete the hike out [10.5 miles], though Rubbert carried his pack, which was damaged by the bear . . .
>
> "This is a very, very special place because the grizzly is still here," [Cole] said. "I'm in grizzly country quite a bit. You take the precautions, but you've got to accept the risk."[71]

Cole had accepted the risk of hiking once again in grizzly country.

On May 23, 2007, in Yellowstone, he readied his camera equipment to photograph bears. He stepped off the roadside turnout and descended into the vast sweep of mostly treeless Hayden Valley.

What happened next? Five months later, from the Baxter Hotel's lobby in Bozeman, Montana, a recovering Cole was interviewed by Yellowstone special agents Dan Kirschner and Justin Ivary.

> In the interview, James COLE told [us]:
>
> That before he was attacked his plan was to go and glass with binoculars in an area south of Trout Creek where, a few days earlier, he saw a male bear walking in timber line near Trout Creek. He said that his plan was that after he went to Trout Creek he had planned to go to Mary Bay (alongside Yellowstone Lake) where he had previously seen a mother bear who was separated from her cubs . . .
>
> That he parked in the first or second turnout near Trout Creek on east side of the Road. He said he parked north of Trout Creek and pointed on a map approximately ¾ to 1 mile north of Trout Creek where he thought he parked. (His vehicle was found south of Trout

Creek on the west side of the road.) He said he did not walk along the road or cross Trout Creek.

That he hiked from road towards Sulfur Mountain. He hiked through "sand flats" near Sulfur Mountain because that area shows tracks in the sand. Behind Sulfur Mountain he hiked along a "ridge" and glassed area with binoculars. He said his plan was to make loop back to his vehicle and hike about 3 miles in.

That he then hiked south. He hiked in a "zig-zag" pattern for 1.5 miles.

That he then stopped and glassed with binoculars by a "big band of trees." He said that to the west he could see a small pond/group of trees. From this location he said he hiked in a south and southwest direction. He said this location was "way north of Trout Creek." He indicated this area was located 1 to 1.5 miles north of Trout Creek.

That from this point his plan [was] to go [to the] south end of [the vegetation transition] zone to glass Trout Creek.

That the attack came while he was walking down hill. He said that while hiking down a slope, he glanced left then right. He said he saw a bear charging him. He said a "mother bear is point blank charging." He also saw one cub for a split second. He said that there may have been a blind spot, coming down the hill, where mauling took place.

That the bear was in a full charge with no chance to get spray being carried on belt (indicates 2 canisters). During mauling was trying to get to spray but arm was not working—thinks bear injured his shoulder when he was driven to the ground. He said he then saw the bear leave with a cub and they ran away from him in the same direction that the bear had approached and at same speed she had charged.

That after the mauling he remembers a "faint perception of sun" which he used to find way back to road.

That he used the sun and Trout Creek to hike out. He said he crossed Trout Creek 4 or 5 times when hiking out.

After being terribly injured by the grizzly, Cole struggled to walk back to the Grand Loop Road, his parked van, and the hoped-for help of passersby. Those passersby were a couple in a parked car, each of whom handwrote a statement of what they saw.

The husband wrote the following. "[We were at the] Trout Creek pullout looking for animals about 12:30 p.m. Wed. 5/23/07."

We saw a man walking out about 150–250 yards. I figured he was doing research or something. Watching him through binoculars, it looked like he was wearing a mask. Lost sight for awhile. Drove down to Trout Creek, saw him sitting on bank. Just looked through binocs and realized his face [was] covered with blood. As he walked across creek he yelled, "Help. Help. I've been attacked by a bear." I helped him to side of road. My wife called 911. Others stopped to help. He was saying he was hypothermic.

Park Ranger Richard T. Fey responded to the scene. In his report he described what he saw:

Upon arrival I immediately went to the group of perhaps three people who were around a gentleman, approximately 10 yards to the west of the road, just to the south of the Trout Creek pull off (to the east). The gentleman's head was bent slightly forward, supporting himself on his right elbow and covered by an NPS [National Park Service] jacket. He was sitting down. I looked at his face as I was putting on my examination gloves. It was immediately apparent that his face was severely traumatized but [he] could breathe. He was sitting, mostly under his own power, semi-vertically. I immediately looked at Ranger [Frank G.] Deluca who was close by. As I was about to set up command and order resources I could hear that he was already on the radio requesting availability of a life flight and wanted confirmation that an ambulance was dispatched. He confirmed our location as Trout Creek.

I returned to the victim and saw that Medic [Mitch] Copeland was starting an IV via his forehand. I wanted to assess the airway and mental state of the individual and returned to his left side. I asked the person to his left, also sitting down, that was applying pressure to his chin . . . if she was involved in this incident. She responded, "No, but I'm a nurse."

I thanked her for her assistance and asked that she continue giving him support.

His nose and nasal cavity appeared to be gone, so was his mandible and most of the soft tissue around it. It appeared that his eyes were missing. It was difficult for me to recognize facial landmarks! I recognized his eyebrows. Everything below that was unrecognizable. Even though it appeared that he was supporting himself I could not believe that his airway was not compromised. I could not figure out how this individual was able to breathe! I asked the patient his name. He tried to answer me but I could not understand him. His answers were garbled. I asked him again and this time he told me Jim Cole. It sounded that [as if] his tongue was also missing. It was apparent that his jaw was.

I had a camera in my pocket and as I was setting it up I continued to assess his mental and breathing status by asking questions. I asked him "Where did this happen?" (about two to three miles behind me to the west). "How many others are out there?" (none, I was by myself). "What did this to you?" (a grizzly with a cub). "When did this happen?" We paused. I told him it was now 1:00 o'clock, how many hours ago did this happen? (about two hours ago, around 11:00).

At this time I was concerned that the pressure to the bottom of his missing chin could compromise his breathing. I went behind him and slowly removed the jacket covering his head. I started to maintain cervical spine protection. I realized that the patient had walked out, with an assortment of gear, for approximately two hours. However, the cervical spine protection was secondary to maintaining his airway. At this time the ambulance had arrived and the gurney was being brought down to our location. We had a brief discussion if the life flight should be brought directly to the scene. It was decided in an instant that the patient should start his trip west and if necessary could meet the life flight along the road to save time.

"Upon arrival at West Yellowstone Clinic at [2:19 p.m.]," the Supplemental Case/Incident Record stated, "Cole was transferred inside to be stabilized before he was flown to Idaho Falls [Eastern Idaho Regional

Medical Center]. Cole did not give any further information at the clinic. Patient care was transferred to flight paramedics from Idaho Falls."

KSL Television and Radio in Salt Lake City, Utah, reported that "Judy Geiger, a nursing director driving through the park, saw a couple trying to help the [injured] man." The June 20, 2007, report continued:

> She [Judy Geiger] described the situation, saying "My parents had a first aid kit in their car and I think that was really lucky, and it had gloves and everything, which was good with this big, bloody mess."
>
> She covered him, put pressure on his bleeding and kept him talking for 15 minutes before EMTs arrived.
>
> Judy is the director of the pediatric intensive care unit, and over the years, has seen many serious injuries. This one was the most gruesome she has ever seen. "I really couldn't tell at the time when I saw him whether he still had eyes, cause things were sort of rearranged and bloody. His face was just hanging off, basically. I was sort of shocked that he could have walked three miles back from where he was hurt," she said . . .
>
> Judy Geiger says she's not heroic, just glad to be in the right place at the right time. "I really think that if he had not been going in the right direction or this couple hadn't seen him and he'd fallen down and, for some reason, couldn't get back up, I think he could have died."[72]

As for the bear and cub, Yellowstone spokesperson Al Nash said on Thursday, May 24, that "We are not at this time planning any management action against the bear. From the little bit of information that we have, it appears he [Cole] surprised the bear and was attacked."

Cole's emergency surgery on May 23, 2007, at Eastern Idaho Regional Medical Center required seven hours, and he was placed on a ventilator. He was released from the hospital on Sunday, June 3, 2007, but faced the prospect of numerous reconstructive surgeries.

The *Bozeman Daily Chronicle* reported that "Longtime friend Michael Sanders said Cole . . . will spend the next several weeks recovering at an undisclosed location."

Cole's friend Sanders told the Idaho Falls *Post-Register* that "Cole 'is experiencing problems with his vision and speech. His arms are very weak, but he is doing some exercises and feeling better.'"[73]

The *Bozeman Daily Chronicle* reported on July 30, 2010, that "Jim Cole, photographer, author, musician, bear advocate and victim of two grizzly bear maulings, died last week of natural causes, Gallatin County Deputy Coroner Mike Chesnut confirmed Thursday." The Friday report added the following:

> Cole was 60 years old. Concerned friends, unable to reach Cole for several days, alerted the Gallatin County Sheriff's Office on Monday, Chesnut said.
>
> "What can you say? It was too early," Jim Halfpenny, a longtime friend of Cole's and president of A Naturalist's World in Gardiner, said Thursday. "It is a loss to the wildlife community. And to bears."
>
> At times controversial but always passionate in his work on behalf of wild bears, Cole had just published his third book, *Blindsided: Surviving a Grizzly Attack and Still Loving the Great Bear* (St. Martin's Press). The book includes details of his encounter with a grizzly bear in Yellowstone National Park in May 2007.

# PART V— TRENDS?
# OTHER RECENT ATTACKS (1986–2015)

# 18

# BEAR ATTACKS 1986–1992

## 1986: I GRABBED THE BEAR'S HEAD, SPENCER HINKLE

*National Park Service—Yellowstone*

*Case Incident Record Number: 861340*

*Location: East of Divide Picnic Area,*

*North of Road—near Dry Creek Service Road (close to Craig Pass), UTM 4922.28 N 528.54*

*Date/Time: Thursday, July 3, 1986, 1:00 p.m.*

That Fourth of July, 1986, was tomorrow, but Spencer Hinkle was enjoying his holiday early. On July 3rd about 10 a.m., the twenty-six-year-old drove his 1978 yellow Dodge van through the south entrance into Yellowstone Park. Following the Grand Loop Road north past Lewis Lake (elevation 7,779 feet), he passed West Thumb Geyser Basin and then headed west into the heart of Yellowstone: toward Old Faithful. He crossed Craig Pass and the Continental Divide (8,262 feet), and then pulled over and parked at the Divide Picnic Area.

The Divide Trail could be accessed from the parking area. Park Ranger Mark C. Marschall described the Divide Trail in *Yellowstone Trails* (revised in 1984, two years before Spencer arrived). Marschall wrote: "The trail climbs 735 feet through a lodgepole and whitebark pine forest to a

70 foot lookout tower." Marschall described the view, which attracts many hikers:

> You can climb the stairs of the tower, but a locked trap door prevents you from going up to the observation deck. Still, the view from the steps is marvelous. Shoshone Lake and Mt. Sheridan to the southeast, the Teton Range to the south, and Yellowstone Lake to the east are all visible.[74]

First things first. Rather than immediately following the trail, Spencer "took a nap and [then] went out for a hike around 3:00 p.m.," wrote Park Ranger John M. Lounsbury in the Case Incident Record. By the time of Lounsbury's interview with Spencer —4:45 p.m. that same day— Spencer was in Yellowstone Lake Hospital and Lounsbury was at his bedside. Spencer had been the victim of a bear attack.

Spencer told Ranger Lounsbury that he had made a choice not to follow the trail to the lookout tower, but to hike off trail into the back-country. He "walked north, crossed a service road, continued north, he thinks about three miles," the ranger's report added:

> [Spencer] got into some thick timber, turned around, and returned he thinks parallel to his original route. (Much confusion on directions, I wouldn't put much credence on these descriptions). Spencer came to a gully, then a marsh, then up on a knoll. While up on the knoll it got quiet??? and a bear came out of the trees towards Spencer. Spencer's first instincts were to run. He ran for approx. 20 seconds in the direction he was heading. Spencer got tired and stopped. The bear knocked Spencer down with his head (he was not bitten or clawed). Spencer then grabbed the bear's head, then Spencer turned to run again and this is when the bear bit him in the leg. Then Spencer got up and the bear backed up, then Spencer started running, the bear followed momentarily, then departed.
>
> Spencer continued running, came out on the Craig Pass road by a sign that said 17 miles to Old Faithful. Spencer thinks it was a grizzly bear, was a golden brown (he pointed out a dark chocolate brown color,

but admitted he was color blind). Bear was approx. 4 feet high on all four feet. He guessed weight at 1200 lbs. and length about 5 feet long. He dropped keys to his van during this incident.

Injuries were 5 punctures on the back of his right leg. They appeared consistent with the canine teeth of a bear with one incisor tooth puncture.

Ranger Lounsbury contacted Ranger Doug Ridley, who at 4:50 p.m. interviewed the "park visitor who stopped and picked up [Spencer] Hinkle and drove him to the hospital (statement included)."

In the statement, the park visitor related his first sight of Spencer: "We were traveling from Old Faithful back to Grant Village Campground when a man flagged us down approximately 2 miles (east) this side of the 2nd Continental [Divide] line." The park visitor continued his account:

> The man stated he had just been attacked by a bear. His right leg was injured with dried blood that had run down his leg. We asked him where the incident occurred and he stated just awhile ago and that he had run for a long time. He stated he didn't know where he was. We put him in our truck and took him to the hospital. During the travel with him he stated the bear came out of nowhere and he ran for a distance but knew the bear was right behind him so he turned and the bear stopped. He said he ("man") started to turn and run when the bear bit him knocking him down. He stated he got up screaming and yelling and the bear backed off. He stated he then ran from the bear and didn't stop until he came to the paved road.
>
> He stated his van was located plus or minus 11 miles from Old Faithful. He stated he lost his keys while running.

After being lucky enough to be picked up by this good Samaritan and his family, Spencer found himself lucky for a second time. Ranger Lounsbury's report described what happened next:

> A nurse and EMT also stopped, cleaned Spencer's injuries and put ice on them, and [name withheld] transported Spencer in the back of his

pick-up on a bed inside a camper shell to the Lake Hospital where he was treated and interviewed by myself . . .

After Rangers Ridley and Les Inafuku located Spencer's Dodge van at the Divide Picnic Area, Ridley wrote that "The area was searched for any sign of tracks or bear sign of any kind." Ridley's "Investigative Report" concluded; "None were found." The rangers then placed bear warning signs in the area:

The picnic area and adjacent roadside pullouts were signed (Bear Warnings – No travel beyond this point). Ridley contacted [Spencer] at [7:30 p.m.] concerning the disposition of his vehicle and plans for the evening. [Spencer] would stay at the Hospital for the night and send for another set of keys in the morning (keys lost in flight from the bear).

[Spencer] departed Lake Hospital on 7/4/86. Arrangements were made to get new set of keys from parents in Salt Lake City. Vehicle picked up at approximately 1900 hours [7:00 p.m.].

NOTE: [name withheld], researcher, sighted black bear sow and cub tracks and single grizzly tracks in this area on 7/8/86. Bear sighting reports filled out.

Bear information reported by [Spencer] did not provide conclusive evidence as to whether the bear involved in this incident was a grizzly or black. The information provided by [researcher] allowed that possibly both species frequent the area.

Exact distances covered by [Spencer] were also skewed by the excitement of the confrontation. Given the time from the beginning of the hike to time of pick up and delivery to Lake Hospital, it is reasonable to believe that the incident occurred within one mile of the Craig Pass road and very near the Dry Creek service road in the area adjacent the Divide Picnic Area.

Some grizzly tracks were found a few days later, but park personnel could not identify the bear that attacked Hinkle.

Ranger Ridley concluded his report: "Investigation closed. Bear activity being carefully monitored in this area as well as off road visitor access and use."

## 1986: BEAR STARTED BITING HIM, ALAIN FOEGLE

*National Park Service—Yellowstone*

*Case Incident Record Number: 861864*

*Location: Turbid Lake, northeast of Yellowstone Lake*

*(off Turbid Lake Trail near Turbid Creek)*

*Date/Time: Sunday, July 20, 1986, 12:30 p.m.*

Sunday, July 20, 1986, was a good-weather day to be sightseeing in Yellowstone—and just in case a visitor got lucky, to be carrying a camera. Alain Foegle, twenty-nine years old, had traveled to Yellowstone from Bitche, France. He understood little English, but hoped to capture photographs of those who spoke to him in other ways—Yellowstone's wild creatures in their native habitat.

At the Pelican Valley Trailhead at half past noon, he hoisted his shoulder bag containing camera equipment but no food, only water. He was hiking alone.

What did Alain see at the trailhead? According to the subsequent Case Incident Record, a trailhead photo "shows trail register box at Pelican trailhead. Sign on left indicates Pelican area open for day use. On left side of register box is BEAR FREQUENTING AREA sign."

Alain signed the trail register for "length of stay: one day or less," and checked his primary activity as "sightseeing." Subsequent hikers following him into that part of Yellowstone included a party of two, a second party of two, and (showing how frequently non-Americans visited Yellowstone) a third party of two from Bremen, Germany.

The trail was not difficult, and was three miles (five kilometers) long. Starting from the Pelican Creek Trailhead, northeast of Yellowstone Lake, the trail led into the backcountry to Turbid Lake.

What did the trail Alain follow look like in 1986, before the great firestorms of 1988 transformed the scenery? "This trail is actually an old dirt road which runs from Pelican Valley Trailhead to Turbid Lake," wrote Yellowstone park ranger Mark C. Marschall in *Yellowstone Trails, A Hiking Guide* (1984). Marschall then warned the reader: "(CHECK SPECIAL RESTRICTIONS DUE TO GRIZZLY BEARS)." Marschall then described the lake at the trail's end:

Turbid Lake is a relatively large backcountry lake which has a group of hot springs located near its east shore. Waterfowl (especially Canada geese), moose, and occasionally bison are seen around the Turbid Lake area. From the trailhead, the road follows the edge of a grass and sage area then climbs gradually through the forest about 8,000 feet from which it descends to the shores of Turbid Lake.[75]

Orville Bach Jr., in his 1991-revised *Exploring the Yellowstone Backcountry*, explains the reason for Turbid Lake's name. "The name is appropriate as thermal features under the 14.3-acre lake cause the water to appear turbid and foamy . . . This is also prime grizzly country; *in fact a man [Alain] was mauled by one here in 1986, so remain alert.*[author's emphasis ]"[76] Alain, in 1986 was now hiking off trail, but he *was* alert. At approximately 12:30 p.m. he was disturbed to hear and see large elk running. Running from what?

All too soon thereafter he would be taken to the emergency room of Yellowstone's Lake Hospital emergency room. With the help of a French interpreter, Alain told Park Ranger Mona Divine what happened next:

[Alain] thought that the elk were chasing him. He ran for an unknown distance along the base of a ridge, thru heavy brush. He intended on climbing a tree but did not see one that was close to his location. After a minute or so, he noted that he could not see the elk. He stopped running and continued walking. [Alain] heard a large crashing noise in brush that was within 10 yds or so of where he was walking. He thought that there was a good possibility of a bear. He dropped down to the ground, glimpsing a large grizzly bear and at least one cub as he went down. The bear then starting biting him as he played dead. [Alain] could not remember much of the attack other than being bitten all over. He did not see the bear as it left the area.

After the attack, [Alain] walked back toward the trail and continued out toward the trailhead. As he approached the trailhead he ran into some fishermen, who were just starting into the Pelican area. They assisted [Alain] to his car and drove him to Lake Hospital for treatment.

Ranger Divine's report dated July 24 described Alain's grievous injuries as follows:

**Punctures to the left thigh;** on superior surface one puncture that completely broke thru skin, with another mark that did not completely break skin located approx. 6 cm proximal inferior surface, two punctures that completely broke skin located approx. 6 cm apart.

**Punctures on back;** located left lower lumbar/kidney area, two punctures approx. 5 and ¾ cm apart. Another two punctures parallel to first on side.

**Gaping wound to left arm;** wound gaping, located lower portion of upper arm from approx. 10 cm above to just below elbow on back of arm, wound approx. 4 cm wide. Appeared to be some portions missing.

**Left shoulder dislocated;** left shoulder area discolored, deformed and loss of range of motion.

[Alain's] treatment included x-rays, shoulder dislocation reduced, wounds irrigated, IV initiated, pain medication. Surgeon on call (Kendall) came in and closed wound and placed in drain.

**Hair fibers;** collected hair fibers from wound area, which were sent to Bear Mgmt.

The above hair fibers, wrote Wildlife Biologist Dan Palmisciano in his report dated July 20, were collected from the wound area and were subsequently verified as belonging to a grizzly bear. The "Description of bear(s)" was listed as "sow with [one or more] cubs," with the cubs believed to be very young, having been born that year.

This same grizzly was "possibly one that treed two TWS [concessionaire] employees," noted the Case Incident Record.

The Park Service's 11 a.m. "CALL-OUT (Turbid Lake Bear Incident)," dated July 21, stated that "Within a short time, the bears left the area. [Alain] hiked out to the road where he was given a ride to the Lake Hospital." The report then described what followed:

> [Alain] was treated, hospitalized overnight for observation, and will be released sometime today.
>
> Pelican Valley and the area surrounding Turbid Lake [11½ square miles] have been closed to all hiking until further notice. Stock parties will continue to be allowed to travel through the area throughout the duration of the closure.
>
> Park officials report that in addition to this closure, the Indian Creek Campground is also temporarily closed until further notice. A female grizzly bear has frequently been observed in the campground and surrounding area. Park officials hope the temporary closure will allow the bear to leave the vicinity without exposure to human foods, as well as to ensure visitors' safety and prevent further incidents between the bear and visitors.

The female grizzly bear in the Alain incident was thought to be protecting its cub or cubs, so no further action was taken against her. "Officials don't plan to trap or relocate the bear," reported park spokesperson Anita Varley.

*Note:* See Chapter 7 (Tesinsky) for another 1986 attack. There were no reported attacks in 1987 or 1988.

# 1989: BITTEN AND CLAWED (NAME WITHHELD)

*National Park Service—Yellowstone*

*Case Incident Record Number: 893442*

*Location: Grizzly Lake Trail to Mt. Holmes, round trip*

*Date/Time: Wednesday, August 16, 1989, approximately 6:00 p.m.*

That night an eclipse of a full moon was expected, but the hiker would not get to see it. On that Wednesday, August 16, 1989, the day hiker was returning from Mt. Holmes, and was three miles down from the summit when his trip was interrupted by a female bear with three cubs.

Investigating Ranger Rick McAdam wrote about the events of August 16: "[The hiker, name withheld] was doing a one-day hike to the summit of Mt. Holmes. He began at approx. 1200 [noon] (according to his trail register entry) at the Grizzly Lake Trailhead. According to Mt. Holmes fire lookout, [the hiker] arrived at the lookout approx. [4:30] p.m. and left at [5:15] p.m." The ranger's report went on to describe the bear attack:

At approximately [6:00 p.m.], having recently passed the 7.0 mile marker, he passed through one of the narrow bands of trees that divide the meadows in this area. Upon leaving the trees he encountered a bear he estimated to be 20 yards away. The bear had 3 cubs with it, which it quickly gathered behind it, then came running at [the hiker]. He dropped to the ground and initially resisted by kicking at the bear. He was bitten on the foot and moved about by the bear. He quit the resistance and after moving him some more, the bear left him. The entire encounter lasted approx. 30 seconds or less. He then stood up, but thought better of it and returned to the ground in a balled up protective posture and waited a few minutes longer. When he finally got up he could no longer see the bear or cubs.

[The hiker] briefly surveyed his injuries then continued down the trail to campsite 1C4 where he received some first aid treatment from camper [name withheld] who was camping at that site. [The victim]

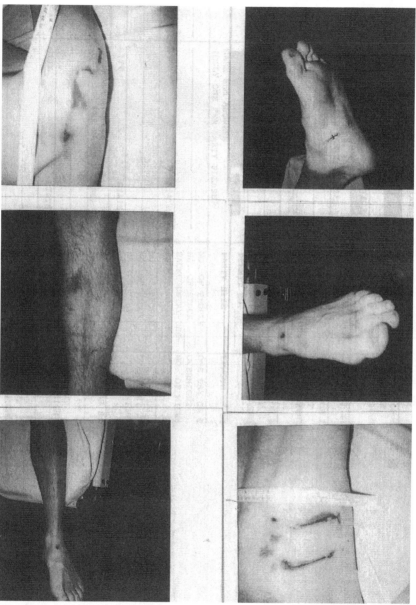

Six Polaroid photographs of hiker attacked by bear, from Case Incident Record #893442

then continued to the Winter Creek Trailhead, arriving around [10:00 p.m.]. He quickly got a ride with visitor [name withheld]. Dr. Dan Hudgings picked [the hiker] up at Mammoth where the [visitor] had taken him.

[The hiker] sustained a puncture wound on the top of his left foot; a 8/10" linear laceration on the instep of the same foot, which was closed by one stitch; 2-6" long straight-line abrasions on the right side rib cage; 1 7" irregular abrasion on the right shoulder; and several bruises on his right leg. He was also given antibiotics for the possibility of infections. He was released after the treatment and transported back to Canyon Village by Steve Frye.

[The hiker] said that he was traveling at a fairly good pace down the trail in order to reach the trailhead before dark. He also reported that he was not making any conscious effort to make noise as he traveled.

[The hiker] was concerned that no negative action be taken against the bear because of its actions and he was assured that nothing would happen since it seemed to be only an entirely natural reaction in defense of the cubs.

According to [the hiker's] description of the bear's coloration, it was probably a grizzly.

Ranger McAdam reported that trails and campsites near the scene of the attack were closed on August 17. He and Mammoth ranger Kevin Ulery later found one set of bear paw prints on August 28 that was one to two days old, but no scat or other evidence of bears. They reopened the trails and campsites and added a "Warning, Bear Frequenting Area" sign near the Winter Creek Patrol Cabin. The Backcountry Office issued a recommendation that hikers and campers travel in groups of four or more in the area.

*Note:* There were no reported attacks in 1990, 1991, and 1993. See Chapter 14 (Muller) and Chapter 15 (Matheny and Bahnson) for 1992 attacks.

# 19

# BEAR ATTACKS 1994–1997

## 1994: TWO CANINE-TOOTH PUNCTURE WOUNDS, GLEN LACEY

*National Park Service—Yellowstone*

*Case Incident Record Number: 941498*

*Location: Old Dry Creek Road northwest of West Thumb, UTM 527.9 E 4922.0 N*

*Date/Time: Wednesday, June 15, 1994, 10:00 a.m.*

One of the reasons employees choose to work in Yellowstone Park is to enjoy their free time hiking and exploring. That Wednesday morning, June 15, 1994, Glen Lacey, a Lake area maintenance worker, parked his car and set out hiking the Old Dry Creek Road (shown on some maps as an unmaintained trail). The campsite-free area—its tall trees untouched by the great fires of 1988—offered relaxation and solitude. Glen, thirty-nine years old, started at about 10:00 a.m. and hiked alone.

Just five miles northwest of West Thumb Geyser Basin, the area seemed far from the Basin's crowds of visitors. Glen was also four miles north of the vehicular noise on the Grand Loop Road. He hiked near an old rock quarry to which the service road led. The mostly level dirt surface, decaying into pine-needle duff, cushioned his feet.

He climbed a small hill—just high enough to keep him from seeing what was on the other side—and walked around the path's curve. A grizzly with her two yearling cubs stood there.

Ranger John M. Lounsbury wrote three days later, on June 18, about what happened next. "The sow grizzly saw Glen at the same time." The ranger's Supplementary Case/Incident Record added the mother grizzly's reaction:

> The bear stood up on her hind legs and then charged Glen. He estimated his distance from the bear when he first saw her as 50–60 feet. Glen ran to a tree about 12 feet away. The sow grizzly reached him the same time he reached the tree. The bear bit his arm as she ran past him. Glen circled around the tree. The bear left him and returned to her cubs. The bear did not show any further aggressive behavior. Glen circled carefully around the bear and returned back [to] the Dry Creek road to his vehicle. He then drove to the Lake hospital where his arm was treated and he was released.
>
> Glen suffered a bite to his right forearm near the elbow. There were two puncture wounds from the bear's canine teeth and a slight scratch. Glen estimated the sow grizzly's weight to be about 200 lbs. The area where the incident happened was temporarily closed.

All three bears were described as "light brown" on Bear Management Specialist Kerry A. Gunther's "Bear Sighting and/or Identification Report," with the two cubs weighing 51 to 100 pounds each, and the mother listed as a "medium adult" at 201 to 400 pounds. The sighting location was checked as "In the Wild."

A Yellowstone Park news release of June 21, 1994, stated that "No management action was to be taken against the sow and her cubs."

## 1994: FACE COVERED WITH BLOOD, RANDY INGERSOLL

*National Park Service—Yellowstone*

*Case Incident Record Number: 941582*

*Location: Chaw Pass, Thunderer Cutoff Trail, UTM 575.6 E 4974.3 N*

*Date/Time: June 20, 1994, 3:00 p.m.*

Five days after the previous incident involving Glen Lacey, another off-duty employee, Randy Ingersoll, left his car parked at a turnout, this time in Yellowstone's Lamar Valley. On June 20, 1994, the TW Recreational Services worker started his day hike at the Thunderer Cutoff trailhead. The sun was warm at 12:40 p.m., and the thirty-seven-year-old wore a T-shirt, shorts, and a red daypack containing some food and personal items. [Randy] stopped at the tall wood sign and took out the register book from its cubby space, writing his destination as (the perhaps unfortunately named) Chaw Pass. A framed information sheet was there, too, headlined: "Danger—Entering Bear Country—A Risk."

The day before, the sign-in sheet showed that two hikers from New York had registered at 10:30 a.m. and then out at 3:45 p.m., enjoying their hike without incident. Randy was hiking alone.

He crossed the ford at Soda Butte Creek and followed the trail in the direction of Chaw Pass, and then almost immediately entered fir and spruce forest.

Ranger Colette Daigle-Berg interviewed Randy on July 8. She wrote that before arriving at Chaw Pass, "[Randy] met [a] friend [name withheld] and three other people hiking down the pass back toward the Thunderer trailhead. They had just been on the [Mount] Thunderer side of Chaw Pass and told [Randy] that the view was good from that side."

After Randy's friend and three companions left to hike down, Randy continued climbing up.

Ranger Daigle-Berg, continuing her interview with Randy on July 8, wrote that "[Randy] continued on up the trail to Chaw Pass." He told her that the time had been about 2:30 p.m. Randy described what happened next:

[Randy] said he was wearing a "Walkman" [with headphones] and listening to music since it made the climb up the hill seem easier. Once on Chaw Pass, [Randy] said he left the trail in the opposite direction

Photo showing the Thunderer Cutoff trail mileage sign located at the trailhead parking area with the bear warning sign not normally there. Photo taken on June 21, 1994, by Ranger Bundy Phillips, from Case Incident Record #941582

of the Thunderer (toward the northeast), and hiked off-trail, along the ridge, for approximately 15-20 minutes. [Randy] said the distance he hiked was probably less than a mile. He said he walked through timber and came to a flat, rocky area which overlooked the Amphitheater drainage.

[Randy] stood on the flat, rocky area for approximately two to three minutes, then turned and started to walk back in the direction from which he had come. He said he looked toward his right and noticed a bear sow and two cubs approx. twenty feet away. [Randy] said the sow and cubs were blondish in color and that the cubs appeared to be about one-half the size of the sow. He said he did not see a hump on the sow but, based on his knowledge and experience of black and grizzly bears, thinks that the bears were grizzly. [Randy] said that the sow was standing on all four feet and the cubs were sitting down on either side of the sow. The bears were at the edge of a group of small trees.

[Randy] said when the sow saw him she sent the cubs away and charged. He said the incident happened very quickly and that he turned to a pine tree with no lower branches to his immediate right and attempted to climb the tree. (Abrasions to the inside of both knees appear to confirm this.) When the sow reached him he yelled at it. The bear pulled him away from the tree and started to bite him. He told himself to freeze and immediately played dead. He doesn't recall for sure if his hands were over the back of his head or not, however he was still wearing his day pack.

As soon as he played dead, [Randy] said the bear quit biting, made a huffing noise once and left. He thought the bear went in the direction of Amphitheater Creek. [Randy] said he lay on the ground about a minute thinking about the possibility of the bear returning. He didn't see the bear so he got up and started down the trail toward the trailhead. He did not see the bears again on the hike out.

[Randy] was aware of his injuries but said that they didn't bleed grossly and that he used his shirt sleeve on his left arm to help stop bleeding. He used his right hand to stabilize painful movement of left arm during the hike out.

When [Randy] got to the Thunderer trailhead he received a ride to the Lamar Buffalo Ranch [a historic site inside the park] with passing motorists.

The passing motorists mentioned above handwrote a report on what happened next to Tower Ranger Desi Crider at Buffalo Ranch (currently a classroom and cabins for the Yellowstone Institute). They described having "stopped at parking area at side of road to take picture when we noticed a man walking from his car over to ours." The motorists saw that the man was bloody:

When he got up to us it was obvious that he had been bleeding badly as his face was covered with blood and his shirt was very bloody. He said he had been attacked by a grizzly but he seemed quite coherent and asked us to notify the ranger station up the road. We told him to get into the car and we would take him to the ranger station which we did.

Ranger Bundy Phillips wrote on June 21 that the motorists were "medical professionals and they are familiar with blood-borne pathogens protection." The ranger reported their meticulous actions:

They spread a blanket out in their car to prevent [Randy's] blood from getting blood all over the car. They told me that they were very comfortable with the fact that none of [Randy's] blood had gotten in their car. [Name withheld] did show me a small spot of blood that had gotten on her shirt sleeve. She said that she was going to soak the shirt in cold water then further wash it. I asked if the park could be of any help in cleaning their car and her shirt. Both [motorists] declined any assistance.

Both [motorists] said that [Randy] (unsolicited) made statements to the effect that he had hiked in Yellowstone for 15 years. He had hiked the Thunderer trail before and knew the area. [Randy] told them that he normally would sing to himself while hiking. He was not singing nor making any other noise while hiking this day. He was hiking alone. He saw nobody else while he was hiking. He said that he had done all the wrong things and knew better (should have been making noise and not hiking alone in bear country).

Randy received emergency treatment after being taken by the motorists to the ranger station. Ranger Phillips wrote in his Summary on June 21 that "[Randy] was provided emergency medical care by rangers Daigle-Berg, [Desi] Crider & [Rick] Burrier. He was transported by park ambulance to Lake Hospital where [he] was treated. Later in the night he was transported by Lake Hospital ambulance to Mammoth ambulance to Hall's ambulance and was taken to Bozeman [MT] Deaconess Hospital." Ranger Daigle-Berg wrote on July 8 that Randy was hospitalized because "Follow-up information revealed that [Randy] suffered a fractured left shoulder in addition to the forehead laceration and multiple puncture wounds. He was transferred to Bozeman Deaconess where he underwent surgery to repair his shoulder."

Ranger Phillips wrote on July 20 of the investigatory efforts to piece together what happened and specifically where:

[Ranger Keith Brown and Phillips] went to investigate the scene where the mauling took place. I thought we could find the "Walkman" type cassette player and watch that Ingersoll said that he lost. We went to Chaw Pass, turned and walked in an easterly direction (away from Chaw Pass) for about 15-20 minutes, then turned and went to a small, flat rocky area that overlooked Amphitheater Creek. This is the exact description that [Randy] gave to Ranger Daigle-Berg of the route he had followed just before being mauled. We were not able to find the "Walkman" or watch.

We searched the area through the trees and in the open. We walked a distance farther up the ridge (easterly) but saw no other area that would have overlooked Amphitheater Creek such as [Randy] had described to Daigle-Berg. After making several sweeps of the area in attempt to locate the exact site we gave up and left the area.

I did not see any bear tracks in the soil in the area. I did see an area very close to the approximate attack site where it appeared that a bear(s) had dug up tree bases and rooted around. I saw a green spruce tree about 6–8" in diameter that had been pushed over and uprooted very recently. There appeared to be claw marks on the roots of the tree. This area was unburned and was a rather dense, dark wooded area.

A Yellowstone news release dated June 21 reported "Second Park Employee Injured by Grizzly Bear." As to the fate of the bears, Yellowstone superintendent Bob Barbee was quoted as saying that "The Thunderer Cutoff Trail has been closed to all hiking until further notice. No management action will be taken against the sow and her yearlings."

## 1994: BEAR BIT THE BACK OF HIS HEAD, KIRK VON MEETEREN

*National Park Service—Yellowstone*

*Case Incident Record Number: 940010*

*Location: Fairy Falls Trail, 200 yds N of falls on trail (he was moving S), UTM 510.5 E 4930.0 N*

*Date/Time: Wednesday, September 21, 1994, 12:00 p.m.*

Kirk Von Meeteren, forty, of California chose to hike the Fairy Falls Trail, which leads to one of the most attractive ribbons of water in the park—a long and delicate spume, more mist than droplets. That September 21, 1994, the time was nearing noon and he was hiking alone.

Orville Bach Jr. described the sights on this trail in his 1991 edition of *Exploring the Yellowstone Backcountry*. "This entire area burned extensively during 1988, but the revegetation on the forest floor is quite colorful and interesting." Bach added the following:

From the old steel bridge the trail passes below the edge of Madison Plateau with Midway Geyser Basin in view to the north. Numerous thermal features are found along the first mile. Look for Canada geese in the meadow just off to your right. Prior to the fires of 1988 about the only way to obtain a good view of Grand Prismatic Spring (the park's largest) was to rent a helicopter. Now you can scramble up the burned ridge above you to gain a breathtaking panorama of this huge and colorful spring. After 1 mi. the trail turns to the west and enters the burned forest. Fairy Falls at a height of 200 ft. is a splendid and graceful waterfall. Views of the falls are much easier to obtain now that the spruce and fir forest canopy has burned away. The pool at the base of the falls was reduced recently when the logjam dam broke loose.[77]

Later that same day, a Wednesday, Ranger Les Inafuku filled out a Bear Sighting Report at Old Faithful, describing what next befell Kirk. "Single male hiking W on trail (Fairy Falls), heard something running at him from the north, saw bear charging," wrote Inafuku:

[Kirk] ran 15–20 ft and ducked behind tree on south side of trail. When he looked up bear was still charging. (Bear charged from flats, man ran uphill.) On his 2nd look he didn't see a bear, then received 2 sets of 2 puncture wounds on left hand's dorsal surface proximal to pinky and ring finger from 2 bites. Also a ½ in. laceration along medial side of left thumb as well as another abrasion. Bear then bit the back of his head—there was a ½ in. diameter skin abrasion with swelling. There were also 4 tears in his daypack. [At] left rear of upper arm (near armpit) shirt was torn, bear slobber and small abrasion on his back. Man falls down and hears bear run away.

When other hikers saw the bloodied Kirk, they hurried to the trailhead near the Midway Geyser Basin parking lot to notify rangers. Ranger Mike Murray wrote of actions taken in the September 22 National Park Service Morning Report:

[Kirk] was able to hike out to the trailhead on his own, where he was met by rangers responding to the incident, which had been reported by other hikers. [Kirk] received basic first aid treatment from the rangers, who cleansed and bandaged the wounds, before leaving the area.

In his report Ranger Inafuku noted that there were "Bear tracks on N and S side of trail but on poor substrate, possibly grizzly. Tracks also circled tree man was behind. No tracks on trail because too much foot traffic; no hair found. Posted as 'Bear Frequenting Area.'"

The Yellowstone news release of September 22 reported that "[Kirk] believed it was a grizzly bear." The release described the efforts to determine whether the bear was a grizzly or a black, and why it may have attacked, as below:

> Park rangers investigating the area found partial tracks suggesting it was a sub-adult grizzly bear in the 200–250 pound size range. Rangers found no signs of a carcass or other food sources that would attract the bear to the area, so it is believed that the bear was simply passing through the area when the encounter occurred. The Fairy Falls Trail has been posted with bear warning signs. The trail has not been closed; rangers will continue to monitor the area for bear activity.
>
> This is the fourth bear incident this season.

*Note*: For another 1994 attack, see Chapter 16 (O'Connell). No attacks were reported in 1995 and 1996.

## 1997: BEAR CUFFED AND BIT HIM, JOSHUA BEATTIE

*National Park Service—Yellowstone*

*Case Incident Record Number: 974244*

*Location: Near Tern Lake, UTM 4945.2 N 557.9 E*

*Date/Time: Thursday, August 21, 1997, 3:00 p.m.*

The park visitor from Indiana, twenty-two, left his Broad Creek campsite to day hike south to the two joined parts of Tern Lake. The surrounding backcountry appeared empty of other people that Thursday, August 21, 1997, about 3:00 p.m. He carried a *Trails Illustrated* "Tower/Canyon" map and followed the Astringent Creek Trail. Joshua later told an investigating ranger that he had "never hiked in Yellowstone or bear country prior to this trip." He hiked alone.

Joshua was enjoying the backcountry sights. Orville Bach Jr., in 1991's *Exploring the Yellowstone Backcountry*, wrote that the "Astringent Creek Trail from Broad Creek near Fern Lake down to Pelican Creek, offers wild and beautiful scenery." Bach then described Joshua's destination: Tern Lake.

> At 1.2 mi. you come to Tern Lake, which teems with various forms of birdlife—duck, goose, and quite probably trumpeter swan. The lake is very shallow, with marshy areas all around. (There are few, if any, fish in Fern, Tern, or White lakes.) Beyond the lake to the west is a ridge that has been burned over by a forest fire. The trail continues to follow Broad Creek through mostly open country. At 2.5 mi., White Lake will be only partially visible to the west of the trail. . . . White Lake is the source for Broad Creek. In 1984 a young woman was tragically killed by a grizzly bear in this vicinity. She apparently did nothing to invite or provoke the attack, though she was camping alone in prime grizzly habitat. Despite intense efforts, the bear was never trapped or located.[78]

Brigitta Fredenhagen (see Chapter 6) died in the White Lake tragedy mentioned above. Thirteen years had passed since then. Joshua had chosen the same general area Brigitta did for his first Yellowstone backcountry trip.

Park Ranger Tim C. Reid, who subsequently interviewed Joshua and investigated the bear-mauling incident, wrote in the Case Incident Record that Joshua obtained a backcountry permit from the Tower Backcountry Office on August 19:

> [Joshua] completed the backcountry campsite request worksheet and viewed the backcountry orientation video in its entirety. The permit was issued by NPS employee David Rothenburger. [Joshua's] itinerary was:
> 8/20   M2 Moss Creek
> 8/21   5B1 Broad Creek
> 8/22   4M2 Moss Creek
> 8/23   4R1 Ribbon Lake

On 8/20/97 [Joshua] parked his vehicle at the Wapiti Lake trail-head (4K7) and hiked to his campsite 4M2 at Moss Creek. [Joshua] stated that he observed no bear sign during his hike or in the vicinity of the campsite and that his night was uneventful with no animal activity of any kind.

On the morning of 8/21 [Joshua] stated that he broke camp at 4M2 and hiked to the campsite at Broad Creek—5B1. [Joshua] stated that he arrived early and made camp at approximately noon or 1300 hours [1:00 p.m.]. [Joshua] stated that he did not have his watch and that all stated times are estimates. [Joshua] stated that he decided to day hike. Sans pack or daypack, [he] hiked the trail south up Broad Creek, past the Fern Lake junction and toward Tern Lake. [He] stated that when he reached the confluence of Broad Creek and Tern Lake he left the established trail and traveled west on a game trail, following the North shoreline of Tern Lake. [He] stated that when he reached the peninsula that separates the two Tern Lake bodies, he traveled south, crossed the connecting drainage, and then followed the south shoreline of west Tern Lake. [He] stated that when he reached the southernmost tip of west Tern Lake he topped a small rise.

As he looked downslope he observed two bears approximately 25 yards beneath his position on the rise, one larger than the other, both light "dirt" brown in color. [Joshua] stated that while he was unsure of species or gender, the bears impressed him as being a grizzly sow and yearling. At [his] first observation the larger bear was in full run upslope toward his position, growling with its mouth open as it progressed. The smaller bear was turning around to look at him. [Joshua's] impression was that the bears were "messing" with something, though he was unable to visualize or smell anything.

The larger bear veered to [Joshua's] right (north), passing within five feet. [Joshua] stated that he stood completely still, not moving his head to track the bear's movements. He heard the bear move to his rear and then the bear knocked him down into a prone position. [Joshua] stated that he felt the bear cuffing and biting him. [He] felt the bear cease its activities and then heard both bears leaving the area, moving toward White Lake to the WSW. [Joshua] states that he lay motionless for approximately 1.5 minutes before getting to his feet and inspecting his wounds. [He] estimates that the entire mauling sequence lasted no longer than 30–45 seconds from his first observation.

In addition to numerous scratches and lacerations, [Joshua] sustained six distinct puncture wounds in his left scapula area and at least six distinct puncture wounds in his left thigh area (lateral/anterior aspect). [Joshua] traveled back to his campsite at 5B1, where he self-bandaged his wounds and spent a fitful night. On 8/22 [he] hiked out the Wapiti Lake trailhead and drove his vehicle to the Canyon ranger station where he reported the incident at [1:00 p.m.]. [He] was assessed by ranger/paramedic Dennis Lojko and transported . . . to the Lake Hospital via NPS ambulance.

DETAILS: [Joshua] stated that he has never hiked in Yellowstone or bear country prior to this trip. When asked what inspired him to adopt a passive approach to the bear's aggression, [he] stated that he did so as a direct function of the backcountry video and orientation materials he was exposed to at the Tower backcountry office. [He] also stated that he had remembered reading about "playing dead and not running" in some other literature prior to his Yellowstone trip.

[Joshua] did not carry bear spray nor did he wear/carry any noise making device during his backcountry trip in Yellowstone. [He] stated that "he made a mistake" by not making noise and moving quickly and quietly off trail. [He] stated that he had been exposed to, and understood, the backcountry video recommendation to not travel alone and to proactively make noise while hiking in the Yellowstone backcountry.

[Joshua] stated that his food rations consisted of dry pasta, dry sauce mixes, trail mix and bagels. [He] stated that he had taken care to make his camp away from his cooking area.

[He] was interviewed at the Lake Hospital on 8/21/97 by myself and Ranger Lloyd Kortge. Present during the interview were Lake Hospital staff Dr. LuAnne Hallagan and nurse Brian Putney. No pain medications were administered to Beattie prior to, or during, the interview. The interview took place at approximately [2:45 p.m.] and terminated at approximately [3:30 p.m.].

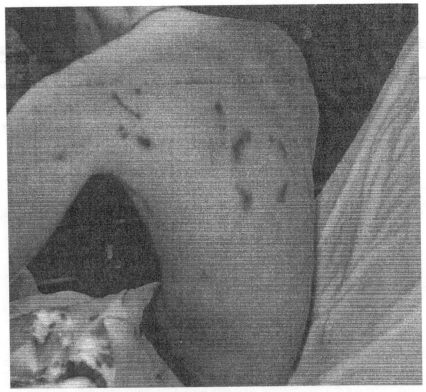

Left scapula bite marks. Photo taken by Park Ranger Tim C. Reid on August 23, 1997, from Case Incident Record #974244

The Bear Management Injury Report (unsigned) described what Joshua did before, during, and after the attack. "He came over a rise S/SE of S end of Tern Lake and surprised a sow grizzly & a yearling at 25 yards."

The larger bear growled w/ its mouth open & bluff charged to within 5 yards. [Joshua] stood still as he had seen to do so in Backcountry video [when he registered for his backcountry trip]. The larger bear then came from behind, cuffed & bit him. He sustained punctures on his left scapula (shoulder blade) & outer left thigh. The incident lasted [approximately] 30 sec. [Joshua] stayed down for 1.5 min after the bears left going W/SW towards the N. part of White Lake. [He] said the bear had no collar & ear tags. He said there was no carrion in the area.

Ranger Reid described the Park Service response in his Supplementary Case/Incident Record. "Trailheads 4K7, 4K8, 5K3 were posted with strong bear warnings the afternoon of 8/23/97. Campsites 5B1 and 5B2 were closed via the Central BC [backcountry] Office."

# 20

# BEAR ATTACKS 1998–2000

## 1998: BLEEDING STRONGLY AT HIS LEG, NAME WITHHELD

*National Park Service—Yellowstone*

*Case Incident Record Number: 984511*

*Location: Trilobite Lake Spur Trail of Mt. Holmes Trail*

*Date/Time: Saturday, September 5, 1998, 2:00 p.m.*

A husband and wife from Belgium [names withheld] were enjoying hiking the rugged Mt. Holmes Trail on September 5, 1998, when the wife, twenty-seven, became tired and stopped to rest. The husband, thirty-one, continued to hike onward. While the couple was separated, a grizzly charged and mauled the husband.

Ranger Colleen Boes soon arrived to help the wife, and wrote the details in her Supplementary Case/Incident Record:

On 9/5/98 at approximately 1700 [5 p.m.] I was on a vehicle stop with Ranger Dennis Lojko just north of the entrance to Norris campground. While on the stop we were approached by a woman who was crying and very upset. I went to speak to the woman while Ranger Lojko kept control over the vehicle stop. She reported to me that her husband had been mauled by a bear. She stated that they were hiking on a trail between Norris and Mammoth and her husband was hiking ahead of her. She stated that at one point he was about 500 meters ahead of her and she was not able to see him.

At that time she heard growling and sounds of her husband being attacked by the bear. She then ran to her spouse's location and found his thigh very bloody and mangled. The woman told me she tied her shirt around his leg and ran back to their vehicle at the trailhead to find help. She stated it had been approximately three hours since she had left her husband's side.

At this time I informed Ranger Lojko of the situation. Ranger Lojko called in the information to the communication center and Mammoth patrol. The woman [name withheld] could not remember what trail they had been hiking.

I took [her] with me in my vehicle to find the trailhead where they had started hiking from earlier that day. When we arrived at the trailhead for Mt. Holmes, [she] stated that this was the area with the trail that they had been hiking on. I called the communication center with the location and proceeded to gather as much information about the incident from [the victim's wife] as I could. I had [her] begin filling out a witness statement and notified Mammoth patrol and the communication center that [the wife] did not feel her husband would be conscious enough to wave his arms or assist in his being located by rescue workers.

[She] also informed me that she believed her spouse was located approximately 10 kilometers up the trail for Mt. Holmes and that she had positioned him under a tree off to the side of the trail. [Name withheld] stated that they had not been talking or making any noise while they were hiking.

Ranger Lojko soon arrived on scene and became incident commander. Ranger Lisa Barracz also arrived on scene shortly after Lojko and took over care of [the victim's wife].

The Witness Statement form instructs the witness to "In your own words, describe who, what, where, when and how." The wife handwrote her witness statement, signed, dated, and returned it to the ranger, as below:

[On the] Trail to Trilobite Lake, we were almost at the end of the trail (I think!). My husband was a little further on the trail. I heard a strong growling noise. A little bit later he came back to me bleeding strongly at his leg. I left him under the tree, tried to stop the bleeding with my t-shirt. I also left a bottle of water with him and his rain coat. Then I returned to the trailhead of Holmes Mountain. It took me 2 h 30 min to get there. I drove to Norris campground to ask help at the ranger station. By that time 3 hours past since I left him. I really hope everybody will do all they can to get him off there in good health. Thanks.

The Yellowstone Park news release of September 5 headlined "Visitor Mauled by Grizzly Bear" and detailed the victim's rescue:

The man was taken by park helicopter to the Mount Holmes Trailhead, where he was then taken by ground transportation to Mammoth Hot Springs and flown to Billings for additional medical care . . .

Both Mount Holmes Trailhead and Grizzly Lake Trailhead have been closed until further notice. No management action will be taken against the sow and her yearling at this time.

This is the first bear mauling this season.

A September 7 news release reported that the injured gentleman's condition "is stable at this time," and described the "short-haul" helicopter rescue:

[Name withheld] was "short-hauled" by helicopter from the mauling site to the park road. The short-haul method is used when a helicopter is unable to land in an area. A rope is put down to the ground from the helicopter where a basket is then used to place the patient in and haul a short distance at the end of the rope. Approximately 20 park staff were involved in the incident.

Park personnel M. Biel interviewed the husband on September 8, and per the husband's description, completed a Bear Sighting Report form.

The husband described seeing "2 bears, sow and yearling," whose color was "dark brown (chocolate)," with one bear weighing "201–400 pounds," and the other "101–200 pounds." The event took "less than 1 minute," during which the larger bear "charged, bit, threw the hiker." The husband then described the events further:

[He] was approximately 500 meters ahead of his wife when he left the trail and walked up a hill to look to see if [he] could see Trilobite Lake. About 15 meters away he saw 2 grizzly bears, one just slightly smaller than the other. The bigger bear immediately charged, he started to back away when the larger bear knocked him down, then picked him up by the leg and threw him down. [Name withheld] then played dead, face pressed down into the ground and the bear immediately left.

## 1999: BEAR INFLICTED TWO GASHES, MAN UNIDENTIFIED

*National Park Service—Yellowstone*

*Case Incident Record Number: 990010*

*Location: 3.5 miles up the Black Butte Trail from trailhead*

*Date/Time: August 27, 1999, 2:00 p.m.*

The two hikers, a woman from New York and a man from Switzerland, began their day hike at the Black Butte Trailhead, 2.4 miles inside Yellowstone's extreme northwest border. That August 27, 1999, their destination was the very scenic Big Horn Peak and Skyrim Trail. They had parked their vehicle at the Black Butte Creek crossing (where Highway 191 narrowly bisected the park) and began to climb the steep trail. They could see to their right the dark lava that formed Black Butte, and were soon far above civilization's roads. They wisely carried bear pepper spray.

Orville Bach Jr. described their strenuous route in his *Exploring the Yellowstone Backcountry*. "Black Butte Creek lies to the northwest of very conspicuous Black Butte." He continued with a warning:

The hike up to the top of Bighorn Peak must rank as one of the most strenuous in the park, as you gain over 3,000 ft. in only 6 mi.—the last 4.5 mi. climbing 2,330 ft. Once the Skyrim Trail is joined, though, your efforts will be rewarded with some very rugged mountain scenery. . . . Follow the trail carefully—one hiker fell to his death here in 1969.[79]

On the trail, the two day-hikers met an iconic figure: a Yellowstone ranger on horseback patrol. A short time later, at approximately 2:00 p.m., the two hikers encountered another icon: Yellowstone's grizzly bears.

Since the two hikers left the park without reporting the mauling that followed, initial information was scarce but was later pieced together after a friend of the hikers notified park officials as to what had happened.

Three days after the mauling, Park Ranger Mona Divine informed her colleagues about the incident in her August 30 memorandum. "Here's the latest and probably the final info on the bear mauling," she wrote.

On Friday August 27th a female hiker from New York age 39 and a male from Switzerland age 28 were day hiking in the northwest corner of the park. They started in from trailhead WK2 to Bighorn Peak. They talked with a ranger on horseback on the trail and continued on their hike. They passed an orange marker which indicated 3.0 [miles] and were approx. .5 past that marker when they had a sudden encounter with a bear and two cubs (by description probably grizzly with 2 yearlings). Female dark in color. Cubs both good size described as about 3 foot when on all fours.

The two hikers were chatting but not making as they described enough noise. They heard what they described as a drawn out moan. Unsure what it was, but thought it farther off. They took only a step or two and when looking to their left onto the slope that comes down to the trail, saw a bear within 10 yds.

The female [hiker] did not initially see the cubs and instantly while stating "It's a bear" stepped one or two steps off the trail, to the right, away from bear, dropping into a ball on her lower legs. The bear charged to her and the hiker could feel breath on her ear and back when the bear huffed a couple of times. The bear did not touch her.

At this same time the male [hiker] stepped uphill in the direction of where the bear came from and was approached by two cubs who did not touch him. The male could not recall the exact sequence but deployed pepper spray, unsure if he hit the yearlings. At this time the adult bear turned and charged toward him, he continued to spray and fell backwards onto his back. The bear did not make contact. He fell as he stepped or was startled. Initially no reaction from the bear. The male hiker put one leg up thinking the bear was going to attack him. The adult bear swatted his leg inflicting two gashes and two shallower marks or scratches (probable claw injury).

The adult bear sniffed at the cloud of spray and ran off—then returned again. Both hikers remained on the ground very still. By this time the male had depleted the can of bear spray. The bears left the area.

Although the hikers knew the ranger was in the area—they chose to return to the trailhead and seek advice from a friend living in Bozeman on which doctor to go to. They saw some RV [recreational vehicles] at the trailhead [and people] that gave them some hydrogen peroxide to wash the wounds. They went to Bozeman and ultimately received medical attention. The wounds although not serious are being monitored for infection and no stitches were made so that they could drain properly.

The Yellowstone news release of September 3 noted the following. "The Skyrim Trail [including Black Butte Trail] has been posted with bear warning signs. The trail has not been closed; rangers will continue to monitor the area for bear activity."

## 1999: SECOND MAULING ON BLACK BUTTE TRAIL, GEORGE LANGLEY JR.

*National Park Service—Yellowstone*

*Case Incident Record Number: 9905916*

*Location: 4.4 miles up the Black Butte Trail from trailhead, UTM 495330 E 4989540 N*

*Date/Time: Wednesday, September 22, 1999, 3:30 p.m.*

Less than one month later and again on Black Butte Trail—this time 4.4 miles from the trailhead—a second, much more injurious bear attack occurred. That Wednesday, September 22, 1999, was a crisp, sunny, early afternoon, and backpacker George Langley Jr. wore sunglasses and a black fleece jacket. Nicknamed "T.J.," the thirty-two-year-old from Washington carried binoculars, a compass, and a canister of bear pepper spray with the safety lock on. He was hiking alone.

For the past two days, George had been hiking and camping in the same area of the Yellowstone backcountry. Earlier, he had obtained the necessary camping permits, parked his blue Volkswagen Super Beetle, and begun his trip at the head of Daly Creek Trail, which was west of and roughly parallel to, the Black Butte Trail where the earlier mauling had occurred.

The park's winter newsletter, *Yellowstone Discovery*,[80] reported that at approximately 3:30 p.m. George "was hiking alone through a heavily forested whitebark pine area. (Whitebark pine nuts are an important food source for grizzlies in the autumn)."[81]

The Case Incident Record noted that the four-foot-wide trail, cushioned with pine duff, angled across the steep hillside which, on both uphill and downhill slopes, was thickly timbered and crosshatched with fallen trees. The Record reported that just ahead was "bear sign," consisting of "freshly dug logs" and a "heavily timbered hillside w/squirrel caches [of pine nuts] recently dug and shredded up." George was "walking quietly down the trail" when it curved to his right, obstructing his view ahead.

Investigator Les Brunton wrote the following day that: "[George] [had] spent that first night camped at site #WF2 in the Daly Creek drainage. The second day of his trip [he] began by hiking across the Skyrim Trail to Bighorn Peak, and then ultimately back to the Black Butte trail head on highway U.S. 191 near mile post 28." The report described the investigation and what happened next:

## *Investigation*

At approximately the 4.0 mile mark on the trail (4 miles east of the Black Butte trail head), [George] heard a branch snap, looked up, and observed a grizzly bear running through the trees in his direction. On first glance, [he] observed two other bears, both thought to be two year old cubs, in the vicinity. As the grizzly charged in his direction, [George] dropped to the ground in the classic move to protect against injury. The bear, a suspected sow grizzly, ran straight to his head, where she bit him at least twice before moving down to his unprotected lower right side. She bit [George] again, causing a long and deep laceration on his side. At this time, [he] was attempting to deploy bear spray (pepper spray), but under the circumstances could not release the safety from the canister. At one point during the struggle, [George's] pack was torn away from him. The bear briefly backed away, then again attacked, knocking [George] from the trail into trees and downfall. As [George] tried to fend off the animal, both of his arms were bitten. The bear backed away again briefly, but returned to attempt to swipe at him with a paw.

At this point, [George] observed the sow grizzly with her two cubs retreating uphill through timber. He then got to his feet and began to hike the remaining four miles to the trailhead. [He] explained that he felt numbness, and had the use of only one eye. He once stopped for water at a creek crossing, before reaching the trail head. At this point, he walked into the roadway to flag down a passing motorist. Two vehicles passed by without stopping before a third did stop. They in turn flagged another motorist who was carrying a cellular phone. The ensuing 911 phone call initiated the EMS response to the scene.

## *Report of Incident*

On September 22, 1999, at 1633 hours [4:33 p.m.], the West Yellowstone Police Department received a 911 cellular phone call reporting a man on the ground near milepost 28 on U.S. highway 191. The report also included that this man had been mauled by a bear. The West Yellowstone PD immediately dispatched their ambulance and rescue vehicle to the scene. Ranger Dave Schneider was within 10 miles of the scene at the time of the call. He responded directly to the scene, as well as myself and ranger John Piastuck from the West Yellowstone area.

### Scene of Incident

Ranger Dave Schneider arrived at the Black Butte trail head, first on scene, at [4:39 p.m.]. Ranger Schneider reported a man seriously injured, with numerous lacerations to the head, lower right side, possible skull fracture, arm injury, and losing a lot of blood.

Ranger Schneider began initial efforts to control bleeding and provided oxygen for the patient.

At [4:57 p.m.], ranger John Piastuck and the West Yellowstone ambulance arrived at the scene. Ranger Piastuck assumed the role of medical unit leader, assisted by ranger Schneider and the West Yellowstone ambulance crew. I arrived at the scene directly behind the ambulance, assuming the role of incident command.

A life flight helicopter was summoned from Eastern Idaho Regional Medical Center for patient transport, and the park helicopter was requested to fly the trail in an effort to clear any other hikers from the area of the bear attack.

The life flight ship was on the ground at the scene at [5:49 p.m.], and was again in the air enroute to EIRMC with the patient at [6:07 p.m.].

Investigative Ranger Bonnie Gaffney described the aftermath of the attack in her report:

I arrived on scene at approx. [7:00 p.m.]. [I] spoke very briefly with the victim, T.J. [nickname] [George] Langley, as he was being loaded into the Life Flight. [George] was able to specifically describe some landmarks to me, assisting in the rapid location of his backpack at the scene of the incident. I flew in the park helicopter to the scene and retrieved [his] pack just before darkness. On the walk up the trail, bear scat and pine nuts were readily noted.

Initial on scene observation showed [George's] pack lying on the side of the trail approx. 4.1 miles from the trailhead. The back of the

Freshly dug log at the point sow was believed to be at when she first noted Lang-ley below. Photo taken on September 22, 1999 by Park Ranger Bonnie Gafney, from Case Incident Record #9905916

pack was covered with blood and long human hair, which was stuck to the shoulder straps. A blood soaked black fleece jacket was located next to the pack. Also in the immediate area on the trail was: a can of bear spray with blood on the body (not discharged), a fuel bottle, binoculars and a pair of sunglasses with one lens gone. Due to time constraints, we loaded the pack and left the area. The location was marked with pink flagging for my return trip the next day. There was no indication that the bears were still in the immediate area, or that they had come back prior to our arrival.

On 9/24/99 myself and NPS employee Ellen Andrews returned to the scene at approx. [3:00 p.m.]. Drops of blood were noted from the creek 3 miles in, to the incident location. We noted recent bear diggings on the hillside above the trail just below the incident location. This hillside was covered with heavy timber and obvious squirrel caches which had been dug up. We continued to the scene and immediately noted half-eaten pine bark cones lying in the trail. We retrieved an older pile of bear scat, full of pine nuts, which was on the trail just below the incident. A number of logs along the trail had also recently been torn up, such as bears do when looking for food.

Closer observation of the actual contact point showed a 10" pool of blood located on the trail where the pack had been retrieved. We noted a large disturbance in the deadfall to the north (downhill) side of the trail. Numerous branches were broken, pools of blood, pieces of human clothing and bloody stubs were easily located. We collected both human and bear hairs from this area, stuck to the logs. Also located here were [George's] compass, sunglass lens and chunks of hair. According to [George], the second and third attacks from the bear took place in this deadfall area.

Further investigation showed where the adult bear had come down to make contact with [George]. It appeared that she had been 30' above the trail, digging on a rotted log. Due to heavy timber in the area, neither bear nor human would have seen the other until they were almost directly in line. Slide marks in the dirt and broken branches indicate where she came straight down the steep slope to contact him on the trail. [George] stated that he only had time to fall down before she appeared, but it seemed that she had paused before striking him. Slide marks in the dirt above the trail support that possibility that she had attempted to stop her momentum. There were no distinguishable tracks in the area.

Ranger Brunton attempted to identify the bear's motivation in his Summary in the Case Incident Record. "Through our conversations with George Langley, both at the scene and a follow-up telephone conversation, we believe the action taken by the sow grizzly was simply a defensive reaction." The summary explained further:

A lone hiker, making very little noise, walked up on a sow grizzly with two cubs, and her apparent response was to protect her young. The Black Butte trail to Bighorn Peak has been closed, and will probably remain closed through the remainder of the season. The Daly Creek trail head has been posted closed, as well as associated trail junctions on the Skyrim Trail indefinitely. (Daly Creek Trail re-opened w/posted warnings 9/24/99.)

George T. Langley will remain hospitalized at Eastern Idaho Regional Medical Center for approximately ten days. Injuries he incurred include the following: A skull fracture near the right eye orbit, lacerations of the scalp, forehead and nose, a deep laceration on his lower right side, lacerations to both arms, and a hip fracture.

Response to this incident was a multi-agency effort. Responding agencies included the National Park Service, West Yellowstone ambulance and rescue, Gallatin Co. sheriff's deputies, and EIRMC life flight.

Describing the bear's actions, Bear Management Specialist Kerry A. Gunther wrote on September 22 that, as reported, the sow and two yearlings were grizzlies, with no markers, and that they were engaged in "ripping open logs and digging pine middens in area," for food when they were surprised by the hiker.

A Yellowstone news release dated September 23 described the Park Service's response. "No management action will be taken against the female grizzly bear, which was displaying natural protective behavior when [George] came between the adult bear and cubs."

## 2000: BEAR BIT HIM ON THE HAND, MARTIN OSTMANN

*National Park Service—Yellowstone*

*Case Incident Record Number: 003694*

*Location: Avalanche Peak Trail, near tree-line, UTM 568741 E 4925797 N*

*Date/Time: July 30, 2000, 9:45 a.m.*

Two Yellowstone hikers had *two* encounters with the *same* two bears, resulting in injuries to one of the hikers on that same warm morning of July 30, 2000.

Martin Ostmann, eighteen, and his friend Matthew Ramey felt hot, especially after climbing half a mile up the steep trail toward Avalanche Peak. The two day-hikers from Missouri had started at about 9:00 a.m., but the temperature now was on its way into the 80s. At 9:45 a.m., reaching an area of open lodgepole pine forest directly below a ridge, the two paused just long enough to remove their long-sleeved shirts. They were talking, and looking forward to the view from the summit.

Orville Bach Jr. described the hike to Avalanche Peak in *Exploring the Yellowstone Backcountry*. "Although there is no maintained trail, a well-worn path winds its way up to the summit and offers some magnificent scenery." He described the hike below:

> From the road you climb about 2,000 feet in 2 mi. to the summit at 10,566 ft., passing through flower-laden alpine meadows along the way. Yellowstone Lake dominates the view from the summit, with distant mountain ranges visible on clear days.
>
> This hike is best after mid-July when the snowfields have subsided and flowers are blooming in the meadows. Once above timberline it will be necessary to ascend steep scree slopes to reach the summit.[82]

After removing their long-sleeved shirts, Martin and Matthew remained standing on the trail. Investigator Arthur Jawad wrote in the Case Incident Record on July 31 that "While standing there talking they heard a rustling sound and turned and looked up and saw a bear on all four paws at the top of the hill looking down at them." The report detailed what happened next.

> The bear stood on its hind feet [20–30 yards away] and another smaller bear appeared. The larger bear came down the hill toward [Martin and Matthew] and the smaller bear moved away.
>
> [Martin and Matthew] said that they both went down on the ground as the bear approached and curled up into defensive positions with their hands covering their heads and knees tucked into their stomachs. [Martin] said that the larger bear then came up to him and bit him on the hand (right) and moved away. The bear then circled around and

sniffed [Matthew] and circled them both a couple of times and walked away in a downhill direction. They did not think that the smaller bear came forward during the incident but thought that they could hear the smaller bear rustling or moving around. Both [men] stated that after the bears moved off that they stayed down on the ground for a couple of minutes until they did not hear anything and then got up and began walking down the trail toward the Trailhead.

Less than five minutes later they were walking around a bend in the trail in smaller dense vegetation and saw both bears again. Both individuals immediately went back down to the ground and assumed defensive positions. The larger bear was five to ten feet away and the smaller bear was fifteen to thirty feet away. The larger bear approached and circled them but did not come close enough to touch. Both [men] agreed that the bears were present only briefly during this second encounter. After hearing no more noise they got up and stayed at this site for about fifteen minutes and dressed [Martin's] wounds. At about 1025 hours [10:25 a.m.], 860 Dixon [Dave, a Yellowstone Park employee assigned to the Canyon Maintenance Shop] arrived.

Meanwhile, Investigator Jawad wrote that he was "patrolling the East Entrance Road three miles east of the Avalanche Peak Trailhead [when] 860 [Dave] Dixon . . . reported by radio to the Communication Center that a person on the Avalanche Peak Trail had been bitten on the hand by a grizzly bear." The investigator's report continued:

I called Dixon on the radio and he stated that the persons were on the trail about three-fourths of a mile from the road and that they were hiking out toward the Trailhead. I asked Dixon if the individuals would need help walking out and he replied that they should be fine hiking out without help. I advised Dixon that I would be waiting at the Trailhead for their arrival and Dixon should come out to the Trailhead also.

I arrived at the Trailhead at [10:25 a.m.] and called the Communication Center and requested that they notify my Supervisor Jessie Farias Jr., and the Bear Management Office. At [10:45 a.m.] two individuals,

[Martin and Matthew] arrived at the Trailhead. [Martin] stated that he was the individual who had been bitten by the bear and [Matthew] denied any injury. I examined [Martin's] right hand and found puncture wounds and scratches with no significant deformity and no loss of function or feeling (see EMS report). After cleaning the injuries to [Martin's] right hand I interviewed both [men] . . .

[They] described the larger bear as a normal medium brown color and the smaller bear as a little darker. They estimated the larger bear to be about three hundred pounds and the smaller bear to be about two-thirds the size of the larger bear. [Matthew] described the larger bear as healthy looking, with a large hump and said it looked like a bear in a picture. He described the hump on the smaller bear as not as big and the muscles not quite as defined. At [11:45 a.m.] I concluded my interview with [both men]. They then departed the Avalanche Trailhead by private vehicle to go to Lake Hospital to have [Martin's] injuries cleaned and treated by a doctor.

By [11:45 a.m.] Rangers Farias and Riegelmayer had closed the Avalanche Peak trail and marked the trailhead with closure signs and flagging. Riegelmayer and I then prepared to sweep the trail for persons and search for the incident site. At [12:15 p.m.] we started our sweep. At [1:24 p.m.] we found the incident site. It was just below the head of a dry ravine about one mile from the trailhead and seventeen paces below the ridgeline (see Diagram) [below]. At the site we collected scat and fur samples and measured one clear bear print we found next to site on the trail where [the men] had assumed defensive postures. The print measured four inches wide by five inches long. We then photographed the area with a thirty-five millimeter camera. On the ridgetop which was seventeen paces uphill from the site where [Martin] was bit on the hand we found extensive digging where the bears had been rooting up squirrel caches and eating pine nuts. At [2:19 p.m.] we finished at the site and continued our sweep for people. By [4:18 p.m. we] had returned to the trailhead after finding no individuals on the trail . . .

The Avalanche trail will remain closed until Ranger Farias determines the area is safe to reopen to the public.

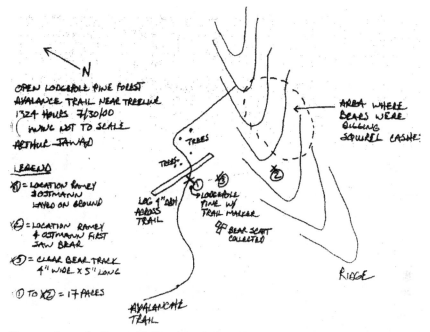

OPEN LODGEPOLE PINE FOREST
AVALANCHE TRAIL NEAR TREELINE
1324 HOURS 7/30/00
( DRAWING NOT TO SCALE
ARTHUR JAWAD

LEGEND

X① = LOCATION RAMEY
JOSTMANN
LAYED ON GROUND

X② = LOCATION RAMEY
& OSTMANN FIRST
SAW BEAR

X③ = CLEAR BEAR TRACK
4" WIDE X 5" LONG

① TO X② = 17 PACES

N

· TREES

TREES

LOG 4" DBH
ACROSS
TRAIL

LODGEPOLE
PINE W/
TRAIL MARKER

BEAR SCAT
COLLECTED

AREA WHERE
BEARS WERE
DIGGING
SQUIREL CASHE:

RIDGE

AVALANCHE
TRAIL

Diagram drawn by Ranger Arthur Jawad, from Case Incident Record #003694

The Bear Management Report noted that the bears involved in the incident were described as grizzlies, a sow and her yearling, with no markers. No action was taken against the two bears.

## 2000: SWATTED IN FACE AND CHEST, RICHARD ROMANO

*National Park Service—Yellowstone*

*Case Incident Record Number: 004917*

*Location: 200 yards from Black Butte Trail along cutoff between*

*Daly Creek and Black Butte Trails, estimated UTM 492000 E 4990700 N*

*Date/Time: September 1, 2000, 1:30 p.m.*

Riders on horseback are rarely charged by bears, but sixty-one-year-old Richard D. Romano had dismounted from his buckskin quarter horse, Dusty.

His horse was not dusty that day, September 1, 2000, because rain was pouring down. Despite the wet skies, Richard was enjoying exploring Yellowstone's northwest corner. Richard, from Montana, was an experienced backcountry traveler in all kinds of weather, both in his home state and in Alaska.

This northwestern "thumb" of the park poked out into Montana, and was an area in which Richard had never been. Ironically, it was Level Five drought conditions that had closed the Gallatin National Forest to his use, and sent him instead to Yellowstone. When riding in the Gallatin, Richard packed a 44-caliber pistol. But this was Yellowstone Park: no guns were allowed [at that time, in 2000].

The day before, Richard had talked with Ranger Bob Siebert about his proposed "loop" day ride. The ranger described the trail, and told him that bears were feeding actively to put on weight for hibernation. So Richard bought his first canister of bear pepper spray.

He parked his truck and horse trailer at the Daly Creek trailhead, put on his rain jacket and rain pants, and attached the bear spray canister to one of his suspenders. Then he and Dusty started off and up—into the high country in the rain.

Richard was riding along the cutoff trail connecting Daly Creek to Black Butte Trail, about 1:30 p.m., when he decided to stop for lunch. Still in the saddle, he looked around for any signs of bears, but saw nothing. He was hard of hearing, though, and was not wearing his hearing aid. He then dismounted, put leather hobbles on Dusty, and sought shelter from the rain under a large tree. He unwrapped his Black Forest ham and provolone cheese sandwich, and began eating it.

Then, "he heard his horse snort alerting him of something wrong," wrote Yellowstone ranger Carl R. "Rick" Bennett in his memo (subject line: "Bear Mauling 09-01-00"):

[Richard] reported he turned to his left and saw a bear practically "on top of him" as he described. The bear then swatted him in the face and chest area knocking him into a tree. [Richard] reported he was face down getting his bear spray and rolled over giving the bear a full spray in the mouth. The bear rolled off him coughing, etc., and [Richard] caught his horse and immediately left the area via Black Butte Trail back to his vehicle which was parked at Daly Creek Trailhead. He then drove north to Big Sky Exxon where he reported the incident.

I was notified of the incident by the Forest Service. [Richard] received lacerations to the right side of his face and forehead. He was transported to Bozeman Deaconess Hospital by Big Sky Fire and Rescue. At the time I interviewed him over the telephone, he was at the emergency room and he thought he would be released from the hospital.

At this point, the Daly Creek/Black Butte trails are closed including the Skyrim Loop. Also, the Skyrim Trail is closed past Shelf Lake. Visitors can still get to Shelf Lake and use the designated campsites at the lake. George [Kittrell] and I will check the area tomorrow in the AM for evidence, etc. at the scene. The closures will remain in effect for 10 days at which time the area will be checked for bear activity and re-evaluated. [Richard] did report the bear got his sandwich. He described the bear as a definite grizzly weighing approximately 300 pounds—sex unknown. There were no other bears observed.

The bear incidents which occurred along Black Butte last year were described as cubs being with a sow at the time of the encounters. This incident appears to be an encounter where person and bear were at the wrong place at the wrong time. [Richard] reported neither he nor the bear did anything wrong.

Ranger Bennett told of locating the bear mauling scene in his Supplementary Case/Incident Record dated September 5. He wrote that "[Richard] described the area as a large tree on the east side of the trail and within sight of the Black Butte Trail." The scene of the attack was described below:

Ranger George Kittrell and I patrolled the area on 9/2/2000 and located the scene. There is a large ravine located just to the east of the scene. It is believed that the bear was in this ravine at the time when [Richard] took his lunch break. There were several logs, which had been disturbed, as well as numerous broken branches. [Richard] was positive the bear was a grizzly. He described the bear as weighing approximately 300 pounds, dark in color, and having a very large head. He was sure there was only one animal. The sex of the bear is unknown . . .

He told me he hunts black bears and is well versed in identifying black and grizzly bears. He also reported when he hunts bears that he uses his horse. When his horse snorted prior to the attack, that he knew there was a bear present by the alert his horse gave . . . [Richard] reported he didn't think the bear was "stalking him or anything like that." He thought he and the bear were at the wrong place at the wrong time and that the incident was an unfortunate encounter. He was released from the hospital that afternoon with facial lacerations.

According to the *Jackson Hole News* on September 6, Richard said of his pepper-spraying experience: "The only reason I saved my ass was because I got him right in the lungs."

"Now that he is safely at home," the news report ended, "[Richard] said he will continue to travel solo into grizzly bear country and that he will always carry pepper spray."[83]

*Note*: No attacks were reported in 2001.

# 21

# BEAR ATTACKS 2002–2004

## 2002: BITTEN WHILE JOGGING, ABIGAIL THOMAS

*National Park Service—Yellowstone*

*Case Incident Record Number: 026035*

*Location: Lake Lodge Cabins area, UTM 547725 E 4933736 N*

*Date/Time: Sunday, May 26, 2002, 7:15 a.m.*

Park Post Office worker Abigail Thomas was ready to go for her early morning run in the area developed for visitors that bordered Yellowstone Lake. The date was May 26, 2002, and Lake Lodge hadn't opened for the season yet. The thirty-two-year-old pulled on dark, elastic-waist, athletic-type pants, and hung her "bear bell" around her neck on its silver-colored cord. Grabbing a water bottle, she decided to take the "loop" road which accessed the dark and silent Lake Lodge Cabins. Thomas was alert and aware of her surroundings, having no desire to encounter wildlife. But that day events would happen otherwise.

After she encountered the bear, she gave a statement to rangers describing what happened:

> At 6:52 a.m. on Sunday, May 26, I left our car which I'd parked in the lot at Lake Station Post Office. I walked for about 3 min to warm up, then began jogging toward Lake Lodge, which I hadn't jogged near this season. I ran past the Lodge building, and turned left into the parking

lot/driveway for the cabins, looking around me to avoid encountering animals. I also didn't wear my CD player so I could hear anything approaching. I wore a small bell as well.

I reached the mid-back portion of the western cabins when I suddenly caught a glimpse of a light brown grizzly bear. This was at about 7:04 a.m. He was approximately 45 degrees to my right and about 20 ft away from me when I spotted him, and sitting or standing stationary inside the fence line on the parking lot side.

I stopped running immediately, took 2–3 slow steps, then froze in a standing position with arms at sides and hands open. It was clear that the bear had seen me, so I decided not to lay face down with hands over the back of my neck. The bear took two to three steps toward me and then raised up briefly on his hind legs to sniff the air. I tried not to look at him for long as not to provoke him, but estimate he weighed 350–450 lb. and was 5'3"–5'5" on his hind legs. He then got back down on all fours and continued to slowly approach, making no noises. I also said nothing at first, thinking he might decide to leave.

He reached my right side, then came (or stretched his neck) around to sniff my crotch area (I didn't have my period). At this point I started talking to the bear in a normal voice, saying "Go away bear," thinking he would realize I was a human and go away. He looked interested but didn't stop investigating. He moved on to sniffing my right fingers, so I slowly balled my hands up and drew them up a bit so he wouldn't try to bite them. I continued talking to him as he started sniffing my jogging pants, possibly interested by the smell of the dog I have at home. He then experimentally put his mouth around the front of my right thigh, and it was either in withdrawing his mouth from this position or in a subsequent mouthing that I felt him nip my right thigh about 8–10 in. above the knee.

At that point I decided he wouldn't leave me alone and might bite me again and inflict worse damage, so I started yelling "Go away bear," repeatedly, and grabbed the water bottle I wore and turned to squirt him in the face 2–3 times. He looked startled and turned away from me to walk away down the parking lot in the direction I had just come from. He did not run or hurry.

I backed away from him, keeping him in sight, then turned down a street going through the cabins toward the area of the employee pub & housing. I walked behind the pub and through the housing back to the road to Lake Hotel. I looked to the left to see the bear crossing the road from the cabin driveway to the meadow. He walked toward some bison there, then paused and began chasing them. 3–4 cars of people were pulled over to observe him.

I turned left to go to the Lake Ranger Station to report the incident, but the office wasn't yet open, so I turned up the next road to the right and went up through the hotel cabins to the hotel gift shop where my father works. We phoned a report in to the Fishing Bridge Ranger Station at about 7:35 a.m.

Ranger Richard T. Fey reported that he was "finishing up a medical run to the Lake Hospital," when "Dr. Sam Smith, emergency room doctor at the Lake Hospital told me that his next patient, currently waiting in the lobby, is claiming she was 'bitten by a bear.'" In his report in the Case Incident Record, Ranger Fey continued his account:

I immediately responded to the lobby of the hospital to find victim Abigail Thomas. [Abigail] later told me she is trained as a Veterinarian Technician but currently works at the U.S. Post Office at Lake as a mail handler. She did not appear to me to be traumatized in any way. She was in no apparent pain, sitting upright on a chair, with another lady introduced as her mother.

After introducing myself, she told me that she was jogging in the Lake Lodge cabin area (the road and cabin area is open to public traffic, beyond the road is closed due to bear management). She was not wearing a cd player, nor was she wearing any perfume or lotion. She was wearing a small "bear bell" necklace. She was at the western most apex of the road when out of the corner of her right eye she spotted a light brown grizzly bear. She froze in place after taking a few steps away from the bear. The bear was "inside the fence line" near the road. The bear was approximately twenty feet away from her and off to her right side. She believes they saw each other at the same time. The bear took a few steps towards her then rose briefly on his hind feet. It appeared to her that it was trying to identify her. Its nose reached for the sky attempting to get a scent. The bear quickly returned to all four feet and slowly began to approach her from her right side. [Abigail] did not look at the bear as it approached, fearing it would be considered an aggressive act. The animal approached her from her right side and began to investigate her. The bear began smelling her, starting at her pants. She spoke to it with a monotone voice hoping that the bear would recognize her as a human and flee. It did not.

She believes the bear was about 5 feet three inches to five feet five inches tall when on its back legs. She thought its estimated weight to be about 350–450 pounds.

As the bear began to sniff her fingers she made a fist thinking her fingers could be bitten. The bear continued to sniff her pants, possibly more interested in the scent of the dog (a 2-year-old fox terrier) rather than her. The bear then "experimentally" opened its mouth and gently clamped on her right thigh. See attached photographs [of too poor quality to reproduce]. The area was photographed on May 28, 2002 and shows black and blue marks with a small red mark toward her inner thigh. It appears the bear made a pressure contusion. A clamping motion of its mouth against her thigh possibly made the black and blue marks. The red mark was possibly made by a top front canine tooth. Fearing further injury, she began to yell at the bear and drew her water bottle from her right side hip and sprayed it several times between the eyes. The bear quickly withdrew and walked away.

The bear walked down the northeast cabin road to the Lake Lodge meadow and began to chase some bison. The bear eventually ran past the Lake Hamilton Store where it had an encounter with a dog inside a propane yard. The two ran, chased, growled and attempted to strike and fight each other, however the locked cyclone fence prevented contact or injury to either party. The bear left the area with 612's (Alice Siebecker, Acting Lake Sub-district Ranger) noise distraction from her patrol car where it found "Lake Shore Drive in the middle of Downtown Lake." It was now heading straight towards the lakeside of the Lake Hotel. Several folks were out for their morning coffee stroll when the bear came running through east to west. The bear now in a gentle loping stride, continued past the hotel without incident and towards the Lake Hospital. It continued to run without an encounter or incident towards the old fish hatchery-building boathouse and down the hatchery trail (closed for bear management) and out of the area. Near the western side of the hospital parking lot however, 612 fired two cracker rounds to encourage its egress out of Lake Village. An hour later the bear was seen running south, through the Bridge Bay Campground [which was] alerted to the possibility of such a track by 612 and 615 (R. Fey) without incident. The bear was last believed to be in the area of Natural Bridge trail, closed [by] bear management.

Further investigation of the victim's pants reveal that there was no rip, tear, indentation, or any visible mark to her pants she was reportedly wearing at the time of the incident.

Yellowstone Park's news release of May 30, 2002, concluded: "Park officials praised [Abigail] for how well she handled the potentially life-threatening bear encounter, remaining calm and focused throughout the ordeal." No information is present in the record as to what happened to the bear.

## 2002: SHAKEN IN BEAR'S JAWS, LEG BROKEN, THOMAS CROSSON

*National Park Service—Yellowstone*

*Case Incident Record Number: 026785*

*Location: Off trail, close to Columbine Creek, near southeast arm of Yellowstone Lake, UTM 563544 E 4917975 N*

*Date/Time: Monday, September 2, 2002, 11:00 a.m.*

The two men's trip was meant to be a relaxing backcountry stay of four nights, with tent camping and day hikes from, and back to, each campsite. That Sunday evening, September 1, 2002, Thomas Crosson from Massachusetts and Nils Wygant from New Hampshire set up their tent south of Columbine Creek, at campsite 5E4, between the Thorofare Trail and Yellowstone Lake. The area they chose lay beside the lakeshore and was little visited, green, and densely forested, untouched by the firestorms of 1988. It was quiet: The infrequent boats in this area had a speed limit of five miles per hour. Farther south the zoning was for hand-propelled craft only. The sun set behind The Promontory, an isthmus of land pointing like a finger across the lake's deep and cold water.

The next morning, Monday, September 2nd, Tom and Nils set out for a hike from their campsite, to which they planned to return that night. The two friends, one a veterinarian and the other a software engineer, each carried bear pepper spray. From their campsite 5E4, they hiked three miles northeast. They were walking up the Alluvium Creek drainage, off trail, at a spot where two creeks—the Alluvium and the Columbine—ran parallel, when the unexpected occurred.

Tom turned away to relieve himself. Hearing a commotion, he looked up to see, less than twenty yards away, a grizzly bear charging him at top speed. She had three cubs running alongside.

According to Ranger Trevor R. Clark "Tom was in the lead and spotted the bear with three cubs first." His report described what happened next:

> The bear then charged and Tom stepped closer towards [Nils]. They then laid down face first on the ground. [Nils] stated that this probably provoked the bear to actually bite Tom on the leg. After the bite, the bear backed off from Tom and circled around towards [Nils]. [Nils] positioned himself so that he was facing the bear. With his bear spray in hand, [Nils] gave the bear a good spray in the face. The bear then took off in a rage and was absent for several minutes. The bear did return but did not attack or get close enough to be sprayed by [Nils].

Now, far from help, Tom was staring at two four-inch gashes on his left calf, and—perhaps when the bear picked him up in its jaws and shook him—a fractured tibia, the larger leg bone, on his left side. He was in pain and shock. Using his skills as a veterinarian, and with his friend helping him, he tended to his injuries as best he could.

But he would have to endure almost twenty-four hours before being rescued. During that period, Tom said that Nils had saved him a total of three times. The first time Nils saved him had been spraying the bear and finally getting it to leave, with cubs in tow.

But the bears had run off in the direction of the two men's campsite, and the men did not want to follow the bears. What were they to do now? The previous day, a park boat had let them off at a lakeside ramp, from which they had hiked three miles south. Their best bet seemed to be to go back to the boat ramp and seek help. So, with Nils' help, Tom leaned on him and they headed back to the boat ramp—three miles of bushwhacking with no trail.

This was the second time his friend saved him, Tom said.

No boat was at the boat ramp, and none was in sight on the lake. Then darkness was setting in, and the men realized they would have to spend the night.

That night, Tom said, his friend saved him for the third time. They had left emergency supplies at the ramp, including a sleeping bag and pad, a first-aid kit and food. Scott McMillion reported in the *Bozeman Daily Chronicle* on September 5, that "At the boat site, [Nils] made a log structure, covered it with garbage bags and used the sleeping pad and some pine boughs as a mattress. He kept a fire going all night. Tuesday morning, a boat dropped off some people across the bay, but didn't see the men and soon departed. 'It was pretty shocking to watch that boat go away,' [Tom] said."[84]

Fortunately, research was underway on the elusive lynx of Yellowstone, and the researcher was crossing the lake, heading for campsite 5E5 (next to Tom's and Nils' abandoned camp at 5E4).

In the researcher's boat was Ranger Clark, who wrote in the Case Incident Record that "At around 8 [a.m.] on 9/3/02, I was transporting Tiffany Potter [a lynx researcher] to Columbine Creek to the campsite known as 5E5." The ranger then described finding the two hikers:

On the way into the site a hiker was waving me in. His name was [Nils] Wygant. This hiker was not injured in the attack. [Nils] told me that his hiking partner was attacked by a bear and was in need of medical attention. The injured individual, Tom Crosson, is a veterinarian and was able to stabilize his wounds on his own . . .

Tiffany Potter, being a first responder, performed a first and secondary assessment over Tom. As she was doing this [Ranger] Dave Hill responded to the scene. We then proceeded to load Tom onto the *Warwood* [boat] where Dave transported Tom to the Lake Marina where Lake Patrol and Lake Hospital took control of the situation.

Tom was treated and sent to Jackson Hospital.

Pete Dalton has ordered that the nine-mile trailhead will be closed to off-trail travel until Friday. Also 5E5, 5E6 and 5E4 [campsites] will be closed to foot travel but will be open to stock.

There have been reports of three sows with cubs in the areas of these sites, so warning to the public should be addressed.

A Yellowstone Park news release of September 4, 2002, noted that "Strong bear warnings have been posted along the Thorofare Trail near Columbine Creek. No off-trail travel is currently allowed in the area, and some backcountry campsites in the vicinity of the incident are temporarily closed."

No action was expected against the chocolate-colored female grizzly, which was determined to have been surprised by Tom and his friend while shepherding her three cubs.

## 2002: PRESUMED PREDATORY, MIKE BARBIC

*National Park Service—Yellowstone*

*Case Incident Record Number: 023193*

*Location: Sportsman Lake Trail area, northwest section of park*

*Date/Time: Friday, August 30, 2002, approximately 10:00 p.m.*

The ABC News television program *Good Morning America* told viewers on September 3, 2002, that "If last year [2001] was the 'Summer of the Shark,' then this season could be called the 'Summer of the Bear.' In one of the most recent encounters, a camper woke up to find a bear nibbling on his butt."

That camper, in Yellowstone Park, had just crawled into his tent for the night at his designated backcountry site. It was August 30, and Mike Barbic of Texas had a two-day permit and was enjoying the sights, smells, and sounds of his Sportsman Lake Trail backpacking trip. He thought he would enjoy a good night's sleep even more. That night, in the remote northwest section of Yellowstone, Mike zipped tight the somewhat porous security of his tent door.

The Park News Release of September 1 reported that "Visitors hiking or camping in Yellowstone National Park should be aware that an unusually high number of bears may be seen in lower elevations because of lack of normal food sources for this time of year." The release specifically mentioned a lack of whitebark pine nuts, as follows:

> One of the bears' main food sources, whitebark pine, a tree that typically occurs above 8000 feet, has produced very few cones this year. Grizzly bears have already been observed coming down to lower elevations in search of food, where they are more likely to encounter visitors along roadsides, in campgrounds and picnic areas, along trails, and near homes and ranches both inside and outside the park's perimeter.

At about 10:00 p.m., a bear exhibiting probable predatory behavior approached Mike's tent. Suddenly Mike awakened to the indescribable experience of feeling, through the side of his tent, a bear biting him in his right buttock. The bear ripped a hole in the fabric of the tent, which partially collapsed around Mike. Mike screamed into the night and the bear ran off.

The September 1 news release, headlined "Visitor Injured by Bear in Yellowstone National Park," then continued. "[Mike] laid [sic] quite still for roughly an hour, listening for bear activity before exiting the tent."

> [Mike] then put his partially collapsed tent back up and spent the remainder of the night there. At one point during the night, he heard scratching noises near the tree where he had hung his food. At daybreak, [Mike] packed up his camp and hiked to the Glen Creek Trailhead where his vehicle was parked. He then drove to Mammoth Hot Springs and reported the incident to park rangers.

[Mike] received a puncture wound and a one-inch laceration to the right side of his buttocks. He was treated and released at the Mammoth Hot Springs Clinic.

ABC News' *Good Morning America*, again on September 3, reported that "Gary Alt, a wildlife biologist with the Pennsylvania Game Commission, has personally handled more than 3,000 bears during his career."

[Alt] says most encounters aren't deadly, but if a bear is looking for a food source, a meeting can become dangerous.

"Less than one in a million encounters results in a fatality," Alt said. "When we have the predatory attack, where the bear seeks you out as a piece of food, you should fight the bear. You don't have to kill it, but convince it you are not easy prey."

The news release concluded that "Because [Mike] did not actually see the bear, it is unknown whether it was a black or a grizzly bear . . . Strong bear warnings have been posted along the Sportsman Lake Trail and no overnight camping is currently allowed in this area."

## 2003: BITTEN TWICE ON BOARDWALK, NAME WITHHELD

*National Park Service—Yellowstone*

*Case Incident Record Number: Not given*

*Location: West Thumb Geyser Basin at Bluebell Pool, UTM 534214 E 4918167 N*

*Date/Time: Monday, June 2, 2003, 7:30 p.m.*

The weather was pleasant at 7:30 p.m. that June 2, 2003, and so the family—a wife, husband, and two children—left their car in the parking lot to sightsee at the West Thumb Geyser Basin. West Thumb, bordering Yellowstone Lake, was so named by the early explorers of the 1870

Washburn party, who thought that the lake resembled a giant hand, and this westernmost part of the lake, its thumb.

Hamilton's *Guide to Yellowstone National Park* described what the family saw. "You can marvel at all the thermal features at West Thumb walking along the constructed walks." Hamilton's *Guide* detailed the thermal feature called the Thumb Paint Pots:

> Chemically, the Thumb Paint Pots are similar to the Fountain Paint Pots at the Lower Geyser Basin. Some consider the colors more vivid. The colors change and the intensity is greater some months than others.
>
> Some of the thermal activity is actually in the lake. Lakeshore Geyser, when its crater is not submerged by water, may erupt to heights of 60 feet for several minutes at intervals of 25 to 35 minutes.
>
> Fishing Cone is a hot spring whose geyserite mound and crater are surrounded by lake water. Abyss Pool, its deep crater filled with hot, clear water, reflects a remarkable blue color.[85]

Not only was the thermal area interesting, but present also were the comforting sounds and sights of other visitors in the popular area. The family's stroll drew them toward the immense blue of Yellowstone Lake, where the boardwalk, marked by a convenient bench to sit on, took a turn to the left down to the lakeshore. Beside them Blueberry Pool was steaming hot, but the elevated boardwalk, winding among this and the other thermal features, was there to keep you safe.

Just ahead, the family's mother noticed a group of visitors photographing and video recording something out of sight in the trees. Curious, the mother walked several feet in front of her husband and children, around the boardwalk's turn, to see what the visitors were photographing.

That something became suddenly apparent. A medium brown grizzly walked out of the trees to the woman's right, and stepped up onto the wooden boards in front of her.

Deputy Chief Ranger Mona Divine described what happened next in an undated e-mail to her colleagues. "[The woman] said she didn't see the bear until it was near." The e-mail then reported the woman's reaction to the bear:

She did not know whether to be still or retreat. The bear approached her and stood on its hind legs (reportedly it appeared to be 6–7 feet tall at the head). She said the bear did not hit her but that she fell to the ground. Once she was lying on the boardwalk, the bear bit her twice then stood over her for a moment and she could feel its breath on her face. She laid still. When her husband screamed at the bear, it ran off.

In an unsigned Bear Sighting Report dated September 2, 2003, the author described the bear as a grizzly with no markers, medium brown in color, and weighing 201–400 pounds. Under "Activities of Bear(s)" the author wrote: "Confrontation/Attack." Under "Detailed description of incident, and area of incident," the author wrote as below:

2 Xanterra [concessionaire] employees were in the West Thumb Geyser Basin. They heard a woman scream, looked towards the scream and saw a woman down on the boardwalk with a bear standing over her. The woman's kids (2) and husband were screaming at the bear. The woman's husband ran up to within 5 ft of the bear and yelled. The bear then ran off along the shore of Yellowstone Lake. The woman got up and ran to her car and the family drove off.

The woman was bitten twice, neither bite broke the skin, but she received 8 deep contusions from the bear's 4 canines, from the two bites.

The woman stated that she saw a group of people photographing something off of the boardwalk. She walked around the corner of the boardwalk to see what they were photographing. The grizzly came from approximately 50 ft away, approached her, and stood up on its back legs in front of her. She was afraid the bear would swat her and knock her off of the boardwalk in the thermal pool, so she laid down on the boardwalk. The bear then jumped on her and bit her twice, once on the arm, once on the back. Her husband then ran at the bear yelling and chased it off. The bear ran down the lake shore.

Mgmt Actions: Area Closure.

An unsigned report in the Case Incident Record stated that a "Xanterra employee and park visitor [names withheld] reported the incident to park dispatch. Sub-district ranger Gary Haynes and Resource Management ranger Eric Reinertson responded to the scene."The report continued:

The injured party had already departed the scene on route to Old Faithful, but the reporting parties were still there. They reported being at Bluebell Pool on the boardwalk when they heard a lot of screaming. They turned and saw a person's feet lying on the boardwalk and a dark bear over the individual. A man (presumably the victim's husband) approached the bear to within 5 feet yelling loudly. The bear jumped off the boardwalk and ran parallel to the Lake away from the scene (534214 /4918167 NAD 83) to the north toward Lake. The victim was seen running on her own from the scene to the parking lot. The extent of the injuries and the nature of the initial encounter were unknown to these reporting parties. In addition, they reported that an individual did capture the bear on video tape, but not the incident. The video recording party has not been in contact with rangers at this point (6/3/03-11 a.m.). Haynes and Reinertson accessed the scene. The bear was no longer in the area. Grizzly bear tracks were located leaving the scene in the direction reported (pictures are attached). [Photos of too poor quality to reproduce.] Upon further investigation, a small scattering of elk hair was observed in the area, which could have possibly been the remnants of an elk calf carcass. No blood, bones or other evidence of a recent carcass was observed, so the carcass aspect of this incident is only speculation at this time.

Commenting on the boardwalk bear attack and other bear activity, Park Superintendent Suzanne Lewis, in a Yellowstone news release of June 3, 2003, "reminds park visitors that bear activity has increased over the past several weeks due to [trout] spawning and [elk] calving activity and an abundance of wildlife jams along roadways." She continued:

Currently, Pebble Creek Campground and West Thumb Geyser Basin are temporarily closed due to bear activity, and bear warnings have been posted in Lamar and Slough Creek backcountry areas. Other restrictions could be implemented as necessary.

A sub-adult grizzly bear (unknown sex) entered Pebble Creek Campground on Sunday, June 1, 2003, and bounced on an unoccupied tent, crushing the tent to the ground and rolling around on it. The bear then left the area. Owners of the tent were not present during the incident, but the incident was witnessed and reported by other Pebble Creek campers. There were no injuries, and the bear did not obtain any human food. Video footage taken of the bear indicates it could be the same bear park staff unsuccessfully tried to capture in 2002 after receiving several reports of a bear crushing tents and being chased out of backcountry campsites in the Lamar area. Park staff have temporarily closed Pebble Creek Campground (it was only partially open due to high water levels) and are attempting to capture the bear at this time.

On Monday evening, June 2, 2003, a woman on the West Thumb Geyser Basin boardwalk had an encounter with a probable grizzly bear (sex unknown).

Deputy Chief Ranger Mona Divine concluded her e-mail, quoted earlier, with the following words: "In addition to bears every employee needs to exercise the usual caution around wildlife. Cow elk with babies (most recently in the Mammoth area) and bison may be close to buildings or vehicles. There are certain risks and rewards to working in a wilderness area."

## 2004: HE WAS GUSHING BLOOD, DENTON TURNER

*National Park Service—Yellowstone*

*Case Incident Record Number: 042108*

*Location: Hayden Valley off the Mary Mountain Trail*

*Date/Time: Saturday, June 18, 2004, 8:45 p.m.*

When Denton Turner drove to Yellowstone's Canyon area on June 18, 2004, he learned the road he would use to get to his planned trailhead was closed. He had wanted to hike to the summit of Mount Washburn. But the frustration of that plan didn't discourage him for long. While driving back south, the way he had come, he saw another trailhead and pulled his car over. It was still early evening. He chose to hike Hayden Valley's Mary Mountain Trail instead.

That Friday was Denton's day off from his summer job in Old Faithful Lodge's kitchen, and he wanted to make every free hour count. A twenty-year-old sophomore at Appalachian State University in North Carolina, he loved the outdoors and all that Yellowstone offered: hiking, camping, bird watching. He spent so much time in the backcountry he even had a Frequent User Card, issued by the Old Faithful Backcountry Office after he attended a safe-hiking-camping lecture.

Denton parked his car and started out on the Mary Mountain Trail (which roughly paralleled Alum Creek). The sun had slipped behind the trees, cooling the day's heat. He carried no pack, just his binoculars and a bird-identifying book. He was looking for birds when he saw a bluebird.

As for bears, Denton later reported that he had seen them three times before in Hayden Valley, but he carried no bear spray. When interviewed later, Denton remarked: "I didn't have time to use it."

Park Ranger Matt Vandzura interviewed Denton that evening at 11:30 p.m. in the Lake Clinic emergency room. The ranger noted that "[Denton] hiked west past the power lines." The ranger's report continued:

[Denton] followed a blue bird off of the trail and up a hill. He stopped near the top of the hill and watched the bird through his binoculars. When he took his binoculars away from his face he saw two bears 30 yards away. The bears immediately charged. [Denton] dropped to the ground and assumed a fetal position. The bear or bears, [he] did not know if both participated, swatted him, rolled him over, and bit him. [He] was unaware of the bites until treated at the Clinic. [He] said the attack lasted less than two minutes. He said the attack stopped suddenly. [He] waited a few minutes then began to look around from his position on the ground. Several minutes later he stood up and saw the bears 100 to 150 yards away grazing on a hillside. [Denton] then walked back to the trailhead and his vehicle. At the roadside [he] realized the extent of his injuries. He flagged down a visitor, who drove [him], in [Denton's] vehicle, north toward Canyon Junction.

This use of Denton's own car to drive him to get help may have been because he described himself to Ranger Vandzura as "gushing blood." He also described feeling lightheaded, having pain in his shoulder, and finding his jacket was ripped.

Ranger Vandzura wrote in his Emergency Response statement that "Park Ranger Ryan Adrian was working a wildlife jam just south of Canyon Junction." The statement then continued:

> The attack was reported to [Ranger] Adrian at 2100 [9:00 p.m.]. Adrian provided emergency medical service to [Denton]. MS-81 (the Canyon ambulance) was summoned. It arrived at [9:05 p.m.]. At that time, Park Ranger Anderson took over primary care of [Denton]. Anderson requested an ALS page, to summon an Advanced Life Support care provider.
>
> In response to the page, I [Vandzura] responded. En route, I notified and called to duty, Park Ranger George Sechrist, established myself as the incident commander, and asked for an ALS page of the Lake Sub district.
>
> I arrived and assumed primary care of [Denton] at [9:19 p.m.]. We were enroute to Lake Clinic in MS-81 [ambulance] at [9:22 p.m.]. At [9:40 p.m.] I transferred care to Park Ranger Mike Cole, Lake ALS. Cole, Anderson, and Park Ranger Liz Voight continued the transport to Lake Clinic, arriving at [10:06 p.m.].
>
> Adrian and I returned to Canyon Junction. Sechrist had posted the Mary Mountain trail as "Closed to Hiking, due to bear danger." As it was after dark there was no immediate investigation at the scene . . .
>
> The Lake Clinic staff decided that [Denton] was to be transferred by ground ambulance to Eastern Idaho Regional Medical Center.

Ranger Matt Vandzura's Emergency Response report then detailed the investigation of the bear attack scene:

> On June 19, 2004 at about [9:10 a.m.] Park Ranger Jesse Teudhope, George Sechrist, [Bear Management Specialist] Kerry Gunther and I hiked to the scene of the attack. We were able to find the general

location based on [Denton's] description: a hill with a single tree south of the Mary Mountain trail just past the power lines.

South and west of the tree we found an area of fresh grizzly bear digging. The bears were foraging on roots.

The approximate scene of the attack is UTM 539453 E, 4946404 N NAD 27. The single tree is about 20 yards south and east of the scene. The edge of the forest to the north is 242 yards from the scene.

We found two grizzly bear tracks at the scene. The most distinct track was 8" from heel to claw. At the scene we also found a lens cap from a Nikon product. When I asked, [Denton] said the lens cap was not his.

About 25 yards north and west of the scene we found another grizzly bear track. This track was 5¼" across the pad. [Bear Specialist] Gunther stated that this was consistent with a female adult bear.

We finished our site inspection at about [10:30 a.m.].

The park's Bear Sighting Report #041021 stated that the two bears were digging up biscuit root, an important grizzly food. See the two maps below, showing the bear mauling site, the area where the two grizzlies dug for biscuit root, the front and hind grizzly tracks, the location of Mary Mountain Trail, and the lone tree—into which the bluebird had alighted as [Denton] followed it through his binocular sights.

Ranger Vandzura concluded that "There are no actions planned against the bear(s). This incident was a surprise encounter between a solo hiker and two grizzly bears. [Bear Management Specialist] Gunther believes that the bears were either a sow with a yearling or 2 year old cub or a mating pair. The hiker reacted in the manner taught by the National Park Service. There is no evidence to suggest that this particular area of the Park is more or less dangerous to the public than any other area of the Park."

As a consequence of this safety assessment, "The Mary Mountain trail was reopened to the public at [noon] on June 19, 2004."

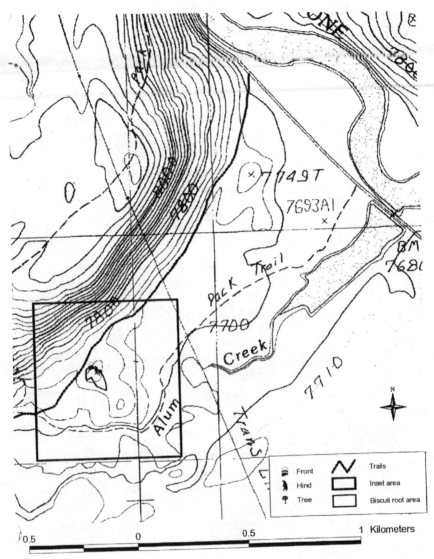

Map of bear mauling site, June 18, 2004, 6/18/04, in Case Incident Record #042108

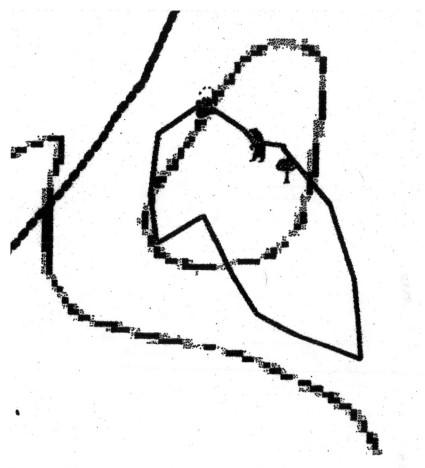

Close-up of inset area, showing bear front track, bear hind track, tree, trails, and biscuit root

In 2006, an update on Denton was posted on the Appalachian State University (Boone, North Carolina) website by Rob Robertson, class of 1996:

> Almost two years ago Appalachian student Denton Turner was hiking alone in Yellowstone National Park when he encountered a fight for his life:
>
> Dusk was settling in as he peered through binoculars at a bluebird, he said. He heard a rustling in the bushes and realized he had company: two grizzly bears.
>
> The larger bear charged . . .
>
> [Denton], who still attends Appalachian, suffered "bruises, cuts, puncture wounds to his back and a bite below his right armpit." His story made national headlines at the time. It's also set to be part of a new show on Animal Planet entitled "After the Attack." According to an e-mail we received today, "Animal Planet flew him back out to Yellowstone Park to revisit and recount the grizzly bear attack that almost took the ASU student's life."[86]

## 2004: PUNCTURE WOUNDS ON HEAD AND SHOULDER, NAME WITHHELD

*National Park Service—Yellowstone*

*Case Incident Record Number: 046750*

*Location: Snake River Trail, south of Heart Lake*

*Date/Time: Sunday, September 26, 2004, 10:30–11:00 a.m.*

A lone backpacker headed up Yellowstone's Snake River Trail that Sunday on September 26, 2004. The forty-one-year-old backpacker (name withheld) was from nearby Montana, and was enjoying hiking the trail, which in this section was forested, with ravines and short rises. But then a grizzly bear interrupted his campsite-to-campsite trip.

After the attack, Park Investigator David Phillips reported that "[the victim] stated that he had camped at backcountry campsite 8C5 along the Heart River on the night of 9/25/04. On the morning of 9/26/04 he left campsite 8C5 and was hiking on the Snake River Trail toward camp-site 6M7 (at Fox Creek) where he was scheduled to camp the night of 9/26/04." The report then described the ensuing bear incident:

After hiking southeast on the trail for approximately 1½–2 miles, he encountered a female grizzly bear with two cubs. He described the size of the cubs as approximately ⅓ the size of the adult female, but said he never really got a good look at the cubs. [He] stated that he was approx-imately ½ mile past the first creek crossing southeast of 8C5 when the encounter occurred. He described the area as forested and full of ravines and moguls. He stated that he had seen bear scat everywhere but had not stopped to check how fresh it was. He was not carrying Bear Pep-per Spray.

He stated that he had been walking slow through a forested section of trail and looking at his map and was just folding up the map when he heard a whoof and looked up to see an adult female grizzly with two cubs on a little hump of ground 15 to 20 feet above the trail and approximately 30 yards ahead of him.

He stated that the adult female looked very agitated and charged, but angled past him. He yelled "No" as the bear charged past. After the sow charged past him, the cubs then started to approach the sow, and in doing that, had to walk past [him]. The bear then turned to look at her cubs. [He] stated that the bear looked real intense, mouth open, grunt-ing and whoofing.

[Name withheld] then turned and started walking away from the bear saying "I'm leaving, I'm leaving." However, as he walked away the bear hit him from behind knocking him down. The bear then ran off.

[Name withheld] initially started to crawl away but heard the bear huffing and so went into a fetal position as the bear came back at him. He was balled up with his back to the bear. The bear bit the top of his pack, biting into his tent and therma-rest that were lashed to the out-side of his pack.

She also batted him hard twice on the top of the head with her paws. He described it as a quick one-two punch. He was also batted hard on the right shoulder. She bit his pack and hit and pawed his pack a few times then ambled off. She then bounded back again, grunting and breathing hard, then left again and did not come back.

He waited a while, then slowly got up and hiked all the way out to the trailhead, arriving at sunset. He had two small holes in the skin on his head and one small hole in the skin on his right shoulder. He did not go to a doctor. He stated that "the wounds all bled a lot which should have cleaned them pretty well." When he came home the evening of the attack, he took a bath to further clean the wounds.

On Thursday (9/30/04) during the interview with him, he stated that the wounds were now all scabbed over and healing well. After getting home he inspected his tent and the contents of his pack. The bear had bitten through multiple layers of his rolled up tent and a notebook with a plastic cover that was inside of his pack had canine bite marks through it, although the fabric of his pack was not torn.

It is considered typical behavior for an adult female grizzly bear to protect her cubs from the perceived threat of a hiker during a surprise encounter at close range, so no management action was taken against the bear . . .

The extent of the injuries sustained by the hiker were probably significantly reduced due to the hiker's coolheadedness and appropriate behavior during the attack. By being passive and going into a fetal position, the hiker appeared as less threatening to the bear. This likely helped defuse the situation and lessen his injuries. In addition, by leaving his pack on during the encounter, the severity of his injuries were probably significantly reduced, as his pack took the brunt of the bear's attack.

# 22

# BEAR ATTACKS 2005–2015

## BEAR GOT ON HIS BACK, PAT MCDONALD, GERALD HOLZER

*National Park Service—Yellowstone*

*Case Incident Record Number: 055640*

*Location: In Yellowstone—North Shore Trail along Shoshone Lake*

*Date/Time: Wednesday, September 14, 2005, 3:15 p.m.*

The two friends started their backcountry camping trip eight miles east of Old Faithful, parking their vehicle at the DeLacy Creek Trailhead. Autumn had arrived that September 14, 2005, when Pat McDonald, fifty-two, of North Dakota, and Gerald Holzer, fifty-one, of Minnesota, headed toward the campsite they had registered for: #8S3 near Shoshone Lake. They had strapped into their backpacks and were now hiking the forested trail, which soon followed the creek into open meadows.

Ranger Mark C. Marschall described Shoshone Lake in *Yellowstone Trails*. "Shoshone Lake, Yellowstone's largest backcountry lake, has attracted backcountry travelers and explorers for hundreds of years. During this time, it's had many names . . . and finally [it was] called Shoshone Lake to acknowledge the earliest name used by the fur trappers." The description continued:

Its cold deep waters hold brown, brook and lake trout. These non-native species were introduced into this once fishless lake during the 1890s. Waterbirds gather on and around the lake to feed on these fish as well as other aquatic animals and plants . . . Sandhill cranes may or may not be seen, but they're often heard for miles as they call out in a voice that's described as a low, loud, musical rattle.[87]

The day was so far uneventful. Pat and Gerald, continuing on the trail to Shoshone Lake, turned west, following the North Shore Trail toward their campsite 8S3. Then they spotted fresh bear scat.

The two men talked together about the scat. But then, the Park news release of September 15 reported, "[They] decided, however, to continue on to their campsite but began making noise in an attempt to deter a possible bear encounter." Then they spotted a bear.

As they came over a knoll, approximately one-fourth of a mile from where they saw the scat, they were charged by a grizzly at full stride. [Gerald], who was walking in front of [Pat], was able to side-step the grizzly. [Pat] stepped behind some trees and dropped to the ground. The bear initially ran by [Pat], but then returned and swatted at him. The bear continued on to [Gerald], who had dropped to the ground and was on his stomach. The bear jumped on [Gerald's] back and also swatted at him. The bear then retreated about 50 feet where they could hear it snorting.

From his position on the ground, [Pat] began removing the wrist straps from his hiking poles in order to retrieve his bear spray from his waist belt. The bear was apparently drawn back to the site by the noise. This time the bear attacked the hiker's leg. The hiker managed to retrieve the pepper spray from his waist belt and doused the bear's face. The bear fled the area.

The men began the four-mile hike back to their vehicle at the DeLacy Creek Trailhead, and proceeded to the Old Faithful Clinic for treatment.

Remarkably, the men were not seriously injured. [Pat] sustained a puncture wound to his lower left leg and was treated and released; his companion was not injured, as he was protected by his backpack during the attack.

Investigating Ranger Mike Hardin wrote, in his undated notes on the multiple attacks: "Hiker #1 [Gerald sustained] minor scratch from swat. Hiker #2 [Pat sustained] bite to leg. While biting leg sprayed with bear spray. Injured group never saw more than one bear. Two others [in another party] saw 2 bears, black and griz."

Personnel from Yellowstone's Bear Management Office, in an unsigned note in the Case Incident Record, wrote that they investigated the scene of the attack. [On] "9/19/05, campsite[s] 8S2 and 8S3 were investigated . . . Travis Wyman, Lisa Coleman, and Tyler Coleman searched the area for any additional information that could be found associated with this incident." The investigators described what they found:

We identified a cow elk carcass very near the trail and very close to campsite 8S3. The UTM for the carcass is 522910 4916893 (83). We found that the carcass cache site was 16 m from the hiking trail and 24 m from the 8S3 trail marker. The carcass was very likely consumed by a bear because there was a large excavation and cache associated with the carcass. There were also several piles of bear meat scat near the site. It is probable that the bear in question was at the carcass when the hikers were attacked on 9/14/05 and *the lone hiker was charged on 9/15/05* [emphasis added. There were two hikers]. The site was investigated by the bear management staff on 9/19/05; at that time we found a mostly consumed carcass and a large excavation site. We also documented large adult grizzly tracks approx .5 mile from the campsites as well as wolf and cougar tracks in the area. . . .

The remains of the carcass were dragged further into the forest by BMO [Bear Management Office] staff.

A Yellowstone news release of September 19, 2005, concluded with the following. "The Delacy Creek, North Shore and Howard Eaton Trails are closed to hiking. Backcountry campsites along the north shore to Shoshone Lake are open to boat access only."

*Note:* There were no reported attacks in 2006. See Chapter 17 (Jim Cole) for 2007 incident.

## 2008: BEAR, MAN, AND FIRE, NAME WITHHELD

*National Park Service—Yellowstone*

*Case Incident Record Number: 083862*

*Location: North of Pelican Valley, East of Le Hardy Rapids/West of Sulphur Hills*

*Date/Time: August 3, 2008, approximately 1:00 p.m.*

Wildland firefighters near Yellowstone's Pelican Valley "observed a sub-adult grizzly bear running around within the Le Hardy fire, seemingly trying to escape flames/fire," reported the unsigned Supplementary Case/Incident Record.

Firefighting crews with the Lewis and Clark "IHC" were conducting a burnout operation on the South flank of the Le Hardy Fire. The date was August 3, 2008. The record continued: "The bear observed the firefighters and ran away. The bear a short time later was observed by another crew of firefighters just east of the original sighting, again seemingly trying to escape active flames and get away from the burnout area and firefighters."

A second report, titled "Le Hardy Fire Bear Encounter Investigation," noted that "The crew [had] started the burning operation at approximately 11 a.m." The investigation report explained further:

> The firefighter involved in the incident was first in line with a drip torch. A Squad Boss was in front and four torches behind. At one point during the operation, a grizzly bear was sighted on the line. Crew members called out the bear on the line and the operation was suspended until crew members lost sight of the bear. The bear was located between the burn-out operation and the fire's edge. A few minutes later, the burn-out operation continued. Crew members shouted and whistled their locations throughout the operation due to being spread out and in thick timber.

At approximately [3:00 p.m.], the firefighter [involved] had his head down, laying fire with the drip torch, when he heard a sound like a branch breaking. The firefighter looked up and saw a grizzly bear approximately 50–60 feet away. The firefighter turned away, which was towards his Squad Boss in front and started walking. The firefighter took two or three steps and looked over his shoulder to see the bear running at him. The firefighter started running and ran approximately eight feet to three downed logs on the ground. The firefighter cleared the logs and attempted to get under the logs.

As soon as the firefighter laid down on the ground, the bear was on top of him. The bear swatted several times, striking the firefighter's pack and upper back. The firefighter screamed loudly and then realized that he should lay there quiet and not move. The bear then stood up on the back of the firefighter's legs and pounced down, with great force, on the firefighter's upper back area. Shortly thereafter the bear left.

The Supplementary Case/Incident Record reported what happened next. The investigator noted that "The firefighter was evacuated from the scene and flown via helicopter to the Lake Clinic where he was examined. The bear inflicted minor wounds (skin abrasions and bruising), and the firefighter was released after a short period of time." The Results and Description of Incident report continued:

Park Bear Management was notified immediately. Travis Wyman from the Bear Management Office assisted Lake Area Rangers with the investigation and determined that the situation was much like a surprise encounter. The bear was most likely agitated by trying to escape the fire and the continual running into firefighters over a distance of approximately 1 mile along the burnout operation on the South flank of the fire . . .

The bear was not seen again. During the fire briefing the next morning, a strengthened bear safety message was stressed, and firefighters were required to work in pairs closely together, report immediately any bear activity they witnessed, and all carry bear pepper spray.

# 2008: SWATTED INSIDE VEHICLE, NAME WITHHELD

*National Park Service—Yellowstone*

*Case Incident Record Number: 082965*

*Location of incident: Madison subdistrict, power-line corridor behind Mesa Pit carcass dump*

*Date/Time: Wednesday, September 24, 2008, approximately 4:30 p.m.*

A Yellowstone Park document entitled "Detailed Description of Incident" (unsigned), reported a bear incident involving an electric-power-line worker. "On Wednesday, September 24, 2008, at approximately 1630 hours [4:30 p.m.], Northwestern Energy employee [name withheld] was swatted and slightly injured by a large adult grizzly bear." The report then described what occurred:

> [Name withheld] and co-worker [name withheld] were driving the power-line corridor in a UTV [vehicle] . . . [The victim] saw a large adult grizzly bear charging at him. [He] hit the gas and accelerated, and stood up as the bear swatted at him. The bear's paw hit him on the hip and thigh, but was partially blocked by the roll cage. As they sped off in the UTV, [the worker] in the passenger seat sprayed the bear with bear spray.
>
> The incident happened where the power-line passes closest to the wildlife carcass dump where road-killed ungulates are dumped.
>
> [The victim] received two small puncture wounds from the bear's claws, and a large contusion from his hip to his thigh. He was wearing his chain-saw safety chaps at the time of the incident. The chaps likely prevented injury from the bear's claws. [The victim] said that in the future he will load his UTV in the back of his pickup and drive 1½–2 miles past the carcass dump, then unload and drive the UTV.

A Yellowstone Bear Sighting Report, gave the description of the above referenced grizzly as "Dark Brown (Chocolate)" and weighing

"Over 400 pounds." What was the distance between observer and bear? "0 ft." How long did you observe the bear(s)? "10 seconds." Bear's reaction? "Charged, then swatted."

*Note*: There were no reported attacks in 2009 or 2012. For 2010, see Chapter 4 (Evert) and Chapter 5 (Kammer). For 2011, see Chapter 2 (Matayoshi) and Chapter 3 (Wallace).

## 2013: BITE AND CLAW WOUNDS, NAMES WITHHELD

A Yellowstone Park news release on August 15, 2013, detailed bear-inflicted injuries to two hikers:

### *Two Hikers Injured In Yellowstone Bear Encounter*

Two people were treated for injuries after a backcountry bear encounter Thursday morning in Yellowstone National Park.

A group of four people was a few miles down the Cygnet Lakes Trail southwest of Canyon Village when they saw an approaching grizzly bear cub-of-the-year about 11:30 Thursday morning. A sow grizzly then appeared at very close range and charged the group.

Two of the hikers immediately discharged their canisters of bear spray and the sow and cub left the area after an encounter which lasted about a minute.

All four members of the group hiked out to the trailhead under their own power. One person was treated at the scene, while the second injured hiker was transported by ambulance to an area hospital with bite and claw wounds. All four have asked that their identities not be released.

Yellowstone bear biologists say the sow's behavior is consistent with purely defensive actions taken after a surprise encounter with people. This was the first report of any bear-caused human injuries in Yellowstone this year. The incident remains under investigation.

Yellowstone regulations require visitors to stay 100 yards from black and grizzly bears at all times. The best defense is to stay a safe distance from bears and use binoculars, a telescope or telephoto lens to get a closer look. These hikers were heeding the park's advice to hike in groups of three or more, make noise on the trail, keep an eye out for bears and carry bear spray. Bear spray has proven to be a good last line of defense, if kept handy and used according to directions when a bear is approaching within 30 to 60 feet.

There had been no recent reports of grizzly bear activity in the area. As a precaution the Cygnet Lakes Trail and the surrounding area have been temporarily closed. In addition, the park has closed the nearby Mary Mountain area to any off trail travel.

*Note:* 2014: There were no incidents of bear attacks *inside* Yellowstone National Park.

Some media sources, however, have referenced a 2014 bear-caused human fatality as a "Yellowstone fatality." However, the distance to Yellowstone Park is farther than the six-mile limit I chose to use in this book. Although this fatality occurred southeast of Yellowstone Park, it is mentioned here for the sake of clarity.

## 2014: BEAR RESEARCHER CONSUMED AND "CACHED": ADAM THOMAS STEWART

According to the multiagency "Board Of Review Report—Stewart 2014" the "31-year-old Stewart, working for a contractor doing vegetation plots, was killed by a bear in Cub Creek on the Bridger Teton National Forest on September 4, 2014. The remains of Mr. Stewart were found by searchers on September 12, 2014."

Mr. Stewart was from Virgin, Utah, and had been alone, camping and hiking to and from the vegetation plots for his work contracted by the US Forest Service. No improperly stored or disturbed food was found at his campsite.

"Mr. Stewart's remains," the report continued, "were almost totally consumed and scattered in a food cache typical of a bear. Such food caches are composed of a pile of dirt and vegetation that covers the food remains. . . No bears were seen at the fatality site but it was evident that both grizzly and black bears had been in the area because of the caching of the remains, several evident bear beds, bear hair, bear tracks, and multiple bear scats."

"There was no evidence of firearms or bear spray near Stewart."

In the area of the fatality, two grizzly bears were trapped, a subadult male (#792) and a female. "Neither bear #792 nor the female grizzly bear," the report noted, "had been captured previously and neither bear was identified from hair obtained at the fatality site as determined by DNA analysis."

*Note:* 2015: See Chapter One, "Victims: Human and Bear: Lance Crosby."

# 23

# WHAT ABOUT THE BLACK BEARS?

*As we came into camp a black bear kindly vacated the premises.*
—NATHANIEL PITT LANGFORD, MEMBER OF THE WASHBURN
YELLOWSTONE EXPEDITION, 1870

## LIVING IN BLACK-BEAR COUNTRY

Black-bear country, which covers most of America, includes Yellowstone Park, where visitors once saw many black bears near or on the roads. "Where are all the black bears?" visitors commonly ask now, according to park rangers. The rangers answer, "They're back in the *back*-country, where they're supposed to be."

Yellowstone's black bears, to the respect of some, the entertainment of some, and the concern of park management, are the quintessential political animal. At one time the public favored their front-country cavortings and roadside beggings, if not their picnic-basket nabbings. Now management policy has returned the bears to a more natural state.

Black bears were a problem in camp as early as 1870. Of Yellowstone then [before it was made a national park], Nathaniel Pitt Langford wrote in his diary the following:

Monday, August 29. Washburn Yellowstone Expedition
    Descending the mountain on the southwest side, we came upon the trail of the pack train, which we followed to our camp at the head of a small stream running into the Yellowstone, which is about five

A black bear in Yellowstone's backcountry.

miles distant. As we came into camp a black bear kindly vacated the premises.[88]

In Yellowstone Park's more recent past, it was not grizzlies but black bears that dealt out the most human injuries (though no fatalities are noted). That has changed, although black bears still occasionally cause problems ranging from the severe to the humorous, even if it's just snoring too loud. The following incident may remind some of the good/bad old days.

## 1959: "THE NIGHT OF THE BEAR"

In 1959 Edmund Jay Williams worked in Yellowstone on a forest survey crew, and lived with his wife, Arlene, in a trailer house in Canyon Village. "That summer we had several close encounters with a large black bear we named 'Meathead.' This was a time when bears were a common sight in Yellowstone." Later a geology professor at Ricks College in Idaho, Edmund described in 1999's International Yellowstone Association newsletter what Meathead did next:

In earlier days, park visitors treated bears like tame animals, but no one had told the bears about that or how they were supposed to act . . .

Meathead would sleep under our trailer house and we had to be careful when we were outside since the bear felt like that was his home and was quite protective. Arlene chased the bear away several times beating it with a broom when Meathead would become a nuisance. She would not do such a dangerous thing now and looks back on that time with fear and trembling.

Another problem with Meathead is that a 400-pound black bear can snore very loud. This method of bagging "Zs" would wake us up often. I would get up and stomp on the floor and wake him up so we could sleep. Meathead also had another bad habit of scratching his back on the underside of the trailer house at night causing the house to shake. Another stomp accompanied by mild cussing and he would quit.

That night of August 17, 1959 was a beautiful moonlit night in Yellowstone. At 11:37 the house started shaking and I jumped up and repeated the ritual of cussing Meathead. By then the house was shaking so hard that it flipped me back on the bed. I could not even sit up so I laid back and bounced around on the bed. My first thought was, "man, that bear sure has an itchy spot tonight." But after a few seconds we realized it was an earthquake.[89]

As it turned out, the event above was *the* earthquake. It was the big one—the 7.5 magnitude Hebgen Lake Earthquake that caused a mountain to fall, and killed twenty-eight people. Meathead probably slept through it all.

## HUMAN INJURIES

Yellowstone Bear Management Specialist Kerry A. Gunther reported in March 1991 that "Human injuries from black bears have decreased from averages of 46 per year from 1931 through 1969. Undoubtedly, some minor injuries were not reported by park visitors," he wrote.[90]

Gunther pointed out in 2002 that, as opposed to Yellowstone grizzlies, which are most active during nocturnal and crepuscular times (night, dawn, and dusk), Yellowstone's black bears are diurnal (foraging in the daytime).[91] That is probably one reason so many past visitors saw so many black bears in the broad light of day, and got too up-close-and-personal.

Also in his 1991 report, Gunther wrote that "Human injuries from black bears have decreased from averages of 46 per year . . . to 4 per year during the 1970's and 0.2 per year from 1980 through 1990." He added the following:

Only 4 of the 42 injuries from 1970 through 1990 were in backcountry areas, and 2 of these were from females "defending cubs." Thirty-four injuries were from bears along roadsides as a result of visitors getting too close while attempting to feed, take pictures, or get a better view of bears. Three injuries were from bears in developed areas, and 1 injury was during a bear-relocation accident.

Gunther's 1991 report includes a table illustrating the decrease in black-bear–caused injuries to humans. See the table below.

| Year | Injuries |
|------|----------|
| 1969 | 21 |
| 1970 | 6 |
| 1971 | 9 |
| 1972 | 5 |
| 1973 | 5 |
| 1974 | 7 |
| 1975 | 1 |
| 1976 | 4 |
| 1977 | 2 |
| 1978 | 1 |
| 1979 | 0 |
| 1980 | 0 |
| 1981 | 1 |
| 1982 | 0 |
| 1983 | 1 |
| 1984– | 0 |
| 1990 | 0[92] |

Injuries have declined in recent years. In Yellowstone Park, a black bear injuring a person "occurs only once every five to ten years," Gunther reported by telephone call to this author on November 7, 2007. This is welcome news.

## 2006: THE BEAR ON THE CAR ROOF

More recently, black bears have occasionally posed a problem, mostly to property. The following Yellowstone park news release of June 18, 2006, described a typical "problem" bear:

> ### Aggressive Black Bear Captured and Removed From Canyon Area
> Rangers in Yellowstone National Park trapped and removed a black bear late Saturday afternoon because its aggressive behavior posed a continuing threat to the safety of park visitors and employees.
>
> The bear charged multiple visitors while raiding campsites in Canyon Campground Saturday morning. The adult male bear broke into one vehicle and attempted to break in to several others. At one point it was observed walking on top of several vehicles in an attempt to gain access. The animal was successful in getting large quantities of human food.
>
> The bear was sprayed several times with pepper spray and was hazed repeatedly by park staff in an attempt to get him to move away from people in the campground. While these efforts failed, eventually the bear left on his own and was seen grazing on clover in a meadow near Canyon Lodge for several hours.
>
> Based on the animal's aggressive behavior, lack of fear of people, and its success at getting human food, the decision was made to capture and remove the bear. As capture operations were being set-up Saturday afternoon, the bear returned to the campground and began rummaging through campsites and acquiring human food from picnic tables, tents, coolers and fire grates. As he entered C Loop, the bear was attracted by an elk hind quarter used as bait and captured in a steel culvert-type trap.
>
> The bear was transported to park headquarters at Mammoth Hot Springs where, based on his aggressive and threatening behavior, the decision was made to euthanize the animal . . .

Note: A stock digital image of two steel culvert-type traps similar to that used to capture the black bear at Canyon Saturday can be found online at nps.gov/yell/slidefile/mammals/blackbear/Images/01758.jpg.

Concerning the black bear above, the *West Yellowstone News* quoted Bear Management Specialist Kerry A. Gunther on June 23, 2006. Gunther "said this week that the bear had 'no known previous history of involvement in bear-human conflicts.' Gunther also said that this was a rare case where 'a bear went bad very quickly.'"[93]

## HOW DO BLACK BEARS DIFFER FROM GRIZZLIES?

Like grizzlies, black bears are born naked and helpless, with eyes sealed shut. But black bears differ from grizzlies in a number of characteristics.

"Bear Characteristics," a 2007 Yellowstone information paper, noted that "The park does not have a current estimate of the black bear population; black bears are considered to be common in the park. The color varies from pure black to brown, cinnamon, or blonde; in the Rocky Mountains, approximately 50% are black with a light brown muzzle."

Bear Characteristics noted that black-bear weight (half a pound at birth) increases so that male Yellowstone black bears grow to weigh "210–315 pounds," while females weigh "135 to 160 pounds." The information paper described black bears further:

Black bears are primarily adapted to use forested areas and their edges and clearings. Although grizzly bears make substantial use of forested areas, they also make much more use of large, non-forested meadows and valleys than do black bears. Black bears have short, curved claws better suited to climbing trees than digging. This enables black bears to forage for certain foods, such as mast [nuts], by climbing trees. In contrast, grizzly bears have longer, less curved claws and a larger shoulder muscle mass better suited to digging than climbing. This enables grizzly bears to efficiently forage for foods which must be dug from the soil such as roots, bulbs, corms, and tubers, as well as rodents and their caches. The primary difference between the food habits of black bears and grizzly bears in the Yellowstone ecosystem is the absence of roots in the diet of black bears (Knight et al. 1988).

Behaviorally, black bears are generally much less aggressive than grizzly bears and rely on their ability to climb trees to allow themselves and their cubs to escape predators such as wolves, grizzly bears, or other black bears. Grizzly bears are generally one and one-half to two times larger than black bears of the same sex and age class within the same geographic region. Grizzly bears are also more aggressive than black bears and more likely to rely on their size and aggressiveness to protect themselves and their cubs from predators or other perceived threats.[94]

## DO BLACK BEARS ATTACK AND/OR PREY ON HUMANS?

Bear experts Stephen Herrero and Susan Fleck wrote that "The black bear (*ursus americanus*) is normally tolerant of people and reclusively dwells in the forest." It too [like the grizzly] will occasionally injure people and much more rarely will prey on them." Herrero and Fleck's report noted black-bear–caused injuries and fatalities to people:

Herrero (1985) concluded that between 1960–1980 more than 500 people were injured by black bears [in North America]; at least 90% of these injuries were minor and inflicted by bears that were conditioned to people's food and habituated to human beings. He stressed that because of the large number of black bears in North America and the very large exposure rate of people to them, injury rates were low . . .

Also, Herrero (1985) identified another type of black bear-inflicted injury, often leading to major injury or death. In these cases, he inferred that the motivation of the attacking bear was predation. This was based on the behavior of the bear before and during the attack, often including the death and partial consumption of one or even several persons . . .

It should be noted that no attempted or actual predatory behavior by black bears has been recognized in national parks, which are typically heavily used by people.[95]

In an article entitled "Black Bear Attack," the author (name not given) commented on black-bear–caused deaths to people. "In his book *Bear Attacks*, Dr. Stephen Herrero of the University of Calgary documented a total of 26 deaths in North America from 1900 to 1983 resulting from Black Bear attacks . . . No two attacks were the same in all respects, but Dr. Herrero was able to detect some general trends. The attacks took place throughout the non-denning season (almost always during the day), and more often involved male bears. Only one case involved a female possibly trying to protect her cubs. Whenever the offending bear was killed and examined it was found to be free of rabies or any other factor that might predispose it toward aggressive behavior."[96]

More recently, in 2013 Dr. Herrero updated this information when he was interviewed by Brian Platt of *The Globe and Mail*, Vancouver, Canada, on June 18. When asked, "What kind of bear behavior leads to an attack," Herrero replied as follows. "The most recent research I published analyzed 63 fatal attacks by black bears throughout North America between 1900 and 2009. There, the male bears, single bears, were the primary perpetrators. And the majority of fatal attacks were predacious. The person was stalked, charged, killed, partly eaten and dragged off. Not the kind of thing you like to think about bears doing, and fortunately they don't do it very often. We're talking perhaps a million black bears in North America, and a couple of people being killed each year. From a statistical point of view it's nothing, but if you're on the receiving end it's everything."

In Yellowstone Park, by contrast, there has been past uncertainty about whether a bear encountered was a black or a grizzly, but there have been no known human fatalities caused by black bears.

May it remain so.

# 24

# THE LATEST ON SAFER TRAVEL IN BEAR COUNTRY

Yellowstone Park personnel—including bear management specialists—are the most informed, experienced resource from whom to learn about safer travel in bear country. Safety cannot be guaranteed. The information below is reproduced from the Yellowstone Park website.

## REDUCING THE RISK OF A BEAR ENCOUNTER

### Be Alert

See the bear before you surprise it. Watch for bear sign such as tracks, scat, and feeding sites (diggings, rolled rocks, torn up logs, ripped open ant hills).

### Avoid Hiking at Dawn, Dusk, or at Night

Whenever possible avoid hiking at dawn, dusk, or at night. During the hot summer season these are the periods when grizzly bears are most active.

### Hike Close Together or in Groups

Whenever possible hike in groups of three or more people—91% of the people injured by bears in Yellowstone since 1970 were hiking alone or with only one hiking partner, only 9% of the people injured by bears were in groups of three or more people.

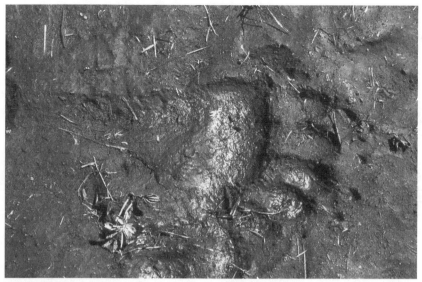

JIM PEACO, NPS

### *Don't Expect Bears to Notice You First*

In Yellowstone National park bears hibernate for approximately 5 months each year and have only 7 months of active time to obtain all of their nutritional needs. Therefore a bear with its head down feeding may not see you as quickly as you would think. Pay attention and see the bear before it sees you and before you surprise it.

### *Make Noise, Alert Bears to Your Presence*

When hiking, periodically yell "Hey Bear" especially when walking through dense vegetation or blind spots, or when traveling upwind, near loud streams, or on windy days. Avoid thick brush whenever possible.

### *Avoid Carcasses*

Ungulate carcasses are a highly preferred bear food that bears will guard and defend against other scavengers or humans. Dead ungulates will attract and hold many bears near the carcass site. It is risky to approach a carcass; many bears may be bedded nearby just out of sight. If you find a fresh dead ungulate carcass that still has a lot of meat remaining, leave the immediate area by the same route you approached the carcass from. If you walked to the carcass without encountering a bear you should be able to back out the same way without surprising a bear. Report all carcasses to the nearest ranger station or visitor center.

### Stay with Your Gear

Don't leave your packs, lunches, food, or beverages unattended as they may attract and hold bears at the site. If you surprise a bear that's eating your stashed food you may lose more than your lunch.

### Safety Tip

When hiking, stay alert and aware of your surroundings. Frequently look ahead, off to the sides, and behind you. See the bear before you surprise it!

## REACTING TO A BEAR ENCOUNTER

### How to React to a Bear Encounter at a Distance

If a bear doesn't see you, keep out of sight and detour as far as possible behind and downwind of the bear. If the bear sees you, retreat slowly and leave the area. If possible slowly walk upwind to let your scent reach the bear. Regardless of the distance, never approach the bear.

If a bear stands up on two legs, it is most likely trying to gather information and not being aggressive. In this situation, don't panic and slowly back away.

### Reacting to a Surprise Encounter with a Bear

If the bear clacks its teeth, sticks out its lips, huffs, woofs, or slaps the ground with its paws, it is warning you that you are too close and are making it nervous. Heed this warning and slowly back away. Do not run, shout, or make sudden movements. You don't want to startle the bear. Don't run because you can't outrun a bear. Running may trigger a chase

JIM PEACO, NPS

response in the bear. Bears in Yellowstone chase down elk calves all the time. You do not want to look like a slow elk calf.

Often times, slowly putting distance between yourself and the bear will defuse the situation. Draw your bear spray from the holster, remove the safety tab, and prepare to use it if the bear charges.

Should you climb a tree? Climbing a tree to avoid an attack might be an option but is often impractical. Remember all black bears and most grizzly bears can climb trees (if there is something up the tree that the bear really wants). Running to a tree or frantically climbing a tree may provoke a nonaggressive bear to chase you. Many people have been pulled from trees before they can get high enough to get away. Remember, you have probably not climbed a tree since you were ten years old and it is harder than you remember. In most cases climbing a tree is a poor decision.

### How to React to a Charging Bear

If a bear charges you after a surprise encounter, stay still and stand your ground. Most of the time, if you do this, the bear is likely to break off the charge or veer away (a bluff charge). If you run it is likely to trigger a chase response from the bear.

If you are charged by a bear and have bear pepper spray, this is the time to use it. Start spraying the charging bear when it is about 40 feet away.

If the bear continues to charge, it is important, not to drop to the ground and "play dead" too early. Wait until the bear makes contact or the nano-second just before the bear makes contact. Remember, by standing your ground, the bear is likely to break off the charge or veer away. If the bear makes contact, this is the point where you become passive and "play dead." Drop to the ground; keep your pack on to protect your back. Lie on your stomach, face down and clasp your hands over the back of your neck with your elbows protecting the sides of your face. Remain still and stay silent to convince the bear that you are not a threat to it or its cubs.

After the bear leaves, wait several minutes before moving. Listen and look around cautiously before you get up to make certain the bear is no longer nearby. If the bear is gone, get up and walk (don't run) out of the area. Remember, the sow grizzly needs time to gather up her cubs which may have climbed trees or hidden in nearby brush. If you get up too soon, before the sow has had time to gather up her cubs and leave, she may attack again.

During a surprise encounter where the bear is reacting defensively, you should not fight back. Fighting back will only prolong the attack and will likely result in more serious injuries. Since 1970, in Yellowstone National Park, those that played dead when attacked by a bear during a surprise encounter received only minor injuries 75% of the time. However, those that fought back during surprise encounters received very severe injuries 80% of the time.

If a bear has not reacted aggressively, and has not initiated a charge or otherwise acted defensively, you should back away. Never drop to the ground and "play dead" with a bear that has not been aggressive or defensive. Being submissive or "playing dead" with a curious bear could cause the bear to become predatory. A defensive bear will charge almost immediately during a surprise encounter, and will charge with its head low and ears laid back. A curious or predatory bear will persistently approach with its head up and ears erect. When approached by a curious or predatory bear you should be aggressive and fight back.

## USING BEAR SPRAY TO DETER AN AGGRESSIVE BEAR

Bear spray is a non-lethal bear deterrent designed to stop aggressive behavior in bears. Capsicum, the active ingredient in bear spray is a strong irritant to the eyes, nose, mouth, throat, and lungs of bears. Bear spray has been proven to be a good defense against charging bears and has been effective in most reported cases where it has been used. Remember, no bear deterrent is 100% effective. Use proper bear encounter avoidance techniques as your first line of defense! We have a great video on using pepper spray on our Wildlife Safety Videos page.

*Bear Spray Tips*

- **Bear Spray Has Been Proven Effective**
  In a study in Alaska, bear pepper spray was effective in stopping aggressive behavior in grizzly bears in 92% of the incidents where it was used.

- **Easy to Use**
  You don't have to be a good shot with bear spray. All you need to do is put up a cloud of bear spray between you and the charging bear. Precise aiming is not necessary.

- **Practice First**
  Use an inert bear spray to practice quick drawing bear spray from its holster, removing the safety tab with your thumb, and firing.

JIM PEACO, NPS

Practice firing inert bear spray with the wind at your back, into a head wind, and with a cross-wind so that you understand how bear spray is affected by the wind.

- **Bear Spray Is Not a Substitute for Common Sense**
  Be vigilant and use bear encounter prevention methods, body language, and bear safety protocols as your first line of defense.

- **Keep It Readily Accessible**
  Bear spray must be immediately accessible in a quick draw holster, not stored in your pack. If your bear spray is not quickly accessible you will not have time to use it. Think of surprising a bear at a distance of 50 feet. The bear is charging at you at approximately 44 feet per second. You would not have time to pull your bear spray out of your pack. Be sure to remove the zip-tie securing the safety clip before heading out on the trail.

- **When to Spray**
  Start to spray the charging bear when it is about 30–60 feet away.

- **How to Spray**
  Hold the can firmly in one or both hands to prevent it from tilting upward upon discharge. Holding the bear spray with two hands gives better control. Point the bear spray nozzle toward the charging bear, aim slightly downward and using a slight side to side motion spray a 2–3 second blast so that the bear must pass through the cloud of bear spray before it gets to you. If the bear continues to charge, keep spraying until the bear changes direction. It is better to aim slightly low so the spray billows up off of the ground, than to aim too high possibly allowing the bear to run underneath the spray. If you have a strong cross-wind you will have to aim slightly up-wind so the spray drifts back in front of you. If you have a strong tail-wind it will carry the bear spray further giving you an added margin of safety. If you have a strong head-wind the spray will blow into your own face and incapacitate you. With a strong head-wind you may consider not using your bear spray until the bear makes contact.

- **Use Body Language**
  Remember, when using bear spray you have made the decision to confront an agitated or aggressive bear in an effort to stop its

charge or attack. Bears respond to body language and sounds. When dispersing your bear spray, take a firm stance, thrust your bear spray out in front of you, and yell loudly at the bear. By doing this you are letting the bear know that you are taking a stand.

- **Leave the Area Promptly After Use**
  After you spray a bear with bear spray you should promptly leave the area as the effects of the bear spray will eventually wear off.
- **Know Its Limitations**
  Bear spray is adversely affected by freezing temperatures, strong winds, heavy rain or snow, and age. These factors may reduce the distance and duration that bear spray will spray. Check the expiration date on your bear spray. Properly dispose of expired bear spray.

Learn more about selecting the proper bear spray, what bear spray doesn't do, and proper storage of bear spray.

Dispose of expired and unused bear spray properly. Yellowstone has a recycling program with designated bins that can be found at campgrounds throughout the park.

## UNDERSTANDING THE BEAR'S MINDSET

One of your best defenses against bear attack is your brain. Your reaction to an encounter with a bear should be based on the bear's behavior and the cause of that behavior. Therefore, it is important that you "understand the bear's mindset" as much as possible. A good knowledge and understanding of bears, bear behavior, bear aggression, bear food habits, and bear ecology can empower you to decrease the chances of having encounters with bears, and to diffuse aggressive encounters when they occur.

There are two main types of bear attacks on people: defensive, and predatory. You should respond very differently to each type of attack, therefore you must be able to tell the difference between a defensive attack and a predatory attack.

### Defensive Attacks & Aggression

Defensive attacks are the most common cause of bear-inflicted human injury. In almost all bear attacks, bears are reacting defensively to a perceived threat to themselves, their cubs, or a coveted food source during a surprise encounter with people. In these incidents, the bear wants to neutralize the threat (you), gather up their cubs (if present), and leave. In Yellowstone National Park the chances of being injured by a bear in a defensive attack, are very low, approximately 1 in 3 million.

## Recognizing Defensive Aggression

If you are attacked after any sudden, surprise encounter with a bear, you can assume that it is a defensive attack. If the bear hop-charges toward you, clacks its teeth, sticks out its lips, huffs, woofs, or rushes a few steps toward you and slaps the ground with its paws, it is warning you that it is nervous about your presence and that you are too close. Heed this warning and back away. If these warning signs precede an attack, you can assume that the attack is defensive in nature. In a defensive attack, the bear will charge toward you with its ears laid back. A bear that rears up onto its hind legs is trying to gather more information through scent, sight, and sound to determine what you are and what your intentions are. To get a better scent, the bear may circle down-wind of you.

## How to React to Defensive Attacks

Once a bear that is displaying defensive aggression has made physical contact with you, you should be passive and play dead to diffuse the situation and minimize injury.

## Predatory Attacks

Many people think that the reason for most bear attacks is that the bear wants to kill and eat you. In reality this is almost never true! In the vast majority of confrontations between bears and people, the bear is only trying to defend itself or its cubs from a perceived threat (you), and the bear's reaction is entirely defensive. Actual predatory attacks do occasionally occur, but are extremely rare. In Yellowstone National Park the chances of being involved in a predatory bear attack are extremely low. Behaviorally, it can be difficult to distinguish a predatory bear from a bear that is just curious or food conditioned.

### Recognizing Predatory Attacks

Predatory bears don't give warning signals or use threat displays or vocalize, there is no huffing, blowing, barking, jaw-popping, hop charging, ground slapping, or bluff charging during a predatory attack. Predatory bears ears will be erect and forward (not laid back). Predatory bears will be intensely interested in their victim, visually locked on. Predatory bears will keep bearing in on you.

### How To React To Predatory Attacks

During a predatory attack you should be aggressive and fight back using any available weapon (bear spray, rocks, sticks) to stop the aggression by the bear. Fight back as if your life depends on it, because it does. Predatory attacks usually persist until the bear is scared away, overpowered, injured, or killed.

### Safety Tip

Play dead if a defensive bear makes contact; always fight back against a predatory bear.

# AFTERWORD

# PEOPLE AND BEARS: WHAT BOTH NEED

What is the future for people and bears in Yellowstone Park?

Were those people injured (or who lost their lives) reckless to be in Yellowstone, especially its backcountry, a place with more and more grizzlies? Should offending grizzlies be shot immediately and not relocated? Should visitors sign a waiver form that states: "The park will assist you, but if you are injured or killed, we are not responsible."?

This book's message is *not* "Don't go into the park." Nor is it "bears are evil or visitors are stupid." As has been said, "You play outdoors, you pay outdoors." People and bears are to each other (to use the legal term for an unfenced swimming pool) "an attractive nuisance." Some conflict is inevitable, and there is no guarantee for your safety.

## WHAT PEOPLE NEED—MORE EDUCATION

Bear researchers and managers have learned exponentially how better to analyze bear attacks, determine what causes them, and hopefully reduce their occurrence. We, the public, need proactively to become part of this educational process. We need to practice, embody, and show others the experts' guidelines for safer travel in Yellowstone bear country. See Chapter 24 for detailed advice, but also visit the Yellowstone Park website *before* you arrive in the park for its most up-to-date advice. When you do arrive in the park, be sure to check with the Backcountry Office for the latest reported bear information on the area you are going to.

## WHAT BEARS NEED—REDUCTION OF HUMAN/ BEAR CONFLICTS

Experts in the Greater Yellowstone area are reporting the presence of more grizzlies, and "grizzlies moving out of core habitats into fringe areas, conflicting with humans." We, the public, need to learn from wildlife professionals about the causes of bear/human conflict, and then work to reduce these conflicts. We need to do this not only for our own safety, but for that of the grizzlies. When human/bear conflicts increase, more grizzlies, and significantly more reproductive-age females and their young, die.

## IMPLEMENTING THE RECOMMENDATIONS

Is putting these measures into practice a simple task? No. Many of the world's human conflicts are present in the microcosm that is the world's first national park.

- Limited resources (such as money, time, and staffing within the shifting political, National Park Service, Interior Department, and bordering states' priorities)
- Intolerance of differences (including differences in attitudes and values held toward wild places and predators)
- Competing interests nearby (agriculture, hunting, extractive industries)
- Pleasure and use versus preservation (motorized vehicles versus roadless areas)
- Safety versus adventure (snow coach versus cross-country skiing into a geyser basin)
- Survival of species (limited habitat to begin with, and in the future decreased habitat, plus human-caused mortality and climate change)

Each of us, while only an individual within the larger park mosaic, can try his or her best to implement these recommendations, so grizzlies at Yellowstone will not become a distant memory.

# ANOTHER YELLOWSTONE DAY PASSES, AND NIGHT COMES AGAIN

"It was one hell of a long night," wrote former backcountry ranger James N. "Nick" Herring in the Fern Lake patrol cabin log book on August 2, 1984. Herring (by 2011 Yellowstone's deputy chief ranger of operations) was alone that night in 1984 and remained barricaded inside the cabin, listening to the noise.

A grizzly, perhaps the same one that had just killed Brigitta Fredenhagen at her White Lake campsite, tried all night to enter the locked door and wood-shuttered windows of the nearby patrol cabin. The day before, Herring had had the sad task of writing up the "Inventory— Tent and Contents" for the Fredenhagen investigation. The tent contents included "Number 8) Various books and Yellowstone topo map, Number 9) Strap with 2 'bear bells,' and Number 18) . . . passport and visa identification [with her photo]." In the morning he hoped to further assist the investigation in any way he could. In the morning the bear was gone, leaving behind tracks that circled the cabin.

"May God rest her soul," he wrote in the patrol cabin log book during that long night. "I feel for the pain she must have felt."

This book is dedicated to all those injured in the attempt to coexist— people and bears.

# ENDNOTES

1. Terry Everard quoted twenty-one years after he was attacked by a grizzly bear sow while hunting bighorn sheep in northwestern Wyoming. Reported by Brett French in *Billings Gazette*, picked up by the *Missoulian*, October 13, 2013.

2. *Yellowstone Science*, Vol. 23, Issue 1, March 2015. The Yellowstone Association, Yellowstone National Park, Wyoming.

3. Copyright Keith R. Crowley. Comments about and photographs of the Yellowstone grizzly known as "Blaze." Posted on the Internet August 13, 2015. Lodgetrail.com.

4. Les Seago, "Investigative Activity Report," in Case Incident Record Number 112587, Department of the Interior, National Park Service, Yellowstone National Park, 2011, unbound, 1–2, paginated only within an individual ranger's report, nps.gov/aboutus/foia/foia-frd.htm.

5. Case Incident Record Number 112587, Department of the Interior, National Park Service, Yellowstone National Park, 2011, unbound, paginated only within an individual ranger's report, nps.gov/aboutus/foia/foia-frd.htm.

6. *Investigation Team Report dated September 9, 2011, Fatality of Mr. Brian Matayoshi from a bear attack on the Wapiti Lake Trail in Yellowstone National Park on July 6, 2011*, with contributing personnel from Montana Fish, Wildlife and Parks, US Forest Service, Interagency Grizzly Bear Study Team, US Fish and Wildlife Service, Wyoming Game and Fish Department, and experts from Yellowstone National Park, fws.gov/mountain-prairie/species/mammals/grizzly/yellowstone.htm.

7. Kerry A. Gunther, Bryan Aber, Mark T. Bruscino, Steven L. Cain, Kevin Frey, and Mark A. Haroldson and Charles C. Schwartz, 2011. "Grizzly Bear-Human Conflicts in the Greater Yellowstone Ecosystem," in C.C. Schwartz, M.A. Haroldson, and K. West, eds., *Yellowstone Grizzly Bear Investigations: Annual Report of the Interagency Grizzly Bear Study Team* (Bozeman, MT: US Geological Survey, 2010), 43–44.

8. Bill Schneider, *Hiking Yellowstone National Park* (Helena, MT: Falcon Publishing/Globe Pequot Press, 1997), 163.

9. Mary Meagher and Jerry R. Phillips, "Restoration of Natural Populations of Grizzly and Black Bears in Yellowstone National Park," International Conference on Bear Research and Management, 5:152–58, quoted in *Grizzly Bear Ecology and Management: 603, Background Readings*, Paul Schullery, Course Coordinator, Yellowstone Institute, 1991, Table 4, Section 6, 5.

10. Federal and state interagency members, *Investigation Team Report dated January 30, 2012* (aka "Board of Review report on the death of Mr. John L. Wallace on August 25, 2011") with contributing personnel from Montana Fish, Wildlife and Parks, US Forest

Service, Interagency Grizzly Bear Study Team, US Fish and Wildlife Service, Wyoming Game and Fish Department, and experts from Yellowstone National Park, fws.gov/mountain-prairie/species/mammals/grizzly/yellowstone.htm.

11. Case Incident Record Number 114555, Department of the Interior, National Park Service, Yellowstone National Park, 2011, unbound, paginated only within an individual ranger's report, nps.gov/aboutus/foia/foia-frd.htm.

12. *Investigation Team Report dated January 30, 2012*, with contributing personnel from Montana Fish, Wildlife and Parks, US Forest Service, Interagency Grizzly Bear Study Team, US Fish and Wildlife Service, Wyoming Game and Fish Department, and experts from Yellowstone National Park, fws.gov/mountain-prairie/species/mammals/grizzly/yellowstone.htm.

13. Bill Schneider, *Hiking Yellowstone National Park* (Helena, MT: Falcon Publishing / Globe Pequot, 1997), 204.

14. Ranger Mark Plona, Report in Yellowstone Case Incident Record Number 114555, unpaginated, nps.gov/aboutus/foia/foia-frd.htm.

15. Werner Herzog in an interview by David Holbrooke, *Outside* magazine, August 2011, 70.

16. Interagency federal and state panel's *Investigation Team Report dated July 16, 2010— Fatality of Erwin Evert from a bear attack in Kitty Creek on the Shoshone National Forest on June 17, 2010.* With contributing personnel from Montana Fish, Wildlife and Parks, US Forest Service, Interagency Grizzly Bear Study Team, US Fish and Wildlife Service, Wyoming Game and Fish Department, and experts from Yellowstone National Park, fws.gov/mountain-prairie/species/mammals/grizzly/yellowstone.htm.

17. *Recommendations of the Investigation Team Based on the Investigation of the Fatality of Erwin Evert from a Bear Attack on June 17, 2010*, fws.gov/mountain-prairie/species/mammals/grizzly/yellowstone.htm.

18. *Ibid.*

19. Paul Schullery 1997. Second edition 1999. *Searching For Yellowstone—Ecology and Wonder in the Last Wilderness* (Boston and New York: Mariner Books, Houghton Mifflin Company, 1999), 85.

20. Federal and state interagency panel, *Investigation Team Report dated August 13, 2010—Bear Attacks in the Soda Butte Campground on July 28, 2010* (released to the public). With contributing personnel from Montana Fish, Wildlife and Parks, US Forest Service, Interagency Grizzly Bear Study Team, US Fish and Wildlife Service, Wyoming Game and Fish Department, and experts from Yellowstone National Park, fws.gov/mountain-prairie/species/mammals/grizzly/yellowstone.htm.

21. Ibid.

22. Mark C. Marschall, *Yellowstone Trails, A Hiking Guide* (Yellowstone National Park, WY: The Yellowstone Association, 1984), 61.

23. Orville E. Bach Jr., *Hiking the Yellowstone Backcountry* (San Francisco: Sierra Club Books, 1979), 199–200.

24. Kerry A. Gunther, "Bears and Menstruating Women," Yell 707, Information Paper BMO-7, Yellowstone National Park, WY, May 2002.

25. Lee H. Whittlesey, *Yellowstone Place Names* (Helena, MT: Montana Historical Society Press, 1988), 165.

26. Stephen Herrero, *Bear Attacks: Their Causes and Avoidance* (New York: Nick Lyons Books, 1985), 73.

27. Ken Preston-Mafham, *Practical Wildlife Photography* (London and Boston: Focal Press, 1982), 8.

28. Orville E. Bach Jr., *Hiking the Yellowstone Backcountry* (San Francisco: Sierra Club Books, 1979), 131.

29. Ken Preston-Mafham, *Practical Wildlife Photography* (London and Boston: Focal Press, 1982). 9.

30. Jack Ellis Haynes, *Haynes Guide, Handbook of Yellowstone National Park* (Bozeman, MT: Haynes Studios Inc., 1962, reprint).

31. Frank C. Craighead Jr., *Track of the Grizzly* (San Francisco: Sierra Club Books, 1982), 212.

32. Dennis G. Martin, January 17, 1975. Administrator for the *Estate of Harry Eugene Walker, Deceased, Plaintiff, vs. United States of America, Defendant*, US District Court, Central District of California (Los Angeles), No. 72-3044-AAH.

33. Reporter's Transcript of Proceedings, *Estate of Harry Eugene Walker vs. United States of America*, in "347 u58," Yellowstone National Park Library "9185," Vol. 8 and 9, 1341.

34. Ibid., Vol. 9, 1379–84.

35. Ibid., Vol. 8, 1335–36, 1339.

36. Frank C. Craighead Jr., *Track of the Grizzly* (San Francisco: Sierra Club Books, 1982), 212–13.

37. Reporter's Transcript of Proceedings, *Estate of Harry Eugene Walker vs. United States of America*, in "347 u58," Yellowstone National Park Library "9185," Vol. 6, 1077.

38. Ibid., Vol. 8, 1343.

39. Ibid., Vol. 9, 1393–96.

40. Frank C. Craighead Jr., *Track of the Grizzly* (San Francisco: Sierra Club Books, 1982), 213.

41. Reporter's Transcript of Proceedings, *Estate of Harry Eugene Walker vs. United States of America*, in "347 u58," Yellowstone National Park Library "9185," Vol. 8, 1348.

42. Carl Bechtold, "Local Bear Goes Bad," *Cody Enterprise* (Cody, WY), July 20, 1983.

43. Joel C. Janetski, *Indians of Yellowstone Park* (Salt Lake City: University of Utah Press, 1987), 28, 42.

44. Frank B. Linderman, *Pretty-Shield, Medicine Woman of the Crow* (New York: HarperCollins, 1972), excerpt quoted in *Bears* magazine, Blackfoot, ID, Summer 1996.

45. Aubrey L. Haines, *The Yellowstone Story, Vol. I*, Yellowstone Library and Museum Association in cooperation with Colorado Associated University Press, chap. 5, 104. Copyright 1977 by Yellowstone Library and Museum Association, Yellowstone National Park, Wyoming.

46. Hiram Martin Chittenden, *The Yellowstone National Park* (Norman: University of Oklahoma Press, 1964 reprint of 1895 edition), 111.

47. Quoted and summarized by Aubrey L. Haines, in *The Yellowstone Story, Vol. I,* Yellowstone Library and Museum Association in cooperation with Colorado Associated University Press, chap. 5, 104. Quoted Philetus W. Norris. 1885. *Meanderings of a Mountaineer, or, the Journals and Musings (or Storys) of a Rambler over Prairie (or Mountain) and Plain,* manuscript prepared from newspaper clippings (1870–1875) and annotated by Norris about 1885 (original in Huntington Library, San Marino, CA), p. 16.

48. Quoted by Aubrey L. Haines in *The Yellowstone Story, Vol. I,* Yellowstone Library and Museum Association in cooperation with Colorado Associated University Press, chap. 5, 104. Quoted William E. Strong. 1876. *A Trip to the Yellowstone National Park in July, August, and September, 1875* (Washington, D.C., 1876), 92–93. Reprinted 1968, edited by Richard A. Bartlett (Norman: Univ. of Oklahoma Press), Vol. 39 in "Western Frontier Library" series, 104–6.

49. "Speaking of Bear," *Livingston Enterprise* (Livingston, MT), December 12, 1903.

50. *Livingston Enterprise* (Livingston, MT), September 11, 1902.

51. Quoted by Paul Schullery, in *Yellowstone Bear Tales* (Niwot, CO: Roberts Rinehart Inc., 1991), 55–56.

52. *Livingston Enterprise* (Livingston, MT), May 6, 1912, 1.

53. Quoted by Paul Schullery, in *Yellowstone Bear Tales* (Niwot, CO: Roberts Rinehart Inc., 1991), 61. Quoted J. A. McGuire, Editor. Dec. 1916. "The Late Grizzly Bear Attacks in Yellowstone National Park," *Outdoor Life* magazine, pp. 583–84.

54. Quoted by Paul Schullery, in *Yellowstone Bear Tales* (Niwot, CO: Roberts Rinehart Inc., 1991), 64–66.

55. Orville E. Bach Jr., *Exploring the Yellowstone Backcountry, A Guide to the Hiking Trails of Yellowstone with Additional Sections on Canoeing, Bicycling, and Cross-Country Skiing* (San Francisco: Sierra Club Books, 1991), 197–98.

56. Lee H. Whittlesey, *Death in Yellowstone* (Boulder, CO: Roberts Rinehart Inc. 1995), 56–57.

57. Quoted by Lee H. Whittlesey in *Death in Yellowstone* (Boulder, CO: Roberts Rinehart Inc. 1995), 42. Quoted William Rush. *Wild Animals of the Rockies, Adventures of a Forest Ranger.*

58. Frank C. Craighead Jr., *For Everything There Is a Season, The Sequence of Natural Events in the Grand Teton-Yellowstone Area* (Helena and Billings, MT: Falcon Publishing, 1994), 72–73.

59. Mark C. Marschall, *Yellowstone Trails, A Hiking Guide* (Yellowstone National Park, WY: The Yellowstone Association, 1984), 46.

60. Associated Press, July 27, 1993, quoted in The *Missoulian* (Missoula, MT).

61. *Ladies Home Journal,* August 1998.

62. Clyde Ormond, *Outdoor Life Complete Book of Hunting,* drawings by Douglas Allen (New York: Outdoor Life / Harper & Row, 1962), 3–4.

63. Kevin Frey, "Investigative Report" (Bozeman, MT: Montana Fish, Wildlife and Parks, September 25, 1992).

64. "Grizzly Mauls Bow Hunters," Associated Press, September 27, 1992, quoted in The *Missoulian* (Missoula, MT).

65. Quoted by Paul Schullery, Course Coordinator, in *Grizzly Bear Ecology and Management: 603, Background Readings*, Yellowstone Institute, 1991, Section 2, 17–18. Quoted Christopher Servheen, USFWS; Richard Knight, IGBST NPS; David Mattson, IGBST, NPS; Steven Mealey, USFS; Dale Strickland, WYGF; John Varley, NPS, YNP; and John Weaver, USFS, 1986. *Report to the IGBC on the Availability of Foods for Grizzly Bears in the Yellowstone Ecosystem, 1986.*

66. Jack Ellis Haynes, *Haynes Guide, Handbook of Yellowstone National Park* (Bozeman, MT: Haynes Studios Inc., 1962), 128.

67. Bill Schneider, *Hiking Yellowstone National Park* (Helena, MT: Falcon Publishing, 1997), 22–23.

68. Ibid., 202.

69. *Yellowstone Journal*, August/September 1994. Yellowstone International Corp., Lander, WY.

70. Don Schwennesen, The *Missoulian* (Missoula, MT), October 1, 1993.

71. Ibid., October 2, 1993.

72. Carole Mikita, KSL Television and Radio, Salt Lake City, UT, ksl.com, June 20, 2007.

73. *Bozeman Daily Chronicle* (Bozeman, MT), June 6, 2007.

74. Mark C. Marschall, *Yellowstone Trails, A Hiking Guide* (Yellowstone National Park, WY: Yellowstone Library and Museum Association in cooperation with National Park Service, 1984), 94.

75. Ibid., 65.

76. Orville Bach Jr., *Exploring the Yellowstone Backcountry, A Guide to the Hiking Trails of Yellowstone with Additional Sections on Canoeing, Bicycling, and Cross-country Skiing* (San Francisco: Sierra Club Books, 1991), 221–22.

77. Orville Bach Jr., *Exploring the Yellowstone Backcountry, Revised and Updated Edition* (San Francisco: Sierra Club Books, 1991), 108.

78. Ibid., 215–16.

79. Ibid., 153, 156.

80. "Resource Notes," *Yellowstone Discovery*, Winter 1999, Yellowstone Association, Yellowstone National Park, WY.

81. Ibid.

82. Orville Bach Jr., *Exploring the Yellowstone Backcountry, Revised and Updated Edition* (San Francisco: Sierra Club Books, 1991), 221.

83. *Jackson Hole News* (Jackson Hole, WY), September 6, 2000.

84. Scott McMillion, *Bozeman Daily Chronicle* (Bozeman, MT), September 5, 2002.

85. Alan W. Cundall and Herbert T. Lystrup, *Hamilton's Guide to Yellowstone National Park* (West Yellowstone, MT: Hamilton Stores Inc., 1987), 37.

86. Rob Robertson, posted on website of Appalachian State University, Boone, NC, May 2, 2006.

87. Mark C. Marschall, *Yellowstone Trails, A Hiking Guide* (Yellowstone National Park, WY: Yellowstone Library and Museum Association in cooperation with National Park Service, 1984), 91.

88. Nathaniel Pitt Langford, *The Discovery of Yellowstone Park* (Lincoln: University of Nebraska Press, 1972 reprint of 1905 edition), 23.

89. Edmund Jay Williams, "The Night of the Bear," in International Yellowstone Association newsletter, January 5, 1999, 1–2.

90. Kerry A. Gunther, "Information Paper No. 1," Bear Management Office, Yellowstone National Park, WY, March 1991.

91. Kerry A. Gunther, Mark J. Biel, Neil Anderson, and Lisette Waits, "Probable Grizzly Bear Predation on an American Black Bear in Yellowstone National Park," in Ursus 13 (2002), 372.

92. Kerry A. Gunther, "Information Paper No. 1," Bear Management Office, Yellowstone National Park, WY, March 1991.

93. Marlo Pronovost, "Black Bears As Dangerous As Grizzlies," *West Yellowstone News* (West Yellowstone, MT), June 23, 2006.

94. "Yellowstone National Park Bear Characteristics, Updated October 1, 2007," US National Park Service, 1–2.

95. Stephen Herrero and Susan Fleck, "Injury to People Inflicted by Black, Grizzly or Polar Bears: Recent Trends and New Insights," published in Proceedings of the Eighth International Conference on Bear Research and Management, "Bears—Their Biology and Management," held in Victoria, BC, Canada, February 1989, 1989.

96. "Black Bear Attack," in *Bear News*, The Great Bear Foundation, Missoula, MT, Winter/Spring 1994, reprinted from *International Bear News*, Vol. 2, No. 3 (August 1993), which had reprinted it from *The Raven* (Algonquin Park News), Ontario Ministry of Natural Resources, Ontario, Canada, Vol. 33, No. 1, April 23, 1992.

# BIBLIOGRAPHY

Adkison, Ron. *Exploring Beyond Yellowstone: Hiking, Camping, and Vacationing in the National Forests Surrounding Yellowstone and Grand Teton.* Berkeley, CA: Wilderness Press, 1996.

"Animals." Vol. VIII, No. 2, *Parabola, Myth and the Quest for Meaning. 2nd ed.* New York: The Society for the Study of Myth and Tradition, 1989.

Auerbach, Paul S. *Wilderness Medicine: Management of Wilderness and Environmental Emergencies.* 3rd ed. St. Louis, MO: C.V. Mosby Company, 1995.

Bach, Orville E., Jr. *Hiking the Yellowstone Backcountry. 1973;* 2nd rev. ed. San Francisco: Sierra Club Books, 1979.

———. *Exploring the Yellowstone Backcountry*, Revised and Updated Edition. San Francisco: Sierra Club Books, 1991.

———. *Exploring the Yellowstone Backcountry: A Guide to the Hiking Trails of Yellowstone with Additional Sections on Canoeing, Bicycling, and Cross-country Skiing.* San Francisco: Sierra Club Books, 1991.

———. *Tracking the Spirit of Yellowstone: Recollections of Thirty-One Years as a Seasonal Ranger.* Illustrations by Margaret C. Bach. Bozeman, MT: Blue Willow Press, 2005.

Baron, David. *The Beast in the Garden: A Modern Parable of Man and Nature.* New York: W.W. Norton, 2004.

Beal, Merrill D. *The Story of Man in Yellowstone.* 1949; 2nd rev. ed. Yellowstone Park, WY: The Yellowstone Library and Museum Association, 1956.

*Bears: Their Biology and Management.* "Abstracts." Ninth International Conference on Bear Research and Management, February 1992, Missoula, MT. International Association for Bear Research and Management, IBA Publications, c/o Terry D. White, Southern Appalachian Field Laboratory, 274 Ellington Hall, University of Tennessee, Knoxville TN 37996, USA, 1994.

*Bears: Their Biology and Management, A Selection of Papers.* Eighth International Conference on Bear Research and Management, February 1989, Victoria, BC. International Association for Bear Research and Management, IBA Publications, c/o Terry D. White, Southern Appalachian Field Laboratory, 274 Ellington Hall, University of Tennessee, Knoxville TN 37996, USA, 1990.

Berger, Joel. *The Better To Eat You With: Fear in the Animal World.* Chicago: The University of Chicago Press, 2008.

Biel, Alice Wondrak. *Do (Not) Feed the Bears: The Fitful History of Wildlife and Tourists in Yellowstone.* Lawrence: University Press of Kansas, 2006.

# Bibliography

Blanchard, Bonnie M. *Field Techniques Used in the Study of Grizzly Bears.* Bozeman, MT: Interagency Grizzly Bear Study Team, Forestry Sciences Lab, Montana State University, 1985.

Brown, Gary. *Safe Travel in Bear Country.* New York: Lyons and Burford Publishers, 1996.

Busch, Robert H. *The Grizzly Almanac.* New York: The Lyons Press, 2000.

Calabro, Marian. *Operation Grizzly Bear.* New York: Four Winds Press / Macmillan Publishing Company, 1989.

Caputo, Philip. *In the Shadows of the Morning: Essays on Wild Lands, Wild Waters, and a Few Untamed People.* Guilford, CT: The Lyons Press / Globe Pequot Press, 2002.

Caras, Roger. *Roger Caras' Treasury of Classic Nature Tales.* New York: Truman Talley Books / Dutton, 1992.

Carey, Alan. *In the Path of the Grizzly.* Flagstaff, AZ: Northland Publishing, 1986.

Chadwick, Douglas H. *True Grizz: Glimpses of Fernie, Stahr, Easy, Dakota, and Other Real Bears in the Modern World.* San Francisco: Sierra Club Books, 2003.

Chase, Alston. *Playing God in Yellowstone: The Destruction of America's First National Park.* Boston: The Atlantic Monthly Press, 1986.

Cheek, Roland. *Chocolate Legs: Sweet Mother, Savage Killer?* Columbia Falls, MT: Skyline Publishing, 2001.

———. *Learning To Talk Bear, So Bears Can Listen.* Columbia Falls, MT: Skyline Publishing, 1997.

Chittenden, Hiram Martin. 1895; 5th rev. ed., *The Yellowstone National Park: Historical and Descriptive.* Cincinnati, OH: The Robert Clarke Company, 1905.

Clark, Ella E. *Indian Legends from the Northern Rockies.* Norman: University of Oklahoma Press, 1966.

Clark, Tim W. et al. *Carnivores in Ecosystems: The Yellowstone Experience.* New Haven, CT: Yale University Press, 1999.

Clarke, James. *Man Is the Prey.* New York: Stein and Day Publishers, 1969.

Cole, Jim. *Lives of Grizzlies: Montana and Wyoming.* Helena, MT: Farcountry Press, 2004.

Compton, Gail W. *Visitors and Wildlife: Yellowstone National Park: Report of the Eastern Michigan University Research Team.* Missoula, MT: Center for Wildlife Information, in cooperation with Eastern Michigan University, 1993.

Craighead, F. Lance. *Bears of the World* (Worldlife Discovery Guides) McGregor, MN: Voyageur Press, 2002.

Craighead, Frank C., Jr. *For Everything There Is a Season: The Sequence of Natural Events in the Grand Teton–Yellowstone Area.* Helena, MT; Falcon Press, 1994.

———. *Track of the Grizzly.* 1979; reprint San Francisco: Sierra Club Books, 1982.

———, and John J. Craighead. *Grizzly Bear Prehibernation and Denning Activities as Determined by Radiotracking.* Wildlife Monographs series, Louis A. Krumholz, ed. Louisville, KY: The Wildlife Society, Inc. / University of Louisville, 1972.

Craighead, John J., Jay S. Sumner, and John A. Mitchell. *The Grizzly Bears of Yellowstone: Their Ecology in the Yellowstone Ecosystem, 1959–1992.* Washington, D.C.: Island Press, 1995.

———, J. S. Sumner and G.B. Scaggs. *A Definitive System for Analysis of Grizzly Bear Habitat and Other Wilderness Resources.* Pittsburgh, PA: The Richard King Mellon Foundation, 1982.

———, J. S. Sumner and G.B. Scaggs. *A Definitive System for Analysis of Grizzly Bear Habitat and Other Wilderness Resources, Utilizing LANDSAT Multispectral Imagery and Computer Technology.* Wildlife-Wildlands Institute Monograph No. 1. Missoula, MT: U of M Foundation / University of Montana, 1982.

Cramond, Mike. *Killer Bears.* New York: Outdoor Life Books / Scribner's, 1981.

———. *Of Bears and Man.* Norman: University of Oklahoma Press, 1986.

Debruyn, Terry D. *Walking with Bears.* New York: The Lyons Press, 1999.

East, Ben. *Bears: A Veteran Outdoorsman's Account of the Most Fascinating and Dangerous Animals in North America.* New York: Outdoor Life / Crown, 1977.

———. *Outdoor Life, Narrow Escapes and Wilderness Adventures.* Outdoor Life / E.P. Dutton & Co., Inc., 1960.

———. *Survival: 23 True Sportsmen's Adventures.* New York: Outdoor Life Book / E.P. Dutton & Co., 1967.

Etling, Kathy. *Bear Attacks: Classic Tales of Dangerous North American Bears.* 2 vols. Long Beach, CA: Safari Press Inc., 1997.

Fish, Chet, ed. *The Outdoor Life Bear Book.* New York: Outdoor Life Books / Times Mirror Magazines, Inc., 1983.

Fletcher, David. *Hunted: A True Story of Survival.* New York: Carroll & Graf / Avalon Publishing Group, Inc., 2003.

Ford, Barbara. *Black Bear: Spirit of the Wilderness.* Boston: Houghton Mifflin Co., 1981.

French, Steven P. "Bear Attacks," in "Wild and Domestic Animal Attacks," *The Management of Wilderness and Environmental Emergencies.* 3rd ed. St. Louis: The C.V. Mosby Company, 1994.

Garfield, Brad. *Bear vs. Man: Recent Attacks and How to Avoid the Increasing Danger.* Minocqua, WI: Willow Creek Press, 2001.

Gilchrist, Duncan. *All About Bears.* Hamilton, MT: Outdoor Expeditions and Books, 1989.

Godlovitch, Stanley, and Roslind and John Harris, eds. *Animals, Men and Morals: An Enquiry into the Maltreatment of Non-Humans.* New York, Grove Press, 1971.

Grandin, Temple and Catherine Johnson. *Animals in Translation.* New York: Harcourt, Inc., 2005.

Haines, Aubrey L. *The Yellowstone Story: A History of Our First National Park.* 2 vols. Yellowstone National Park, WY: Yellowstone Library and Museum Association in cooperation with Colorado Associated University Press, 1977.

Hart, Donna, and Robert W. Sussman. *Man the Hunted: Primates, Predators, and Human Evolution.* New York: Westview Press, 2005.

Haynes, Bessie Doak, and Edgar Haynes, eds. *The Grizzly Bear: Portraits from Life.* Norman: University of Oklahoma Press, 1966.

Herrero, Stephen. *Bear Attacks: Their Causes and Avoidance.* Piscataway, NJ: Nick Lyons Books / Winchester Press, an imprint of New Century Publishers, Inc., 1985.

————. *Bear Attacks: Their Causes and Avoidance.* 2nd rev. ed. Guilford, CT: The Lyons Press, an imprint of The Globe Pequot Press, 2002.

Hoshino, Michio. *Grizzly.* San Francisco: Chronicle Books, 1987.

————. Karen Colligan-Taylor, trans. *The Grizzly Bear Family Book.* London: Picture Book Studio Ltd., 1993.

Houston, Pam, ed. *Women on Hunting.* New York: The Ecco Press / Penguin Putnam, 1995.

Jenkins, Ken L. *Grizzly Reflections.* Reflections of the Wilderness. Merrillville, IN: ICS Books, Inc., 1995.

Jonkel, Charles. *How to Live in Bear Country.* Missoula, MT: Ursid Research Center, n.d.

Kerasote, Ted. *Bloodties: Nature, Culture, and the Hunt.* New York: Random House, 1995.

Knibb, David G. *Grizzly Wars: The Public Fight over the Great Bear.* Cheney: Eastern Washington University Press, 2008.

Langford, Nathaniel Pitt. *The Discovery of Yellowstone Park: Journal of the Washburn Expedition to the Yellowstone and Firehole Rivers in the Year 1870.* 1905; reprint, Lincoln: University of Nebraska Press, Lincoln, 1972.

Lapinski, Mike. *Self Defense for Nature Lovers: Handling Dangerous Situations with Wild Critters.* Stevensville, MT: Stoneydale Press Publishing Co., 1998.

————. *True Stories of Bear Attacks: Who Survived and Why.* Portland, OR: Westwinds Press / Graphic Arts Center Publishing Co., 2004.

Laycock, George. *Wilderness Legend: Grizzly.* Minocqua, WI: Northword Press, Inc., 1997.

Long, Ben. *Great Montana Bear Stories.* Helena, MT: Riverbend Publishing, 2002.

Long, John, editor. *Attacked! By Beasts of Prey and other Deadly Creatures: True Stories of Survivors.* Camden, ME: Ragged Mountain Press / McGraw-Hill Companies, 1998.

Marschall, Mark C. *Yellowstone Trails: A Hiking Guide.* 1978; 2nd rev. ed., Yellowstone National Park, WY: Yellowstone Library and Museum Association in cooperation with National Park Service, U.S. Department of the Interior, 1984.

————.1999; 2nd rev. ed., *Yellowstone Trails: A Hiking Guide.* Yellowstone National Park, WY: The Yellowstone Association, 2003.

McMillion, Scott. *Mark of the Grizzly.* Helena, MT: Falcon Publishing, 1998.

McNamee, Thomas. *The Grizzly Bear.* New York, Knopf, 1984.

Mills, Enos A. *The Grizzly, Our Greatest Wild Animal.* 1919; reprint, New York: Ballantine Books, Inc., 1973.

Murphy, Bob. *Bears I Have Known: A Park Ranger's True Tales from Yellowstone and Glacier National Parks.* Helena, MT: Riverbend Publishing, 2006.

Neal, Chuck. *Grizzlies in the Mist.* Moose, WY: Homestead Publishing, 2003.

Nelson, Jim. *Bear Encounters: Tales from the Wild.* Auburn, WA: Lone Pine Publishing, 2005.

Olsen, Lance. *Great Bear Foundation Field Guide to the Grizzly Bear.* Seattle: Sasquatch Books, 1992.

Ormond, Clyde. *Bear! Black, Grizzly, Brown, Polar.* Harrisburg, PA: The Stackpole Company, 1961.

Patent, Dorothy Hinshaw. *The Way of the Grizzly*. New York: Clarion Books, 1986.

Peacock, Doug. *Grizzly Years: In Search of the American Wilderness*. New York: Henry Holt & Co, 1990.

Peacock, Doug and Andrea Peacock. *The Essential Grizzly: The Mingled Fates of Men and Bears*. Guilford, CT: The Lyons Press, an imprint of The Globe Pequot Press, 2006.

Preston-Mafham, Ken. *Practical Wildlife Photography*. New York: Focal Press, an imprint of the Butterworth Group, 1982.

Pritchard, James A. *Preserving Yellowstone's Natural Conditions: Science and the Perception of Nature*. Lincoln: University of Nebraska Press, 1999.

Prodgers, Jeanette. *The Only Good Bear Is a Dead Bear: A Collection of the West's Best Bear Stories*. Helena, MT: Jeanette Prodgers / Falcon Press Publishing, 1986.

Reed, Tom. *Great Wyoming Bear Stories*. Helena, MT: Riverbend Publishing, 2003.

Reese, Rick. *Greater Yellowstone: The National Park and Adjacent Wild Lands*. Montana Geographic Series, Number Six. Helena, MT: Montana Magazine, Inc., 1984.

Rezendes, Paul. *The Wild Within: Adventures in Nature and Animal Teachings*. New York: Jeremy P. Tarcher / Putnam / Penguin Putnam, 1998.

Ricciuti, Edward R. *Killer Animals*. New York: Walker and Co., 1976.

Robinson, Michael H. and Lionel Tiger, eds. *Man and Beast Revisited*. Washington: Smithsonian Institution Press, 1991.

Rockwell, David. *Giving Voice to Bear: North American Indian Myths, Rituals, and Images of the Bear*. Niwot, CO: Roberts Rinehart Publishers, 1991.

Rubbert, Tim. *Hiking with Grizzlies: Lessons Learned*. Helena, MT: Riverbend Publishing, 2006.

Russell, Andy, intro. *Great Bear Adventures: True Tales from the Wild*. Stillwater, MN: Voyageur Press, Inc., n.d.

Samson, Jack. *The Bear Book*. Clinton, NJ: Amwell Press, 1979.

———. *The Grizzly Book*. Clinton, NJ: Amwell Press, 1981.

Savage, Candace. *Grizzly Bears*. San Francisco: Sierra Club, 1990.

Schemnitz, Sanford D. *Wildlife Management Techniques Manual*. Washington, D.C.: The Wildlife Society, Inc., 1980.

Schneider, Bill. *Bear Aware: Hiking and Camping in Bear Country*. Helena, MT: Falcon Press, 1996.

———. *Where the Grizzly Walks*. Missoula, MT: Mountain Press Publishing Co., 1977.

Schullery, Paul. *The Bear Hunter's Century: Profiles from the Golden Age of Bear Hunting*. 1988; reprint, Silver City, NM: High-Lonesome Books, 1998.

———. *The Bears of Yellowstone*. 1980; reprint, Boulder, CO: Roberts Rinehart Inc. in cooperation with the National Park Foundation, 1986.

———, Course Coordinator. *Grizzly Bear Ecology and Management 603: Background Readings*. Yellowstone National Park, WY: Yellowstone Institute, 1991.

———. *Lewis and Clark Among the Grizzlies: Legend and Legacy in the American West*. Guilford, CT: Falcon Press / The Globe Pequot Press, 2002.

———, ed. *Mark of the Bear: Legend and Lore of an American Icon*. San Francisco: Sierra Club Books, 1996.

———. *Mountain Time*. New York: Nick Lyons Books / Schocken Books, 1984.

Bibliography

———. *Searching for Yellowstone: Ecology and Wonder in the Last Wilderness*. 1997; reprint, New York: Mariner Books / Houghton Mifflin Co., 1999.

———, ed. *Yellowstone Bear Tales*. Niwot, CO: Roberts Rinehart Inc. Publishers, 1991.

Shelton, James Gary. *Bear Attacks: The Deadly Truth*. Hagensborg, B.C., Canada: Pallister Publishing, 1998.

———. *Bear Attacks II: Myth and Reality*. Hagensborg, B.C., Canada: Pallister Publishing, 2001.

———. *Bear Encounter Survival Guide*. Hagensborg, B.C., Canada: self-published, Box 95, Hagensborg, B.C., 1994.

Shepard, Paul, and Barry Sanders. *The Sacred Paw: The Bear in Nature, Myth, and Literature*. New York: Viking Penguin Inc., 1985.

Sholly, Dan R., with Steven M. Newman. *Guardians of Yellowstone*. New York: William Morrow and Co., Inc., 1991.

Smith, Dave. *The Backcountry Bear Basics: The Definitive Guide to Avoiding Unpleasant Encounters*. Seattle: The Mountaineers, 1997.

Smith, Richard P. *The Book of the Black Bear*. Piscataway, NJ: Winchester Press / New Century Publishers, 1985.

Thomson, David. *In the Shining Mountains: A Would-be Mountain Man in Search of the Wilderness*. New York: Alfred A. Knopf, 1979.

Turner, Jack. *Travels in the Greater Yellowstone*. New York: Thomas Dunne Books / St. Martin's Press, 2008.

Whittlesey, Lee H. *Death in Yellowstone: Accidents and Foolhardiness in the First National Park*. Boulder, CO: Roberts Rinehart Publishers, 1995.

———. *Yellowstone Place Names*. Helena: Montana Historical Society Press, 1988.

Wuerthner, George. *Yellowstone: A Visitor's Companion*. Harrisburg, PA: Stackpole Books, 1992.

# INDEX

# ABOUT THE AUTHOR

Kathleen Snow is a member of the Outdoor Writers Association of America and the Montana Writers Guild. Her nonfiction has appeared in *Harper's Magazine*, *Women in Natural Resources*, and other periodicals. Her novels include the new mystery *Searching for Bear Eyes*, published in 2015 by the University of Montana Press. Visit kathleensnowbooks.com.